D0718547

SPECIAL NEEDS IN ORDINARY SCHOOLS
General editor: Peter Mittler
Associate editors: Mel Ainscow, Brahm Norwich, Peter Pumfrey,
Rosemary Webb and Sheila Wolfendale

New Directions in Special Needs

Titles in the Special Needs in Ordinary Schools series

Meeting Special Needs in Ordinary Schools: An Overview (2nd edition)
Assessing Special Educational Needs
Management for Special Needs
Reappraising Special Needs Education
Special Needs Provision: Assessment, Concern and Action
Working with Parents of Children with Special Needs

Concerning pre- and primary schooling:

Primary Schools and Special Needs: Policy, Planning and Provision
    (2nd edition)
Pre-School Provision for Children with Special Needs
Expressive Arts in the Primary School
Improving Children's Reading in the Junior School

Concerning secondary schooling:

Secondary Schools for All? Strategies for Special Needs (2nd edition)
Secondary Mathematics and Special Educational Needs

Concerning further and higher education:

Further Opportunities: Learning Difficulties and Disabilities in
    Further Education
Opening Doors: Learning Support in Higher Education

Concerning specific needs:

Children with Hearing Difficulties
Children with Learning Difficulties
Children with Speech and Language Difficulties
Educating the Able
Improving Classroom Behaviour: New Directions for Teachers and Pupils
Mobility for Special Needs

Forthcoming:

Spelling

New Directions in Special Needs

Innovations in Mainstream Schools

Catherine Clark
Alan Dyson
Alan Millward
David Skidmore

CASSELL

Cassell
Wellington House   127 West 24th Street
125 Strand   New York
London WC2R 0BB   NY 10011

© C. Clark, A. Dyson, A. Millward, D. Skidmore 1997

First published 1997

British Library Cataloguing-in-Publication Data
A catalogue record for this book is available from the British Library.

ISBN 0-304-70023-1 (hardback)
      0-304-70024-X (paperback)

Typeset by Kenneth Burnley in Irby, Wirral, Cheshire.
Printed and bound in Great Britain by Biddles Ltd, Guildford and King's Lynn

Contents

Acknowledgements

Acknowledgements are due to the following: Joseph Rowntree for Figure 8.1, from A. J. Millward and D. Skidmore (1995) *The Role of Local Education Authorities in the Management of Special Educational Needs.* Routledge for Figure 9.1, from R. Bowe and S. J. Ball with A. Gold (1992) *Reforming Education and Changing Schools.*

Editorial foreword

The decade that has passed since the launch of the present series of books has been a period of unprecedented change for the education system and for pupils, teachers and parents.

Whether pupils with special educational needs have been helped or harmed by the changes of the last ten years is a matter of debate. On the one hand, there is undoubtedly a greater awareness in schools of the needs of pupils who are under-achieving and who experience difficulties in learning, for whatever reason. This is reflected in a commitment to the inclusion of all pupils in the life of the school and a determination to ensure entitlement and access to the whole curriculum.

On the other hand, the 'ethos' of mainstream schools has been undermined by the cold wind of market forces, the obsessive emphasis on examination performance as the sole indicator of achievement and by the increasing fragmentation and divisiveness of the education system. The intolerable pressures inflicted on schools by the constant demands for change and by the need for politicians and the media to target scapegoats has led to a rising number of casualties, particularly the escalating number of pupils who are excluded from school. At the very time when there is a clearer articulation of the case for an inclusive system which caters for diversity, mainstream schools are under pressure to increase selection and segregation, and to concentrate on the raising of standards. Against such a background, schools are working against all the odds to implement the *Code of Practice*.

This book provides an opportunity to learn from the experiences of the past ten years in order to plan more successfully and purposefully for the future. It is based on a detailed study of the response of mainstream schools to the challenge of change posed not only by legislation but by the development of new perspectives and priorities. It examines the process of change in classrooms, in schools and in Local Education Authorities and in the interactions between all of these as they impact on pupils, parents and communities. The book offers no easy, ready-made solutions. But it does illustrate ways in which more schools have been moving towards inclusive policies and practices.

Professor Peter Mittler
University of Manchester
October 1996

Introduction and background

Writing in an earlier volume in the Cassell *Special Needs in Ordinary Schools* series, Wolfendale (1987) suggested that the future of special education in mainstream schools would be about an increasing amalgamation of the best practice present in the two systems. Thinking particularly in terms of primary schools she expressed that future thus:

> An alignment between best practice in primary and in special education is now called for. As schools embrace the equality of opportunity inherent in the anti-discriminatory educational policies espoused by a slowly increasing number of LEAs, so the hard won expertise in devising effective curricula in primary schools needs to be matched by and married to the equally hard won expertise in remedial and special education. . . . Beyond the rhetoric lies the task of translating aims into sound pedagogic practice that provides for the universality of all children's needs as well as for the specificity of each child's needs, and for the overwhelming majority whose paramount educational need is to be educated in local schools. (pp. 1–2)

Offering a secondary school perspective in the same series, Sayer (1994/1987) expressed somewhat similar views:

> . . . we must extend across the continuum to all children the special concerns, insights, and skills that have been most obviously developed to meet the most irrefutable needs, and engage society and its political expression in seeking a new consensus in which all are specially regarded. We must ensure that in taking this turn from the separate treatment for a few towards a continuum of resource according to need, we are building the resource of all to assist each other's learning. We must rebuild attitudes and organizations to

make happen what we say we intend. We may find in doing so that we are at the same time the instruments of social reform in keeping with the human values that have for so long been proclaimed rather than expressed in the realities of living. (pp. 163–4)

Such statements are typical both of the concerns of this series as a whole, and of an optimistic, committed and values-driven perspective that has, to a greater or lesser extent, been a constant theme within the field of special needs education in recent decades. Building on the set of liberal values which had underpinned the emergence of comprehensive schools, the development of integration, the exploration of mixed ability teaching and the curricular experiments which predated the National Curriculum, special needs education has increasingly sought to embody the broad 'human values' to which Sayer refers. Segregated special needs provision has increasingly come to seem discriminatory, inequitable and ineffective. The older forms of special needs provision in mainstream schools – such as special classes and remedial groups – have seemed simply to replicate the patterns of discrimination that were most clearly seen in special education. Not only has the ability of such provision to improve children's attainments been in doubt but it is also seen to have had the effect of stigmatizing children, separating them from their peer group and limiting their curricular opportunities. It has seemed increasingly important, therefore, to find ways of responding to the particular needs and learning characteristics of individual children that will be non-segregatory and non-discriminatory. Values of equity and participation in common educational experiences have thus come to be major driving forces in the development of special needs education in mainstream schools.

It has appeared to many commentators on special needs education that it is only a matter of time until these values will be realized by reconstructing responses to special needs in mainstream schools so that the best of special education and mainstream education would be combined into a seamless whole. By the late 1980s, writers such as Dessent (1987), Sayer (1994/1987) and Wolfendale (1987) could already point to the significant changes that had been wrought in the preceding ten years under the umbrella of the whole school approach. It was reasonable for them to look ahead to a decade of further development in which that approach would be tested, refined and reconstructed to bring the projected merger of special and mainstream education closer still. By the time this book is published, that decade will have run its course. What has happened to this 'bold experiment' in the meantime?

THE HISTORICAL CONTEXT

In order to begin answering this question, it is necessary to sketch in something of the historical context out of which these optimistic and liberal views have sprung. That context, we suggest, has its origins, not where they are commonly placed, with the Warnock Report (DES, 1978), but with the education system created by the 1944 Education Act.

In common with all legislators concerned to establish or consolidate national mass education systems, the creators of the 1944 Act faced a fundamental *dilemma* – a term which will come to have particular significance for us during the course of this book. On the one hand, they were developing a system which would be, to a significant extent, universal. That was a system which would recognize the necessity of offering some form of education to all (or nearly all) children within a common national framework. If nothing else, the nation's children would all attend school for a prescribed minimum period where, it was anticipated, they would all acquire some shared basic learning. In keeping with the traditions of earlier education reformers, the creators of the 1944 Act sought to move still further away from the situation in which education was the prerogative of the few, or in which the form and content of the education which a child received depended solely on the opportunities which existed locally or on the economic resources of the child's family.

On the other hand, the millions of children to whom this common education was to be offered were recognizably not a homogeneous group: some learned quickly, others slowly; some had marked social advantages, some had equally marked disadvantages; and some experienced 'handicaps' whilst others seemed blessed with outstanding abilities and skills. In other words, the national education system had to cope, at one and the same time, with a pupil population in which all children shared some common characteristics and entitlements but in which every child was also significantly different from every other.

The resolution of this dilemma favoured by the 1944 Act was to formalize, within the common educational framework, a system based on segregation and selection – operating both between mainstream and special education and, at secondary level at least, within mainstream provision itself. More-or-less rigid divisions between special schools and mainstream schools were mirrored by equally rigid divisions between the three types of mainstream secondary school – grammar, technical and secondary modern. There were, moreover, divisions *within* those schools as children at both secondary and primary level were commonly segregated into different 'ability' groups. Underpinning the whole system was the notion that powerful assessment techniques were available (such as the 11-plus examination and 'IQ tests') which made it possible to identify different 'types' of learners. Children of the same 'type' (the academic, the practical, the educationally sub-normal, and so on) could then be grouped together in the same learning environment and given the same form of education which would be appropriate to their particular needs and characteristics.

This system facilitated the development of general curricular approaches geared to meet what were regarded as fixed and predetermined learning characteristics. It allowed the tracking of pupils into increasingly academic or vocationally-oriented programmes. It created a differentiated hierarchy akin to a series of steps within and between schools which was later to be carried forward in the streaming systems of many of the comprehensive schools of the 1970s. In creating this ladder it offered the prospect of individuals clambering up to a level which reflected their individual capability, and there was indeed some movement between the various school types. Segregation was, however, effectively reinforced for the majority not just by school type but also by curriculum access. Unless pupils transferred soon after the age of 11, the gaps between the curricula of the schools within the tripartite system were such that the practicalities of transfer were significantly reduced, whilst the gap between mainstream and special education was, to all intents and purposes, unbridgeable.

There was also, however, a sense of stability created by this system: pupils and parents knew broadly what to expect of schools; teachers had a degree of confidence about the aims and purpose of the educational diet that they offered; administrators were responsible for an essentially self-regulating system, and politicians could point to an inherent logic of opportunity-through-achievement as an underpinning rationale. In particular, the structure of the education system could be seen to have a scientific – and, in particular, a psychometric – basis. Since different types of pupil – or, at least, different levels of ability amongst pupils – existed and could be identified with confidence, the maintenance of different types of school and different pupil groupings within schools was a perfectly rational policy response. Moreover, it could be defended as humane: insofar as pupils could be considered to have educational 'rights', then the right to an *appropriate* form of education could justifiably be regarded as much more important than any notional right to participate in *common* educational experiences and settings.

Two factors were, however, to challenge this stability. First, the logic of tightly ordered segregated systems gradually came to be questioned: the failure of the promised technical schools to establish themselves within the education system threw into doubt the notion of different types of schools catering for different types of learners; widely different proportions of pupils were selected for grammar school education in different local education authorities (LEAs); and the capacity of the 11-plus test to discriminate accurately between 'academic' and 'non-academic' pupils came into question – along, indeed, with the whole psychometric project. There were similar destabilizing moves in special needs education: it became evident, for instance, that for every child placed in special education by reason of their learning difficulties, there were many others in mainstream schools whose difficulties were equally great; that the system made it extremely difficult for pupils to move out of special education once placed there, regardless of their progress; and that many children had learning difficulties which might better respond to short-term intervention than to permanent segregation. In both mainstream and special education, then, the certainties of the established system began to crumble.

Second, notions of 'rights', 'equality of opportunity', and 'anti-discrimination' came gradually to inform the broader social agenda, effectively challenging a wide range of social systems based on selection and segregation. Across the fields of workers' rights, race relations, gender issues, criminal justice and sexuality, a concern for social cohesion, participation and tolerance was reflected in 'liberal', and, in particular, anti-discriminatory, legislation. As this movement became translated into the educational arena, the 'scientific' basis of the established system came to seem not merely questionable, but an instrument of social division, maintaining the privileges of the more advantaged members of society at the expense of the life-opportunities of those who were already disadvantaged. The structure of the education system thus came to be seen as the embodiment of a particular set of social values rather than simply as a scientific response to 'real' differences between learners; and it became apparent that what had been created to maintain one set of values could and should be recreated to embody a different value position.

The most obvious manifestations of that recreation were, perhaps, the comprehensive school movement in mainstream education and the integration movement in special needs education. However, integration was just one of a series of examples of the blurring of the rigid boundaries between special and mainstream education established in 1944. The first significant 'chink' in these boundaries was the growth, during the 1960s in particular, of special classes in mainstream schools to maintain 'small groups . . . of children of limited ability and children retarded by other conditions' (DES, 1978, 2.48). That they became a significant feature of special educational provision in the secondary modern schools where they were first established is a powerful testament to the inherent instability of systems based around precise demarcation between supposedly homogeneous groups. These classes are illustrative of an early attempt to bridge the incoherence of the special/mainstream divide by importing the methods and approaches of the special school into the mainstream school. They were described by Tansley and Gulliford (1960) as means of 'extending *special educational treatment* into the ordinary school' (p. 11; our emphases). Furthermore they were justified because: 'the aims and methods of the special school are needed not only for the one per cent who are selected as most in need of special schooling but also for the many backward children who remain in ordinary schools' (p. 11).

The view that mainstream schools could only respond to the full range of pupil diversity by importing the methods of special education was carried forward into the developing comprehensive schools of the 1960s and 1970s, where the special class became an established feature of much provision. Many of these special classes sought to replicate the special school situation: there were relatively small numbers; the curriculum was substantially modified; the staffing was fixed, and imbued with a 'specialism' in the field; they were often managed as an adjunct of the overall provision of the LEA rather than as integral to the school in which they were located. The problem remained however, that, as Tansley and Gulliford had pointed out, there were more pupils unable to respond to the unreconstituted curriculum of the mainstream school than could be accommodated in the special classes that had been established.

The notion of 'remedial' education appeared to offer a solution to this problem. In contrast to the semi-permanent alternative offered by special classes, remedial education was seen as '. . . part-time, relatively short-term and limited to specific objectives such as remedying failures or difficulty in learning certain school subjects, especially in basic educational skills. It is teaching which is additional to normal schooling rather than an alternative form of education' (Gulliford, 1971, p. 7). It was, in other words, based on the assumption that it was possible to correct deficits within the individual pupil through limited interventions in a context where the curriculum itself remained essentially unchanged. At the very least, remedial education offered pupils a more individualized and intensive education than was possible in the mainstream class, and at its best it made available sophisticated teaching techniques that were beyond the scope of mainstream teachers. It thus made it possible to offer a form of education that was recognizably 'special' to a relatively large number of pupils without removing them from the mainstream school – or, indeed, from the mainstream class – for any significant period of time.

Moreover, as remedial education and special classes established themselves through the 1960s and 1970s, many other 'half-way houses' began to spring up, enabling mainstream schools to respond to at least some aspects of the diversity of their pupil populations: 'bottom streams' brought with them some of the supposed advantages of special classes (in terms of modified curriculum and pedagogy) without the same rigid segregation (they might, for instance, be taught by subject specialists rather than special educators); 'alternative curricula' for older pupils allowed them to be maintained in some recognizably mainstream form of education until their disaffection and disruption became too difficult to manage, and then directed them to some more 'relevant' form of provision; burgeoning pastoral systems in the 1970s helped maintain some children in the mainstream whose difficulties might have overwhelmed either themselves or their teachers; and 'on-site units' contained those children who were beyond the capacity even of the pastoral system.

As these interventions and alternative forms of provision continued to blossom, so large secondary schools in particular began to develop complex mixed economies of special or quasi-special education alongside their mainstream provision. It was not uncommon, for instance, for a city comprehensive school in the late 1970s to have one or more special classes, a number of 'lower streams' following a modified curriculum, remedial tuition for significant numbers of pupils, one or more 'disruptive units', a school counsellor, a pastoral team involving, perhaps, a dozen or more teachers on promoted posts, and a series of 'non-examination' groups in the final two years, probably following some sort of 'life-skills' or 'preparation for work' alternative curricular provision.

There is much that could be said about the complex motivations which led to this proliferation of alternatives. What concerns us here, however, is the way in which it constitutes a subtle shift in the resolution of the dilemma which faced the creators of the 1944 Act. The rigid divisions between mainstream and special schooling certainly had not, by the late 1970s, entirely disappeared, but they had been overlain and permeated by a much more flexible system in which 'special' interventions, approaches and forms of provision were imported, replicated or generated within mainstream schools. Sayer (1994/1987) describes responses to diversity such as these as '"garden shed" extensions' (p. 9) and criticizes the failure of mainstream education to develop 'schools for all' where the diversity of the pupil population is seen as the starting point for planning rather than as an afterthought. However, such apparently ramshackle extensions, for all their limitations, enabled schools to find their way pragmatically towards a different resolution of the dilemma created by diversity within a common system – a resolution which realized more fully the increasingly dominant values of equity and participation.

It is out of this context that, from the late 1970s onwards, the form of special needs provision emerged that came to be known as the 'whole school approach' (Dessent, 1987) – that is, an approach which sought to develop means of educating children 'with special needs' alongside their peers in mainstream classrooms and through the mainstream curriculum. This approach will, in the next chapter, form the starting point for our story proper, partly because it continues to dominate much contemporary thinking about special needs education, and partly because it constitutes, we suggest, the first thoroughgoing and explicitly-argued attempt to replace Sayer's 'garden shed extensions' with a structural merger of special and mainstream education. However, it is important to remember that the whole school approach did not appear out of the blue. In seeking to enhance the flexibility and responsiveness of mainstream schools in respect of the diversity of their pupil populations, it was simply the latest in a long line of developments; and in seeking to realize the increasingly dominant values of equity and participation, it was evidence of a shift in social values which had been in train for some time.

As the whole school approach acquired, in the 1980s, something of the status of an orthodoxy in thinking about special needs education, there were good reasons for looking back on the history of this field as one of unbroken progress. The somewhat inflexible categorizations of the 1944 Act had been softened, humanized and liberalized by successive developments which made mainstream schools increasingly flexible and responsive – special classes, remedial education, the proliferation of alternative provisions and interventions and, finally, an apparently coherent whole school approach. Given this history, it was entirely understandable that optimistic commentators in the field should have begun to look forward to the time when that merger would be complete and when, in Dessent's (1987) classic phrase, the 'ordinary' school would become 'special'. Indeed, many of the developments which we shall trace in subsequent chapters of this book will show some elements, at least, of that optimism to have been justified.

However, events have not entirely turned out as many might have hoped. As Sayer somewhat ruefully comments in the second (1994) edition of his book: 'Less political priority has been given to special educational needs in the last decade. . . . Opportunities have been wasted or overlooked' (p. 163). Some might regard this as an understatement of major proportions; special needs education has, they might argue, not so much been overlooked in recent years as thoroughly undermined. They might, with justification, point to the fact that, at the very time that the optimistic accounts of Wolfendale, Sayer and Dessent were being published, the Conservative government was finalizing its 'Great Education Reform Bill'. The latter's introduction of a highly-prescriptive National Curriculum, of a national system of pupil assessment, of local management of schools (LMS), of a quasi-market in education, of increased parental power and of an erosion of the role of the LEA, coupled with years of continuing budgetary constraint and successive waves of educational 'reform', were to have a highly destabilizing effect on special needs education. Far from continuing an inevitable progress towards some ultimate merger of special and mainstream education, pessimists might argue, mainstream schools have become increasingly unwilling or unable to respond to the needs of their most problematic pupils; articulate and well-resourced parents have increasingly manipulated the education system in their own interests, at the expense of more vulnerable children; and schools, rather than committing themselves to the liberal values of equity and participation, have increasingly operated as entrepreneurial and even predatory businesses intent on increasing their market share irrespective of the consequences for their communities or for the education system as a whole.

What has become evident in the years after the 1988 Act is that the apparently inevitable progress towards a merger of special and mainstream education actually depended on the conjunction of a particular set of circumstances. As we have seen, moves towards that merger had gathered momentum at a time when liberal values were increasingly dominant in society, when the economy was growing more or less steadily, and when the education system was exploring the notion of 'comprehensiveness'. By 1988, however, a 'New Right' government was grappling with a recession-hit economy whilst seeking to reconstruct the education system around notions not of participation and equity, but 'choice and diversity'. As the proposed merger has proved highly vulnerable to these changed circumstances, so too have all the previous assumptions about the nature and the inevitability of 'progress' in the field of special needs education.

From the time that Collins (1972) wrote about the 'remedial education hoax', or Galletley (1976) advocated that remedial teachers should 'do away with' themselves, it was possible to believe that, simply by reconstructing itself, special education could embed itself within, and thereby transform, the mainstream. In the 1990s, it is increasingly difficult to hold such views. Special needs provision has certainly contorted itself, over the past thirty years, into a variety of shapes and forms – but it has signally failed to transform the nature of mainstream schools. There are reasons for believing that all that it has achieved by such contortions is the replication and multiplication of special education in a mainstream location, rather than any genuine merger. Certainly, the relationship of special to mainstream education, and the relationship of both to the external social and political environment, are more complex – and more frustrating – than many of us might previously have supposed. If, therefore, we remain committed to the 'old' values of equity and participation, and if we still hold to the ideal of some unspecified and elusive 'merged' form of education, then the task which faces us is daunting indeed. The first step that we need to take may well be to understand the complexities and difficulties of the field within which we work.

THIS BOOK

This book seeks to outline some of the key elements of these complexities and difficulties. In particular, it seeks to trace the fate of the 'bold experiment' which began to be articulated some twenty years ago: that is, the projected realization of 'human values' of equity and participation through a merger of special and mainstream education. In so doing, we hope to reveal something about the nature of special needs education in mainstream schools and, ultimately, about the direction it might take in the next decade or more.

The starting point of our detailed analysis will be the whole school approach as it emerged in the late 1970s and flourished through the 1980s. We shall examine both the promises which the whole school approach held out and the complexities, ambiguities and reversals which accompanied its implementation. We shall see how, as these complexities began to be apparent and as the 1988 Act wrought major changes in the context of special needs education, some schools began to develop more radical, 'innovatory' approaches. Once again, these approaches opened up the possibility of a final merger of special and mainstream education, but, as we shall see, once again they proved to be highly problematic in their implementation. We shall also study the most recent attempt (in the UK context, at least) to merge special and mainstream education – the emergence out of a long tradition of integration of the 'inclusive schools' movement. Although examples of 'inclusive schools' are few and far between in the UK, we shall try to read such straws in the wind as we can find that might indicate the extent to which inclusion is likely finally to realize the values of equity and participation.

The whole school approach, the innovatory approaches of the post-1988 period and inclusive schooling share the characteristic of being largely driven from *within* the field of special needs education itself. However, there have been other, externally-driven changes that have impacted on the possibility of 'progress' – changes such as the rapid emergence of specific learning difficulties as a category of special need, the introduction of the *Code of Practice* (DFE, 1994a) as the most significant government intervention in the field since the 1981 Act, and the reconstruction of the relationship between schools and LEAs. We shall attempt, in later chapters, to analyse the impact and significance of each of these changes for the 'bold experiment', and to understand the relationship between such externally-driven changes and the internal development of the field. Finally, we shall seek to pull the threads of our story together in order to see if it is possible to identify *patterns* of change within special needs education and, if so, what lessons can be learned to help us chart its future.

There have, of course, been many more changes in the field of special needs education in mainstream schools than we have indicated here: one thinks in particular of significant developments in response to 'behaviour difficulties' following from the Elton Report (DES, 1989b) and, more recently, of the government's *Pupils with Problems* circulars (DFE, 1994b); or of the growth of interest in provision for very able learners (Freeman, 1996); or of the impact of vocationalism through, the Technical and Vocational Education Initiative, the introduction of a national system of vocational qualifications and the Dearing reviews of the National Curriculum and post-16 education (DES, 1989a; Dearing, 1994/1996). The omission of these, and many other developments, should not be taken as an indication that we regard them as unimportant. It does, however, reflect a deliberate decision and stance on our part. As we have seen, special needs education is a field which is shot through with questions of ethics and values. The consequence has been, particularly since the advent of the whole school approach, that the literature in the field has been heavily weighted towards the articulation of firmly-held value positions and the advocacy of particular 'approaches' which seem likely to bring about their realization. We readily acknowledge the importance of such advocacy, but feel that it needs to be set alongside empirical evidence. In this way it will be possible to test both the extent to which the advocated approaches succeed in realizing the value positions, and the consequences that follow from attempting value-driven approaches of this kind.

We shall see in the following chapters how, when empirical investigations are undertaken in special needs education, the picture which they reveal is frequently more complex and, indeed, more gloomy than some advocates of 'new' approaches would have us believe. In order, therefore, not to lose this complexity, we have restricted ourselves so far as possible to those aspects of special needs education where we can contribute some empirical data from the various research projects undertaken by the Special Needs Research Centre at Newcastle University and/or some evidence from our own professional experience in schools. Sometimes, those data are rich and substantial – as in the case of the innovatory schools discussed in Chapter 3; at other times, the data are more limited and constitute emerging findings from ongoing work. In every case, however, we regard the empirical element as a touchstone in our attempts to understand the complexities in this field.

Similarly, we have adopted an historical perspective on special needs education. The dominance of advocacy and values in this field has, we suggest, led to an effectively a-historical literature – a literature in which the past is caricatured as embroiled in error and the future is presented unproblematically as a sunlit upland towards which we are inexorably being borne. Our view is perhaps a more sombre one of special needs education in mainstream schools as the outcome of a complex and continuing set of historical processes. Even in this brief introduction, we have seen how the certainties of the post-1944 system became eroded and transformed as social values shifted and as the implications of the forms of provision they created became fully apparent. In much the same way, we will see in the course of this book how values have shifted and forms of provision have emerged and declined over the last decade. In our view, such phenomena are an integral part of this field; the values on which special needs education (however defined) is premised and the context within which it is shaped are constantly changing. There is, therefore, no single end-point towards which we are heading and no blueprint of a form of provision which will be unequivocally 'better' than all others. If we are to make rational and principled decisions about how responses to diversity are to be formulated and managed, we must understand in all their complexity the processes out of which they emerge, the values they embody, and the opportunities for creative action which they contain.

The implication of this is that we will make no attempt in this book to delineate some 'new approach' which will constitute a final resolution of the dilemma of responding to diversity within a common educational framework. Instead, we seek to offer a way of understanding the current situation in special needs education and of learning from its past. As part of this attempt, we will outline in the final chapter a model of what we believe to be the major forces and processes which shape special needs education at any given time. We then believe it is both the responsibility and the prerogative of practitioners, policy-makers and other stakeholders to use this understanding in their own situations in order to make rational, informed and principled decisions.

However, this does not mean that we claim for ourselves some neutral position, detached from the chaotic fray of activity and change within special needs education. Our position as academic researchers and commentators inevitably gives us a particular – and inevitably partial – perspective on that field; our historical and sceptical perspective might well not be so readily available to practitioners who are required to act on a day-by-day, minute-by-minute basis – much less to the 'clients' and 'consumers' of special needs education who are the willing or unwilling 'beneficiaries' of those actions. However, in a values-driven field, a commitment to some set of values is unavoidable – whether that commitment be explicit and explicitly justified, or implicit and assumed. Our explicit commitment is, therefore, to the 'human values' of equity and participation that have enlightened and enlivened so many of our predecessors. In particular, we feel that inclusive education, as it is currently emerging in the UK, offers the best hope at this time of realizing these values more fully, and, in the final chapter in particular, we will say more about what we take the implications of such a commitment to be. However, in line with our mistrust of absolutes and blueprints, we must forewarn readers that we see neither the values nor the forms of inclusive education as being entirely unproblematic.

We therefore welcome and applaud the work of practitioners, policy-makers, 'clients', 'consumers' and other commentators in this field whose task it is to seek and advocate lines of immediate action based on principles of equity and participation. We hope, simply, that this book will help inform those lines of action through a fuller understanding of the difficulties, complexities and ambiguities of the field in which they are located.

A NOTE ON TERMINOLOGY

The language of special needs education is notoriously slippery and, in the view of many, inadequate. For the purposes of this book we have retained, with some unease, much of the traditional terminology within this field, but should, perhaps, clarify the nuances of meaning which we attach to it.

Special needs education we use to designate all those forms of education, both in mainstream and special schools, which are regarded by their practitioners as constituting explicit means of responding to children's 'special' characteristics and 'needs'.

Special education we use to designate those forms of special needs education which are located in special schools and settings.

We prefer to use the term *mainstream education* to indicate those forms of education that are not regarded by their practitioners as 'special'. We prefer stylistically the term *mainstream schools* to the equally acceptable 'regular schools' or 'ordinary schools'. Similarly, for the sake of simplicity in writing about all phases of education, we have tended to use the terms *pupil* and *child* to refer to all learners, though we acknowledge that the terms *student* and *young person* are more appropriate to older learners.

We use the terms *special*, *special needs* and *children with special needs* because these terms are in common usage and have some currency. However, whereas the term 'special education' describes a form of practice and provision which indisputably exists, the term 'children with special needs' is much more contentious. To indicate our unease with this term, and with any lack of an adequate alternative, we have tended to put these terms in quotation marks.

—2

The whole school approach

THE ORIGINS OF THE WHOLE SCHOOL APPROACH

In the first chapter, we saw how the whole school approach arose out of a particular historical context within the education system. The principal elements of that context are vividly illustrated in the *Remedial Teacher's Handbook* – a standard text for practising special educators in mainstream schools, produced by Westwood in 1975. For Westwood, although the 1944 Education Act was premised on humane values of minimal segregation, those values could be further realized by enhancing the capacity of mainstream schools to respond to the diversity of their pupil populations. This effectively meant the importation of special educational techniques into those schools:

> If the standard and scope of special educational help within ordinary schools could only be improved it would probably meet the needs of quite a number of children currently referred for special schooling, as well as more adeqately (*sic*) catering for the needs of slow learners already in the normal school. (p. 150)

For Westwood, such improvement, however, continued to be based on the traditional notion of accurate identification of 'types' of learner and the creation of 'appropriate' forms of provision for each 'type'. He identifies three such categories of children and provision:

i) Children who need 'adaptive education; that is, almost every aspect of the curriculum will be modified to meet their needs and a different methodology employed in their instruction. They will need special provision in terms of accommodation, equipment, and staff wherever the number involved justifies it' (p. 150);

ii) Children 'who need special help only with some aspects of basic skill learning. Their needs can be met either within the normal

class or through withdrawal from the class for special group
work, or through allocation to a special "set" for that subject'
(p. 150); and

iii) '. . . a few children of average or above average mental ability
who have specific learning problems associated with language,
reading, writing, spelling or mathematics, and who require special help. . . . Sometimes this need for remedial help can only be
met by individual tuition' (p. 151).

Such an analysis leads, of course to the 'mixed economy' which was,
as we have seen, typical of the special needs provision increasingly
available within mainstream schools during the 1970s – a mixture of
remedial intervention through withdrawal, placement in special class
or bottom stream or set, and whatever help could be provided within
ordinary classrooms by class teachers. As such, it constituted a blurring of the rigid boundaries established by the 1944 Act between
special and mainstream education and the beginnings of a shift in the
resolution of the major dilemma of how to respond to diversity within a common educational framework. However, it also depended on a
replication of special provision in mainstream schools rather than any
thoroughgoing reconstruction of mainstream education itself. Not
surprisingly, therefore, at the same time as Westwood was writing, this
form of 'remedial education' (as the mixed economy was usually
known) was coming under fire. It had already been pointed out some
years before (Lovell, Johnson and Platts, 1962; Carroll, 1972; Collins,
1972) that the claims of remedial intervention to be able to 'cure' children's learning difficulties to any significant degree were something
of a 'hoax'. Moreover, there was growing awareness that remedial
education as it was practised in the 1970s could, like the rigid special-
mainstream divide itself, be overly 'restrictive' (Brennan, 1974) in
emphasizing pupils' inadequacies, requiring them to focus almost
exclusively on so-called basic skills, and denying them the same social
and cultural opportunities as their peers.

As these criticisms gathered force, the question began to be asked
towards the end of the 1970s, as to whether remedial education could
ever offer a model of provision that would benefit children in the ways
that were claimed. Establishing multiple forms of special provision in
mainstream schools, it appeared, was not only ineffective but also
replicated all the old problems of restriction and segregation. Instead,
therefore, of setting up *alternatives* to mainstream provision, might it
not be better to find ways of *changing* the mainstream so that it became
accessible to a wider range of children? As Golby and Gulliver (1979)
famously asked, was the education system maintaining remedial edu-

cation as an ambulance service when it would be more rational to reform mainstream education so that fewer accidents in learning happened in the first place.

Already, in fact, moves were taking place to develop the alternative form of provision that would come to be known as the 'whole school approach'. As early as 1978, HMI in Scotland (SED, 1978) set forth both a trenchant critique of remedial education as then practised and recommendations for an alternative. Their proposed model differs from remedial education in four crucial respects:

- They start from the assumption that children who have learning difficulties experience those difficulties right across the curriculum; the almost exclusive focus on literacy and 'basic skills' which was characteristic of remedial education is seen as being overly-narrow.
- They identify access to a broad curriculum as a major educational aim; withdrawal, which had been a major strategy of remedial education, is downgraded and schools are explicitly warned against withdrawing children from areas of the curriculum where they might experience success in order to 'remediate' their difficulties.
- Whereas remedial education assumed that children with learning difficulties could only be taught by specialist teachers – and that more such teachers, much better trained – were an essential prerequisite of development in this field – Scottish HMI assume that much teaching of children with learning difficulties could and should be done by class and subject teachers who would learn to incorporate some of the techniques of remedial education within their own repertoires.
- By the same token, remedial teachers, they suppose, would be freed from the sole responsibility of working with children and would be able to become a much more flexible resource within the school, adding 'co-operative teaching' and advisory work with colleagues to their existing repertoire of skills.

Perhaps the most important aspect of Scottish HMI's proposals is the shift in responsibility for the school's response to special needs. Instead of locating that responsibility largely with remedial teachers working outside the mainstream classroom, HMI see it as shared between those teachers and their mainstream colleagues. Working in partnership, they are to create a response to special needs, not in alternative forms of provision and intervention, but within mainstream classrooms, curricula and pedagogies themselves. Special and mainstream education, in other words, are to move a significant step closer together.

Similar developments were also taking place in England (Widlake, 1975; Gains and McNicholas, 1979; Gulliford, 1979; Gains, 1980), where calls grew for the barriers between remedial and mainstream education to be broken down and for a sharing of expertise between teachers in each sector such that pupils with learning difficulties would be enabled to participate more successfully in the mainstream curriculum. By the time Dessent (1987) set out his sophisticated version of a whole school approach which would make 'the ordinary school special' towards the end of the 1980s, that approach had – at the level of rhetoric at least – achieved the status of an orthodoxy. The notion that children with learning difficulties could be educated in mainstream classrooms; that a mixture of in-class support and appropriate teaching techniques adopted by the class teacher together with a judiciously limited amount of withdrawal; that the role of the remedial teacher (now designated 'special educational needs co-ordinator') was to offer support to children and advice to colleagues – all of these tenets were taken largely for granted by policy-makers, LEA advisers and 'well-informed' practitioners alike. Indeed, it is arguable that they continue to be so: the *Code of Practice* (DFE, 1994a), for instance, makes assumptions about the nature of desirable mainstream special needs education that are to all intents and purposes identical with those of Dessent or of the pioneers of the whole school approach.

Given what we saw in Chapter 1 about the values-driven nature of special needs education in mainstream schools, it is significant that Dessent (1987) declared the whole school approach to be essentially 'a question of values' (p. 11). It is, he argues, an attempted 'merger of special education with mainstream education' such that 'ordinary primary and secondary schools can extend the idea of comprehensive education to include those children currently excluded from the mainstream educational system' (p. 1). The values on which it is based, in other words, are those 'human values' of equity and participation that have been so central to special needs education in recent decades. Two questions therefore arise in respect of this 'new' approach. First, how viable has it proved to be? To what extent has it actually proved possible to merge special and mainstream education in the context of ordinary primary and secondary schools? Second – and linked to this – how far has that attempted merger succeeded in overcoming the restrictive and segregatory characteristics of remedial education in order to deliver some recognizable form of 'comprehensive' education to children with special educational needs? How far, in other words, has it realized the values on which it is premised? It is to these questions that we shall now turn.

THE WHOLE SCHOOL APPROACH IN ACTION

Implementation

In response to the first question – the viability of the whole school approach – the picture is far from encouraging. Despite the continued and consistent advocacy of that approach as the way forward for special needs education, it rapidly became obvious that schools were reluctant to abandon their traditional remedial and special class approaches in favour of a whole-hearted commitment to whole school responsibility for special needs (Croll and Moses, 1985; Hinson, 1985). As Dessent (1987) somewhat ruefully pointed out after a decade or more of advocacy: 'Whole school approaches represent the new "Holy Grail" within the field of special education – much talked about, advocated by all but difficult to find in practice' (p. 119).

Although, therefore, certain new forms of organization – notably the use of in-class support and the designation of special needs co-ordinators – were introduced into schools, it seems that they did not so much displace more traditional forms of provision but, rather, were overlain on top of a largely unchanged structure. Even the most recent surveys (Evans *et al.*, 1995; Lewis *et al.*, 1996) continue to show that many schools place a heavy reliance on withdrawal work, 'resource bases' and setting (if not special classes or streams) – that is, on forms of special needs provision which take place outside ordinary classrooms and which seem to offer little by way of a merger of special and mainstream education. This is certainly confirmed by a number of our own ongoing research projects, which suggest that it is the exception rather than the rule for schools to have abandoned withdrawal work – and that, in the few cases where this has happened, this is often simply because the resources to sustain withdrawal are unavailable rather than because of any ideological commitment to including children in mainstream classes.

Moreover, the quality of provision that has been achieved under the aegis of the whole school approach has been, to say the least, patchy. In England and Wales, for instance, the Senior Chief HMI was still able to report as late as 1990 that,

> It is particularly troubling that in some schools some 30%, and in higher and further education some 20%, of what HMI saw was judged poor or very poor. Those figures, if replicated throughout the system, represent a large number of pupils and students getting a raw deal. Furthermore, and sadly, less able pupils and students are much more likely to experience the poor and the shoddy than are the more able: a worryingly persistent feature of English education at all levels. (HMI, 1990, para. 4)

A year later, Senior Chief HMI (HMI, 1991) was, if anything, even more damning:

> There are worryingly poor standards among particular groups and in particular parts of the education service. They are serious, and almost all, regrettably, are of long standing. They include . . . the less academically able who continue to suffer disproportionately from whatever chronic or acute problems affect the education service. (Para. 9)

Or again,

> The quality of work with pupils and students with SEN is variable . . . provision for the wide range of SEN is not in good shape to respond to the needs of the next decade. (Para. 30)

Or again,

> In too many [ordinary] schools, however, the physical, social and academic aspects of integration are less effective than they ought to be, as a result of inadequate planning and monitoring of the day-to-day experience of the pupils involved. (Para. 75)

Many of Senior Chief HMI's comments in the 1990 report were based on a major survey of special needs provision undertaken by HMI in 1988–9 (DES, 1989). This survey continued to advocate many of the strategies of the whole school approach – in-class support rather than withdrawal, differentiated teaching in ordinary classrooms, the central role of the special needs co-ordinator, and so on – but was not at all optimistic about the extent to which these strategies had been adopted effectively by schools. Pupils were still being faced with work which was too demanding or contained too little challenge; withdrawal work persisted to the detriment of the curriculum as a whole and was itself sometimes not appropriately differentiated; communications between SEN specialists and class and subject teachers were poor; curricula were narrow (despite the imminence of the National Curriculum); SENCOs, where they existed, were frequently under-trained, whilst class and subject teachers also had received little training.

To be sure, the reports of HMI in the late 1980s and early 1990s also contain many comments about special needs provision which are positive and point to some areas of improvement. However, the overall picture certainly does not indicate either that the whole school approach had been implemented wholeheartedly or that it had succeeded in addressing the long-standing limitations of special needs provision in ordinary schools.

Interestingly, a not dissimilar picture also emerges in Scotland. Following the seminal HMI progress report (SED, 1978), the Scottish education system embraced a version of the whole school approach – known as 'Learning Support' – which was more heavily supported and planned at national level than was the case in England. Whilst problems with the whole school approach in England might to some extent be attributable to the piecemeal way in which it was developed across the country, this was certainly not the case north of the border. Nonetheless, as late as 1993 (HM Inspectors of Schools: Audit Unit, 1993) we find HMI reporting a series of weaknesses in schools' policies and procedures for Learning Support:

- support in English language and mathematics only;
- inadequate collaboration between class teachers and specialists;
- inadequate matching of pace, resources or tasks to perceived needs;
- inappropriate withdrawal of pupils from mainstream activities. (Section 5.0)

At about the same time, independent research by Allan *et al.* (1991) reported a number of problematic aspects of the implementation of Learning Support approaches: there was no agreement – particularly across phases – as to the definition of learning difficulties or the aims of intervention; the role of learning support teachers was fundamentally different across primary and secondary phases; although HMI recommended that such teachers should adopt a collaborative and consultative role with their mainstream colleagues, in reality they were rarely able to make such a role effective; although learning support staff were expected to collaborate with both parents and external agencies (notably educational psychologists), these collaborations were fraught with misunderstandings and difficulties. Again, neither this research nor HMI reports in Scotland are by any means unequivocally negative; but neither do they point to an unproblematic implementation of the whole school approach, even under these highly favourable circumstances.

There does, then, seem to be good evidence that the whole school approach has proved to be difficult to implement and that the proposed merger of special and mainstream education has not produced the high-quality responses to children's learning needs that were anticipated. Moreover, in addition to problems with the approach overall, there have been difficulties in relation to the preferred forms of provision within it, and it is to these that we now wish to turn.

FORMS OF PROVISION

Support teaching

As the whole school approach has evolved, certain forms of provision have come to be seen as the dominant means whereby the merger of special and mainstream education was to be realized. Foremost amongst these has been in-class support teaching, or co-operative teaching as it was known in Scotland. On the face of it, support teaching is a relatively unproblematical strategy, based on the notion that special needs and mainstream teachers should work together in the same classroom, combining their skills to enable children with learning and other difficulties to be maintained in a mainstream setting. As such, it appears to be an unequivocal realization of the aim of merging previously separate forms of provision.

However, any examination of the way in which support teaching has been defined within the whole school approach reveals that, as a strategy, it is in fact highly ambiguous. As support teaching became established, so commentators began to note the complexities of its aims (Hart, 1986; Visser, 1986; Dyer, 1988; Best, 1991). These, it became clear, could be conceptualized in at least three ways:

- support to individual pupils, enabling them to function within a classroom and curriculum which would otherwise be inimical to their learning;
- support to the class teacher, enabling her/him to manage a class containing problematic pupils who might otherwise make teaching difficult;
- support to the development of appropriate curriculum and pedagogy within which *all* children would be able to learn effectively.

The difficulties which the existence of these alternatives creates are twofold. First, it means that, as Hart (1986) points out, 'no generally agreed definition of support teaching actually exists' (p. 26). The term 'support teaching' in fact encompasses quite different strategies with quite different aims which are simply masked by a common organizational form. More than this, however, the multiple aims of support teaching actually stand in contradiction to one another. As Bines (1986) reports, a strategy which offers support to class teachers in continuing to work in ways which are essentially inappropriate to some children in the class is hardly likely at the same time to persuade those teachers to change their ways of working. There was, therefore, a fundamental contradiction between support teaching as a strategy for change and support teaching as a means of maintaining the status quo.

The consequence was inevitable: support teachers would find the developmental aspect of support teaching increasingly difficult to realize and would therefore find themselves confined to supporting pupils and teachers within an unreconstructed classroom situation. As early as 1982, a study by Ferguson and Adams showed that this is precisely what was happening (Ferguson and Adams, 1982). Working within the Scottish context, where the whole school approach had been formalized relatively early, and where a major emphasis was placed on a developmental relationship between special needs and class teachers, Ferguson and Adams investigated the support teaching practice of some forty-one teachers. Their findings make sobering reading:

- Only five of the forty-one teachers jointly prepared and taught lessons with class teachers, and only eighteen had ever addressed the whole class – and then usually only briefly.
- Support teachers were confined to a somewhat passive, low status role within the classroom, with little prospect of having a catalytic effect on the class teacher's teaching style: 'Nearly all remedial teachers are cast in the role of teachers' aides or more accurately are "the classroom's faithful retainers"' (pp. 26–7).
- By and large, support teachers accepted their limited role, while class teachers defended their dominance over the classroom.
- The majority of both support and class teachers felt that support teaching was of less benefit to pupils with special needs than withdrawal work – an indication of a lack of commitment to the support teaching process, if nothing else.

There is, unfortunately, no reason to suppose that things have improved since the early 1980s. Despite a constant stream of exhortation for schools to deploy support teaching as a major strategy for special needs provision, *empirical* investigations of support teaching in action (Bines, 1986; DES, 1989a; Allan *et al.*, 1991; Thomas, 1992; Best, 1991/1994; HM Inspectors of Schools: Audit Unit, 1993; Lovey, 1996) tend to point to the same problems that Ferguson and Adams highlight. Conflicts between class and support teachers, ambiguities surrounding the support role and uncertainties as to the effectiveness of that role are, it seems, endemic in this aspect of the merger of mainstream and special education.

Differentiation
In the early versions of the whole school approach, the merger of mainstream and special education techniques was conceptualized

principally in terms of 'remedial education across the curriculum' (SED, 1978; Gulliford, 1979). The implication seems to have been that the specialized techniques of remedial teaching would be *imported* into ordinary classrooms so that pupils with special needs would be taught through the specialist approaches which had previously been confined to withdrawal situations. However, the growing interest in notions of a common curriculum meant that the simple importation of remedial techniques gradually came to seem inadequate to meeting the learning needs of the full range of pupils. Instead, the view emerged that teaching – and in particular, learning tasks – had to be adapted, or *differentiated*, in a variety of ways in order to meet these needs. The introduction of a closely-prescribed National Curriculum to which all children were to be given 'access' had the effect of making this notion of differentiation a central plank in most schools' responses to the 'special needs' of their pupils and of leading to its widespread advocacy in official guidance (NCC, 1989; SCCC, 1993) and elsewhere. For writers such as Dessent (1987), for instance, the whole school approach was inseparable from a differentiated curriculum:

> The whole school response will essentially be a response to meeting the *individual needs* of children. As such it is not just about the size and shape of a school's special needs department – although the work of such a department will be vital . . . most importantly, it will affect school curriculum, by which is meant all the opportunities for learning provided by a school. The search for a whole school approach to meeting special needs runs parallel to the search for a 'differentiated curriculum' – a curriculum responsive to individual needs. (pp. 120–1)

Despite this advocacy in both the official and the academic literature, however, the realization of differentiation in practice seems to have been patchy in the extreme. Quite apart from the incessant stream of individual school reports from HMI and (latterly) Ofsted which point out the inadequacies of schools' approaches to differentiation, there has long been evidence of endemic problems in teachers' attempts to match learning activities to pupils' abilities and attainments – particularly where those abilities and attainments are relatively low (Bennett *et al.*, 1984). Part of the problem, at least, seems to be that the concept of differentiation is a somewhat nebulous one. Writers such as Dessent, for instance, are reluctant to tie differentiation down too closely to a specific set of techniques, seeing it instead as more a question of attitudes and values:

The development of a differentiated curriculum – a curriculum adapted to the abilities, backgrounds and interests of all pupils – is the ultimate goal of a whole school approach. Such a curriculum will not arise outside of an educational philosophy which nurtures and facilitates it. The first questions to be addressed are questions of value rather than of educational technology or, indeed, questions concerning the organization of special needs provision. However, prevailing values, attitudes and educational philosophy will not always be conducive to these ends. (1987, p. 137)

If Dessent is right to argue that differentiation goes beyond technology to questions of value, then he is also right to point out the potential for conflicts of value. As Weston (1992) argues,

The real problem goes beyond the clumsiness of the word and the difficulty of pinning down a definition. The problem is that if the inquirer asks a range of education professionals 'Just what do you mean by differentiation? What are the practical implications?' he or she could receive conflicting definitions, each carrying with it a train of educational beliefs and practices. (p. 6)

Weston goes on to cite the work of Stradling and Saunders (1991), who identify two fundamentally different interpretations of differentiation – one which seeks to respond to individual differences within a common setting and framework, and one which seeks to offer different educational experiences to different groups of pupils.

This ambiguity appears to have two major consequences. First, it makes it difficult for schools to know what, precisely, it is that they are supposed to do in order to 'differentiate'. Certainly the palpable confusion of many teachers about differentiation, suggest that this is a continuing problem and the stream of critical HMI and Ofsted reports lends further weight to this view. Differentiation may not be reducible to a technology, but without an agreed and viable set of techniques, how, precisely, are schools to turn their values into practice? Second, some commentators have identified the danger that differentiation may be used to realize values and attitudes that are diametrically opposed to those which it appears to imply. They argue that differentiation in practice is less about giving a wide range of children access to common educational experiences than it is about setting children on separate tracks within the same classroom and under the umbrella of a 'common' curriculum. Thompson and Barton (1992), for instance, suggest that the notion of difference underpinning much differentiation is 'not "different but equal" but "different and unequal"' and that differentiation might, therefore, constitute 'a mechanism for exclusion' (p. 14). They argue that attempts at differentiation have to be seen in the context of a fundamentally inequitable education system in which the 'less able' are held in low esteem, and under-resourced teachers are expected to 'deliver' to them a fundamentally inappropriate curriculum. Similarly, Hart (1992) argues that differentiation is simply a means of introducing a sort of disguised segregation by emphasizing the ways in which children differ rather than the learning needs they have in common: 'The focus on differentiation risks taking us back a stage or more, because it encourages us to focus on individual learners and their differing needs rather than using the links between them as a resource for curriculum adaptation and development' (p. 10). Far from constituting a means of merging special and mainstream education, she argues, differentiation simply reinforces the differences between the two:

> It disregards the most important insight arising from experience of special needs work over the past decade. This is the role which learning difficulties can play in highlighting possibilities for enhancing teaching and learning to the benefit of *all* children. Rather than emphasizing differences, we need a way forward which emphasizes the *links* between special educational needs and the needs of all learners. . . . (p. 10)

The role of the special needs co-ordinator

Proponents of the whole school approach have consistently argued that one of its major implications was a change in role for special needs teachers (SED, 1978; Gains and McNicholas, 1979; NARE, 1985; Dessent, 1987). The direction of this change was outlined by Gains (1980):

> . . . remedial education can only be conceived within the context of the general aims of education. Remedial education, therefore, should be available across the whole curriculum. This opens up exciting prospects for new partnerships between class teacher, subject specialist and remedial exponent. The specialist remedial teacher should be in the business of giving away his or her skills, at the same time being aware of the potential every area of the curriculum has for supporting and reinforcing traditional basic skills. (p. 8)

And again,

> . . . the concept of remedial education across the curriculum may
> open up the most dramatic change of role. This could see an end to
> withdrawal methods, except in the most extreme cases. Here a
> child's needs are met in terms of his total tuition. The remedial
> teacher would act as co-ordinator, catalyst and resource agency. As
> yet there are no clear models for this which must be based on team
> teaching, an idea still foreign to most institutions. (p. 9)

In broad terms, the outline of the new role is relatively clear: the specialist approaches characteristic of remedial education were to be
made available right across the curriculum; in order to achieve this,
the remedial specialist would give away his/her specialist skills so
that they became the common property of all teachers. This meant in
turn that the remedial specialist had to become a catalyst of change in
the pedagogy of the ordinary teacher, a resource-agency for their new
style of teaching, and co-ordinator of their efforts across the school.
Thus understood, the newly-designated 'special educational needs
co-ordinator' would become the central agent in the merger of mainstream and special education. Given, however, that the special needs
co-ordinator was to operate, in part at least, through the management
of support teaching and the promotion of differentiation, it is scarcely
surprising that the operationalization of the role has been fraught with
difficulties. The small number of empirical studies of that operationalization that have been undertaken (Bines, 1986; O'Hanlon, 1988;
Allan *et al.*, 1991; Norwich, 1993), together with some more reflective
pieces on the role in practice written by special needs teachers themselves (Andrews, 1989; Burroughs, 1989) point to two fundamental
problems for co-ordinators.

In the first place, the co-ordinator's role has proved difficult to define
with any precision; Gains' observation that, 'as yet there are no clear
models' of the role probably rings as true in the late 1990s as it did in
1980. Such attempts as there have been have tended to take the form
less of models than of lengthy lists of activities and responsibilities; the
Code of Practice (DFE, 1994a), with its specification of seven major
responsibilities is simply the latest in a long line of such lists (e.g. SED,
1978; NARE, 1985; Gains, 1994). Behind the surface precision of these
lists lies a series of problems. In particular, it is not always clear how
the diverse responsibilities of the co-ordinator are to be managed so
that they form a coherent whole, nor, indeed, whether they are mutually compatible. NARE (1985), for instance, advocated eight 'roles' for
the co-ordinator:

- an assessment role;
- a prescriptive role (in the sense of prescribing teaching programmes for pupils);
- a teaching/pastoral role;
- a supportive role;
- a liaison role (with schools, parents and other professionals);
- a management role;
- a staff development role.

There is, however, no indication as to when each role should come into play, or what sort of balance is to be struck between them. Moreover, it is not at all clear that the prescription and delivery of teaching programmes is compatible with staff development and supportive roles aimed at persuading and enabling mainstream colleagues to teach children with special needs.

This latter problem of mutually incompatible roles centres very much on notions of responsibility and specialist knowledge which seem never to have been fully worked out within the whole school approach. It became common for co-ordinators and commentators to argue along these lines: 'Remedial teachers must disclaim the myth that teaching pupils with special needs requires approaches, methods and techniques not available to, or outside the repertoire of, the subject teacher' (Lewis, 1984, p. 7). Such disclaimers placed special needs teachers in a position to argue that mainstream colleagues should take responsibility for pupils with special needs. However, if they were successful in making this disclaimer, then what purpose did they serve within the school – at least after an interim period of 'giving away' their skills? Why did they not, as Galletley (1976) suggested, simply 'do away with' themselves? If, on the other hand, they did not uphold this disclaimer, and their specialist skills were indeed necessary for the education of children with special needs, then what was the meaning of a whole school approach premised on placing those children in mainstream classrooms to be taught by mainstream subject and class teachers? What seems to have been missing from the 'list' approach to defining the role, in other words, is any coherent rationale underpinned by a fundamental purpose which would resolve such dilemmas and enable the disparate elements of the role to be reconciled (Dyson and Gains, 1995). It is scarcely surprising, therefore, if special needs co-ordinators have interpreted their roles very differently, or have found themselves unable to discharge that role in any balanced manner.

The second problematical aspect of operationalizing the new role was the difficulty which special needs co-ordinators frequently encountered in bringing about the changes in the rest of the school that their redefined role depended upon for its viability. The new role needed, as we have seen, to be interpreted and operationalized; however, the interests of many (if not all) class and subject teachers led them to resist any interpretation which would require fundamental reconstruction of their practice. As Bines (1986) put it,

> Remedial and subject teachers may be able to work together to minimize the effects of . . . demands and constraints upon provision for pupils with learning difficulties, but in some cases there may well be conflict or the remedial teacher may be no more than an 'aide', finding perhaps that although the 'goods' of support are being provided, the 'price', of sharing decisions or instituting change is not being paid. Given the traditional low and marginal status of remedial teachers and the continued dominance of subject hierarchies, the latter outcome may well have to be expected, particularly if the constraints of not having enough remedial staff and time to develop close collaboration are not resolved. (pp. 120–1)

This resistance, of course, does not stop at the level of class teachers; by no means all headteachers have been willing to bring about radical reorganization within their schools and accord the special needs co-ordinator the status and authority which their change-agent role demanded. Moreover, the uncertainties and ambiguities experienced by co-ordinators themselves made it difficult for many of them to push unequivocally for change in any one direction. In particular, many co-ordinators found that their commitment to the well-being of individual disadvantaged children has made them reluctant to abandon those children entirely to the mercies of sometimes hostile class and subject teachers, and therefore constantly drew them back into a more traditional individual-intervention role.

A major consequence of this has been the subversion of the catalytic change-agency aspect of the co-ordinator's role. Co-ordinators constantly found – and continue to find – that those aspects of their role which brought them into closest contact with their mainstream colleagues and apparently provided most opportunities for changing practice within the mainstream of the school were also the aspects which they were least able to carry out (Bines, 1986; Allan *et al.*, 1991; SOED, 1993). Whilst the withdrawal of children with special needs and the provision of some form of in-class support continued to be widely welcomed, attempts at involvement in curriculum planning, at genuinely co-operative teaching, or at whole school development planning were, in many schools, much less easy to get off the ground.

The consequence was, as Bines (1986) pointed out, many special needs co-ordinators finding that, rather than promoting and enabling change in the mainstream of the school, they were simply providing a sort of safety-net service which allowed the mainstream to proceed in an unreconstructed manner. Instead of *merging* mainstream and special education into some new form of provision, they were, if anything, simply *relocating* special services within a mainstream setting.

THE WHOLE SCHOOL APPROACH: PATTERNS OF FAILURE

It is, perhaps, too sweeping a statement to say that the whole school approach has been a 'failure'. If, throughout this chapter, we have emphasized its limitations and shortcomings, that is partly, at least, to redress the imbalance that has been produced in the literature by an almost endless stream of advocacy and exhortation that has taken the whole school approach to be largely unproblematic. It is, therefore, as well to acknowledge, that special needs provision in ordinary schools is different in many significant respects from the sort of provision which Westwood advocated in the mid-1970s, and that these changes have undoubtedly been produced under the umbrella of the whole school approach.

On the other hand, the whole school approach can scarcely be regarded as an unmitigated triumph. We have seen how patchy was its implementation, and how partial its attempted merger of mainstream and special education. If, some twenty years after the first stirrings of the 'new approach', we can still find extensive use of withdrawal for remedial teaching and of the grouping of 'less able' pupils in 'bottom sets' following a somewhat restricted curriculum, then it is fairly evident that no effective and widespread merger has yet taken place. The question that arises, then, is why the whole school approach has failed in at least some of its ambitions. Is this simply an indication of the endemic difficulties of educational change, or is there an underlying pattern of causation which we can identify?

At this stage, it is possible to identify three principal factors that are implicated in this failure:

1. Resistance from the mainstream
The projected 'merger' of mainstream and special education, however forcefully advocated in some quarters, never succeeded in winning over a significant number of mainstream schools and teachers. On the contrary, it seems to have succeeded in some cases only in generating conflict between mainstream and special educators – a conflict which the latter, from their somewhat marginalized position, have never

been likely to win. The consequence of this, of course, was that the 'merger' of mainstream and special education tended to be a somewhat one-sided affair, with the latter reconstructing itself in order to take its place in ordinary schools and classrooms whilst the former remained substantially unchanged.

2. Replication of special education

Whether as a result of overt resistance, covert subversion, or simple failures of understanding, the whole school approach appears to have succeeded less in merging special and mainstream education than in allowing the former to be *replicated* within the latter. Differentiation, in-class support and the work of the special needs co-ordinator all look very different from 'traditional' special education. As we have seen, however, rather traditional notions of segregated and alternative education can sometimes be found beneath these changed forms. Indeed, without the necessary reconstruction of mainstream education, it is difficult to see what else special education could do than fulfil its traditional role of providing a more 'appropriate' alternative for children who were failing in their ordinary classes.

3. Internal ambiguities and contradictions

This in turn points to an essential ambiguity – perhaps, even, contradiction – in the project of the whole school approach. Special education, by the late 1970s, already had a long history based on 'individually-appropriate' forms of provision – alternative curricula, adapted pedagogy, specialist teachers, and so on. All of this was very different from the traditional emphasis of mainstream education on group teaching, the delivery of curriculum content and the development of 'academic' knowledge and skills.

What, then, did the 'merger' of special and mainstream education actually mean? What was the 'new form' of education which was to encompass the other two; indeed, what could it be, given that mainstream and special education had operated under such different circumstances and on the basis of such different aims and assumptions? There have, of course been many attempts to resolve this ambiguity by positing a relationship between special and mainstream education which would make them mutually compatible. The Warnock Report, for instance, characterized special educational provision as something 'additional or supplementary' to mainstream education (DES, 1978, 3.45), whilst Fish (1989) regarded it as a 'variation' of certain aspects of 'everyday education' aimed at meeting the needs of particular children. Such attempts, however, left the ambiguity unresolved: if special education is different from mainstream education (even in being 'more of the same'), then how can the two be merged without one or other giving up its essential characteristics; and if some merger is possible by means of the invention of a 'new form' of education, then what precisely does this new form look like?

It is our contention that the whole school approach failed adequately to answer these questions. There was (as there continues to be in special needs education) much advocacy of the 'human values' of equity and participation, but precious little engagement with the practical issues of how those values could be operationalized, or what happened in schools and classrooms which attempted to put them into practice. Instead, there was an optimistic belief that if these values permeated the education system, the technology for their implementation would materialize in some unspecified way. Even as sophisticated a commentator as Dessent, therefore, could declare: 'Whole school approaches to special needs begin and end with questions of value, philosophy, and the attitude of teachers and headteachers' (1987, p. 121).

It is hardly surprising, therefore, if attempts to adopt the whole school approach proved more problematical and complex than its advocates supposed, if the laudable values of equity and participation seemed somewhat ambiguous in practice, and if the 'merger' of the two forms of education simply resulted in the replication of special education in the mainstream.

The whole school approach was formulated amidst high hopes of a merger of mainstream and special education. There is no doubt that, under its aegis, significant changes were wrought in the surface forms of special needs provision: remedial teachers were indeed replaced by special needs co-ordinators; some level of in-class support became common in many schools; and many class and subject teachers came to see themselves as having an explicit responsibility to 'differentiate the curriculum'. In some schools, these superficial changes may have been indications of a more fundamental change which betokened a response to pupil diversity quite different from anything that would have been possible in, say, the 1970s. However, the extent to which such fundamental reconstructions took place on a widespread basis must be in great doubt. After the initial enthusiasm for the whole school approach, the evidence began to accumulate about its limitations and its complexities. By the late 1980s, as the advocacy of ever-more-radical versions of the approach grew, so did the awareness of many in schools that the whole school approach was failing to live up to its promises. Moreover, the late 1980s were momentous times;

the major changes signalled by the 1988 Education Act posed new challenges and opened up new opportunities. Creative and committed teachers in some schools were only too eager to rethink their approaches in the light of this changed situation – and it is to their attempts to rethink special needs that we now wish to turn.

Beyond the whole school approach?

In the late 1980s, the received wisdom may still have been that the whole school approach offered the best way forward for special needs provision. However, two significant forces for change came into play which led some schools, at least, to develop their approaches in somewhat different directions. The first of these was the awareness amongst special needs teachers and others who had conscientiously sought to implement the whole school approach, of the limitations and difficulties outlined in the previous chapter. Hence, whilst some special needs teachers were still feeling their way towards a whole school approach for the first time, others were becoming sceptical of its ability to deliver the sorts of fundamental changes they believed necessary.

Equally, if not more important, were the implications for special needs provision of the 1988 Education Reform Act. It is no accident that neither the 1988 Act as a whole nor the National Curriculum which it introduced had much to say about special needs provision. The basic framework of the 1981 Act was reiterated and a system for exempting children from National Curriculum requirements was introduced (though the latter was accompanied by guidance which discouraged its use (NCC, 1989)). The main thrust of the reforms, however, was directed towards mainstream provision in ordinary schools – and in particular towards the governance of schools and the nature of the curriculum. Special needs provision would have to wait until the 1993 Act before it received an equally thorough review.

Nonetheless, this relative neglect of special needs provision was precisely what caused the 1988 Act to have such an impact in this area. Whereas special needs had historically been treated as the subject of separate legislation – the 1981 Act is a case in point – and had, therefore, constituted an *administratively* separate system, the 1988 Act effectively treated special needs as part and parcel of mainstream education. On the one hand, this meant that children with special needs were in some danger of losing part of the protection which legislation had hitherto afforded them. On the other hand, it meant that some of the barriers that had separated mainstream and special education were – whether by default or otherwise – removed. There is indeed a case for saying that the 1988 Act did more to promote the 'merger' of special needs and mainstream education by default than the whole school approach had been able to achieve by intent.

This was most obviously the case in terms of the curriculum. For all Warnock's achievements in removing or lowering some of the boundaries between special needs and mainstream education, the commitment of the Warnock Report (DES, 1978) to the notion of a common curriculum was actually rather weak:

> We hold that education has certain long-term goals, that it has a general point or purpose, which can be definitely, though generally, stated. The goals are twofold, different from each other, but by no means incompatible. They are, first, to enlarge a child's knowledge, experience and imaginative understanding, and thus his awareness of moral values and capacity for enjoyment; and secondly, to enable him to enter the world after formal education is over as an active participant in society and a responsible contributor to it, capable of achieving as much independence as possible. The educational needs of every child are determined in relation to these goals. We are fully aware that for some children the first of these goals can be approached only by minute, though for them highly significant steps, while the second may never be achieved. But this does not entail that for these children the goals are different. The purpose of education for all children is the same; the goals are the same. But the help that individual children need in progressing towards them will be different. (1.4)

The rhetoric of common goals is impressive (and, indeed, so it was at a time only shortly after some children had ceased to be regarded as 'ineducable'). However, two features of this commitment are notable. First, the goals are expressed at a level of considerable generality; they take the form of statements of desirable personal attributes rather than a commitment to the teaching of anything in particular. The curriculum is not so much an end in itself, to be specified in sufficient detail to make its delivery possible, as a *means* to achieving broader educational goals. As such, it has to be developed and devised in response to needs and circumstances rather than being predetermined and imposed on schools.

Second, the notion that different children will make different progress towards these goals, and will need different forms of help in pursuing them, opens the way for separate forms of provision, offering 'alternative' or 'modified' curricula that would be quite different from mainstream curricula but that would nonetheless fall under the broad umbrella of Warnock's 'goals'. It is interesting to consider how far the notions first of 'remedial education across the curriculum' and then of the 'whole school approach' did *in themselves* challenge this separation of curricula. Certainly, the whole school approach had the aim of locating children in mainstream classes alongside their peers who were following a mainstream curriculum. However, it was not primarily a curriculum-focused, let alone a curriculum-development, movement. The *nature* of the mainstream curriculum seems to have been a matter that was largely taken for granted, as the approach focused on questions of organization and access.

The National Curriculum, on the other hand, introduced for the first time a curriculum for all (or nearly all) children which was specified at the level of detail rather than generality. Attainment targets and programmes of study set out specific content to be mastered and skills to be acquired, rather than broad goals to be pursued. Although it was technically possible to disapply certain National Curriculum requirements in respect of particular children with special educational needs, such disapplications were relatively infrequent (particularly in mainstream schools) and official guidance was to the effect that they should not be used as a routine response to children's learning difficulties (NCC, 1989a and b). Moreover, in contrast to the situation even in Scotland (SCCC, 1993), the English National Curriculum made no provision for alternative routes through a broad common entitlement, requiring that children with special needs progress up the same curricular ladders as all other children – albeit at a different pace.

It is scarcely surprising, therefore, that HMI reports following the introduction of the National Curriculum (DES, 1989a; HMI, 1990/1992) noted some restructuring of curricular provision in ordinary schools for children with special needs. Interviews which we ourselves conducted with special needs co-ordinators at about this time suggested that the management of this new situation was the major challenge which they faced. On the one hand, they had to come to terms with the implications for their role – how were they to master nine or ten content-heavy subject areas; how were they to manage withdrawal work, or at any rate the teaching that had taken place in withdrawal sessions if participation in all subjects was statutorily required; and what was to happen to the alternative curricula they had offered? On the other hand, they had to manage relations with subject and class teachers who were preoccupied not with special needs pro-

vision, but with 'delivering' the new curriculum and with maximiz-
ing the achievements of their pupils in ways which would manifest
themselves in 'league tables'.

The impact of the National Curriculum cannot be divorced from the
impact of the governance provisions of the 1988 Act. Much has been
made of how the introduction of open enrolment and the local management of schools had the effect, as one group of commentators put
it, of placing 'Warnock in the market place' (Riddell and Brown, 1994).
Hitherto, special needs education was something for which schools
had been resourced (more or less adequately) by their LEAs and which
they had had little choice in undertaking. Whatever the personal feel-
ings of heads and other teachers, children with special needs were, for
the most part, allocated to the school as part of its catchment area by
the LEA, and constituted part of an overall population to which the
school had an unavoidable obligation.

The 1988 Act changed this situation in subtle – and not-so-subtle –
ways. As the notion of catchment areas gave way to parental choice of
schools, so individual schools were able to exercise some control, however marginal, over their intakes, either by openly discouraging some
parents or (more probably) by setting out to recruit certain others.
Schools also gained greater control over their resources. Rather than
receiving the bulk of those resources in the form of staffing – the pattern of which had to be agreed, if not determined, by the LEA – they
began to receive financial resources, enabling them much more readily to determine their own pattern of provision. Since, moreover, the
amount of financial resource was determined by the numbers of
pupils in the school, there were strong incentives for schools to make
themselves as attractive as possible to parents of prospective pupils.

The implication for children with special needs was perhaps not as
simple as has sometimes been portrayed. Certainly, such children
were now increasingly vulnerable to decisions by schools to withdraw
resources from them and devote them to other activities which would
make the school more attractive in the market place (Bowers, 1995;
Vincent *et al.*, 1995). However, this can be seen as part of a somewhat
broader shift which recontextualized special needs provision in mainstream schools. Such provision had previously been made within a
heavily-LEA-determined framework, which left schools with relatively little freedom to determine their priorities and responses.
Post-1988, however, the framework was much more one of school-
level decision-making. If some (indeed, many) schools used their
increased autonomy to relegate special needs provision within their
list of priorities, this should not disguise from us the *requirement* which
schools now had, to consider special needs in the context of whole

school resourcing and the setting of strategic priorities, nor the *opportunities* which this opened up for a rethinking of the place of special needs provision within the school as a whole.

The situation post-1988 was, therefore, a veritable melting pot of contradictory tendencies: on the one hand there was a National Curriculum that was highly prescriptive and designed without reference to children with special needs, together with a system of local management which made such children vulnerable; on the other hand, the National Curriculum and new systems of governance opened up for schools considerable opportunities for refocusing their special needs provision. No doubt there were many schools where the whole school approach may never have gained more than a foothold or where external circumstances were particularly disadvantageous, in which the threats of the post-1988 situation significantly outweighed the opportunities. However, there were others, where dissatisfactions with the whole school approach had already led to explorations of ways in which its limitations might be overcome, and where the opportunities afforded by the new situation acted as a further stimulus to the development of something that would be 'beyond the whole school approach' (Dyson, Millward and Skidmore, 1995). It is to developments in these schools that we wish to direct our attention.

The studies
The studies in the remainder of this chapter took four forms:

- First, and most informally, the authors worked more or less closely with a number of schools which were actively seeking to develop their special needs provision in the light of the 1988 Act.
- Second, they undertook more extended consultancies with a group of secondary special needs co-ordinators who were concerned to find a way through the challenging situation which they saw themselves faced with, both as a result of the 1988 Act and as a result of the underlying tensions within the whole school approach.
- Third, they undertook a national survey aimed at identifying and analysing innovatory special needs practice in ordinary schools. The investigation took the form of a questionnaire survey with follow-up field visits to more than 200 primary and secondary schools nominated by LEAs and other key informants. The work was sponsored initially by the University of Newcastle and subsequently by the DFE, and its detailed outcomes have been published elsewhere (Dyson, 1992; Clark *et al.*,1995).

• Fourth, they undertook more detailed case studies in a small number of schools identified by the national survey, seeking to understand the factors which facilitated innovation in these schools and to understand in more depth the nature and limitations of the approaches to special needs which these schools were seeking to develop. This work was funded by the University of Newcastle. Some of these studies have been reported elsewhere (Dyson, Millward and Skidmore, 1994; Clark *et al.*, 1995), and will be referred to in subsequent chapters.

Varied as this range of studies may be, it cannot, of course, claim to have identified every development that has taken place in schools following the 1988 Act. However, our own findings receive some confirmation from a small but significant body of literature which reports similar developments elsewhere (Luscombe, 1993; Montacute, 1993; Ainscow, 1994; Dyson and Gains, 1995). We therefore believe that it is possible to characterize with some confidence the broad trends of development which took place between the 1988 and 1993 Education Acts.

The emerging model
The expectation, however naïve, with which we started our inquiries was that the combination of the 1988 Act and the working out of tensions within the whole school approach might be leading to the development of some entirely new form of special needs provision in ordinary schools. Certainly, there had been points in the history of special needs education where such new forms – special classes, remedial teaching, in-class support – had emerged as alternatives to preceding ways of organizing provision, and there is no obvious reason why something different should not appear to replace them.

In fact, the situation we found was somewhat more complex than this. Most strikingly, there is no evidence that any single new strategy or form of provision emerged in schools following the 1988 Act. By and large, the established strategies – in particular, in-class support and differentiation – were continuing to flourish even in the most 'innovative' schools and, moreover, continued to form the foundation of those schools' approaches to special needs. There are perhaps two exceptions to this. The first is that in some schools, withdrawal work was falling into disfavour, and indeed, was sometimes being openly opposed as a segregatory form of provision. However, this was by no means a universal phenomenon, was in any case a trend that was evident within the whole school approach, and, indeed, there was some contrary evidence of a resurgence of withdrawal as a form of provision for certain children (see Chapter 6). The second exception is that in some schools, particularly secondary schools and larger primary schools, there was evidence of a reconstruction of the role of the special needs co-ordinator – a theme to which we shall return below. However, in general terms it is true to say that if there were any new developments following the 1988 Act they were not to be found in the surface features of the provision made by schools.

Moreover, not only was there no single 'new' form of provision, but the detailed organization of approaches to special needs varied significantly from school to school. This was certainly true within the primary and secondary phases, but was even more striking *across* those phases. Secondary schools (and, to a certain extent, large primary schools) have a long tradition of being able to sustain specialist teachers and departments which take lead responsibility for pupils with special needs, even within the whole school approach. The presence of in-house specialists has meant, of course, that most secondary schools have historically been in a position to construct responses targeted specifically at pupils with special needs, though the corollary of this is that those responses have had a tendency to be segregatory in effect, if not in intent. The developments which occurred after the 1988 Act, therefore, tended to take the existence of these specialist forms of provision and the problem of overt or covert segregation as their starting point and were, to a significant extent, concerned with redefining their role within the school.

Smaller primary schools on the other hand have, by and large, not had the resources which would enable them to sustain equivalent in-house specialist provision; though, of course, neither have they had the problem of pupils with special needs being segregated into separate classes and departments. They have, therefore, relied much more heavily for their specialist input on external LEA services and there has probably been a greater acceptance that, apart from this, pupils with special needs could only be educated alongside their peers by ordinary class teachers in ordinary classrooms. This formed the starting point for developments in primary schools which, therefore, tended to be much more concerned than secondary schools with how the school might structure a response to pupils with special needs which would both be specific to their particular needs and, so far as possible, owned and managed by the school itself.

These differences between phases once again mean that any search for 'innovation' which is restricted purely to the surface features of provision is less likely to reveal the emergence of a new 'approach' to special needs so much as a diversity of approaches, differing from school to school and phase to phase. Nonetheless, we continue to have some confidence in asserting that the period following the 1988 Act did indeed see the emergence of a new 'approach', that this approach was broadly similar across phases, and that the diversity of forms of provision actually conceals an underlying coherence at the level of aims and broad strategies. Moreover, although this development was clearly derived from the whole school approach, sharing many of its fundamental values and assumptions, and although in many schools it appeared as little more than a cautious evolution of that approach, we nonetheless feel that it was indeed something genuinely 'new' and that, in a number of the more 'radical' schools which we have studied, it can clearly be differentiated from the forms of special needs provision which dominated the 1980s. The question of whether this new approach will go on to dominate the second half of the 1990s and beyond in quite the same way is an intriguing one, complicated as it is by the introduction of a *Code of Practice* (DFE, 1994) which is in some respects out of tune with the more radical developments in schools. This is, therefore, a question to which we shall return in a later chapter.

Given the surface complexity of the new approach, probably the simplest way to represent its underlying coherence is in diagrammatic form. Figure 3.1 presents this approach in terms of a core concern with teaching and learning sustained by four managerial strategies which are essential for its realization. We will deal with each of these elements in turn.

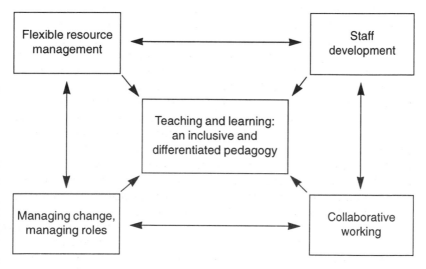

Figure 3.1: The emerging model

Teaching and learning

At the heart of the new approach is a concern for teaching and learning which is derived – but nonetheless subtly different – from that in the whole school approach. It is helpful to remember the origins of the whole school approach's view of teaching and learning in the notion of 'remedial education across the curriculum'. It is also worth remembering that when special classes were developed in ordinary schools, the intention was to deliver special education in mainstream settings (Tansley and Gulliford, 1960). In both cases, the move of children with special needs into the mainstream left the idea that such children needed specialist forms of teaching – and therefore the corollary that mainstream teaching was inappropriate for them – largely intact. The innovation lay in finding ways of delivering that specialist teaching within the mainstream school and classroom without disturbing overmuch the established practices of those settings. It is in this attempt to combine specialist teaching with a mainstream setting that the tensions which we noted earlier in support teaching and differentiation have their origins.

However, as the whole school approach unfolded and, in particular, following the introduction of the National Curriculum as an entitlement for all children, it seems to have become increasingly obvious to some schools that this duality was untenable. Children with special needs would certainly not be enabled to participate meaningfully in that common curriculum if they were simply offered an undifferentiated pedagogy deemed to be appropriate for 'most' of their peers. On the other hand, neither could they participate fully, simply by bolting on to that pedagogy mechanisms of in-class support and limited and segregatory attempts at *post hoc* differentiation. Instead, these schools began to take seriously the need to develop a pedagogy which would be fundamentally and inherently differentiated – that is, one which would be based upon the particular learning characteristics of pupils and which, therefore, would be appropriate both for pupils with special needs and for all the other individuals in the class.

Some schools have gone into print with an explicit commitment to an inclusive but differentiated pedagogy of this kind. Wheal (1995), for instance, in describing his own school's position, goes straight to the heart of some of the tensions within the whole school approach and begins to indicate how this 'new approach' diverges from it:

> I am suspicious of any system which takes the curriculum for granted and which marks out some students as deficient, inadequate or maladjusted, not only because of the deleterious effect on those

students' attitudes, enthusiasms and expectations ('I can't do that Miss, I'm thick'), not only because an unfair proportion of the schools' resources are used on a relatively small number of students, not only because the existence of specialists implicitly encourages teachers to pass on their responsibility ('I can't deal with kids like that, you're paid to know about it. Take him away and do something') but mainly because it reinforces the idea that most students are 'normal' and it therefore supports and legitimates teaching which is, in fact, inappropriate not merely for the few but also for the many. (p. 84)

However, even in schools where radical rhetoric was somewhat less in evidence, we found a marked movement towards pedagogical development. The particular strategies which such schools were using are not in themselves especially new or remarkable. What was remarkable, however, was the range of such strategies in use both within and across schools – self-study materials, DARTS (Lunzer and Gardiner, 1979), the teaching of thinking skills, the use of word processor and dictating machines, distance learning, individualized teaching programmes, precision teaching, collaborative group work, problem-solving, dramatheraphy, mastery learning, peer tuition, academic counselling. As we noted earlier, no single strategy was dominant in these schools; rather, they were characterized by their tendency to be extremely eclectic in their search for any strategies which might contribute to an inclusive pedagogy.

The rationale for this eclectic approach is well presented by Luscombe (1993):

Mixed ability teaching has suggested that most children in 'Warnock's eighteen percent' probably had a mismatch between their abilities, attitudes, hopes and the diet provided for them by the school. It is our belief that working in mixed ability groups brings about an understanding of abilities, needs and character that cannot begin to be understood in narrow singular environments.

This has implications for teaching methods. We believe that a variety of lesson presentations will reach and satisfy a greater proportion of pupils, hopefully inculcating a desire and will to learn. Across the school, therefore, we use a full range of teaching strategies – group work, paired work, videos, drama, role play, linked cross-curricular topics and, increasingly, flexible learning approaches. (p. 70)

It is, of course, possible to characterize this approach to teaching and learning as simply a sophisticated version of differentiation.

However, it is evidently *not* the sort of limited and ultimately segregatory form of 'separate tracking' that so concerns Thompson and Barton (1992) or Hart (1992). It is not simply an attempt to present 'less able' pupils with simplified materials and tasks. Rather, it is an attempt to diversify the available forms of pedagogy in respect of *all* pupils so that they respond to a *range* of differences in learning attainment, aptitude and style.

Two specific examples may serve to illustrate further the subtle, but, we suggest, important difference between this approach to teaching and learning and that which characterized the whole school approach. The first is in the use of support teaching. We have already seen how there were some ambiguities and tensions in the use of support teaching in the whole school approach. In particular, it was entirely possible to use support teaching as a means of sustaining pupils in what would otherwise be an inappropriate setting and thus to avoid the critical examination of the pedagogy on offer in that setting. No doubt this was also the case in some of the classrooms in the schools we studied. However, we were also able to find evidence of a trend towards a much more developmental use of support teaching: in some schools, for instance, subject teachers and departments were asked to bid for in-class support, not on the grounds that their classes contained large numbers of 'pupils with special needs' but on the grounds that such support would enable them to develop schemes of work and teaching approaches more appropriate to those children; in others, formal partnership teaching schemes were in operation, requiring class and support teachers to plan lessons jointly and work together as closely as possible; in others again, support teachers did not simply 'parachute into' classrooms, but were full members of departments, involved in the team planning of teaching – and so on.

A second illuminating example is the emergence of resource centres. The relative failure of the whole school approach seriously to challenge established pedagogy meant that it always faced something of a dilemma: on the one hand, children could be placed and supported in ordinary classrooms characterized, in many cases, by inappropriate pedagogy; on the other hand, children could receive a (supposedly) more appropriate pedagogy if they were withdrawn from ordinary classrooms and the price of temporary segregation was deemed worth paying. In a number of schools, however, a solution to this dilemma was emerging in the form of an alternative form of provision. Building, in many cases, on the work undertaken in the TVEI Flexible Learning initiative (Employment Department, 1991; Eraut *et al.*, 1991; Nash, 1993), some schools have developed resource centres which allow pupils to work on curriculum tasks independently, outside the classroom, but with a degree of adult supervision and support.

Such centres offer some of the advantages of withdrawal in that they allow pupils to work outside the classroom at their own pace, on their own tasks and with adult support. They also allow that adult support to be located centrally and to be available throughout the school day (and beyond) rather than scattering a limited number of support teachers across a much greater number of classes. However, resource centres overcome the segregatory tendencies of withdrawal in that the tasks on which pupils work are *curriculum* tasks, and the use of the resource centre is by no means restricted to pupils with special needs. Moreover, the proper use of resource centres is only possible if there is a change in classroom pedagogy such that teachers routinely enable their pupils to work independently on extended tasks. At their best, therefore, the combination of the resource centre with a reconstructed pedagogy enables a school to respond to special needs by developing a fundamentally differentiated form of provision of the sort which, we have argued, is characteristic of this emerging approach.

One final point is worth making about this 'new' approach to teaching and learning. As Booth (1983) pointed out when the whole school approach was still relatively young:

> The assumption still is that ordinary schools can only be expected to supply one 'normal' form of education. But if we expect schools to cater routinely for children with diverse needs and interests then our whole approach to the notion of special needs should change. Special needs are those needs to which schools currently do not respond. (p. 41)

It follows that the attempt to develop 'remedial education across the curriculum', even in its later, more sophisticated forms, had negative implications not only for pupils with special needs but also for the 'mainstream' peers. For the former, it implied, as we have seen, the perpetuation of an ultimately segregatory form of teaching. However, for the latter, it also implied that there was a single undifferentiated form of pedagogy which was appropriate for *all* pupils who did not have 'special needs'.

In the schools we studied, the development of an inclusive and differentiated pedagogy certainly meant that pupils with special needs were more likely to receive an appropriate pedagogy in ordinary classrooms. However, it also meant, as Wheal (1995) argues, that all other pupils were likely to receive a pedagogy that was to a greater or lesser extent responsive to their learning characteristics. Increasingly, techniques such as support teaching, the use of resource centres, flexible learning and all the other pedagogical techniques referred to above were being used in these schools not simply for pupils with special needs, but for all pupils. This has two implications. First, the development of particular techniques for pupils with special needs was no longer in itself segregatory; it was simply part of the development of appropriate pedagogy for *all* pupils. It was in this way, for instance, that many primary schools were finding it possible to develop a distinctive approach to special needs without falling into the trap of separate provision which has bedevilled secondary education for so long.

Secondly, for many schools the development of appropriate pedagogy for all meant that the notion of special needs itself was becoming increasingly redundant. In a few cases, the language of special needs was totally eschewed and a conscious attempt was being made to develop an alternative language – a language with the emphasis on individual difference and on the limitations of pedagogy rather than on the limitations of pupils as the source of educational failure. Hence, one school in particular persisted in speaking of 'children who challenge the curriculum' rather than 'children with special needs'. In other schools, the language of special needs continued to be used, but its meaning subtly changed: some children with significant learning difficulties might well be regarded as having special needs; but then able children had needs of their own, many children had mild and temporary learning or emotional difficulties, and all children had difficulties at some point or other. The use of the term 'special needs', therefore, could not be taken to denote a distinct group of children for whom special provision must be made so much as a status which all children occupied to varying degrees and at various times, and which, accordingly, must be dealt with by the development of a flexible pedagogy responsive to their learning characteristics.

Resource management
Traditionally, special needs provision has been sustained by a system of resourcing that is to a significant extent separate from that which sustains mainstream provision. This is at its most obvious where such provision has been delivered through separate facilities and personnel such as special schools and services. However, even as special needs provision has come to be developed within mainstream schools, and even in the relatively sophisticated and integrated whole school approach, separate resourcing remained very much the norm. The Warnock Report (DES, 1978) and subsequent 1981 Education Act, for instance, certainly succeeded in freeing special needs resources from special schools as such, but they did not challenge the notion that chil-

dren with special needs did indeed require their own resources provided through a system different from that which resourced all other children. Similarly, in many – especially primary – schools, resources for special needs came via LEA support services rather than through the establishment of the school, whilst in secondary schools, although Remedial and Special Needs Departments might be staffed from the school's establishment, they constituted clearly-identifiable resources which were allocated exclusively to children with special needs.

The local management of schools (LMS) provisions of the 1988 Act challenged this situation in two major ways. First, the delegation of budgets to schools reduced the capacity of LEAs to sustain substantial special education provision centrally; special schools or support services or both had, to some extent, to be sacrificed in many authorities, with the consequence that ordinary schools were compelled to rely somewhat more on their own resources to meet special needs (Clayton, 1992; Audit Commission and HMI, 1992a and b; Bangs, 1993; Diamond, 1993; Moore, 1993). Second, although most LMS formulae included some 'additional needs' element, this was not hypothecated to special needs provision, and consequently headteachers and governors had to see the resourcing of special needs provision as simply one demand among many in the resourcing of the school as a whole.

It seems entirely possible that, in some cases, these factors provided the basis for a reduction in special needs resourcing in schools (Fletcher-Campbell, 1993; Lunt and Evans, 1994; Vincent *et al.*, 1995). Certainly, our own work in schools immediately after the 1988 Act suggested that some heads and governors were diverting resources away from special needs provision and into more 'urgent' or 'prestigious' areas of work, such as the staffing of the National Curriculum[1]. However, the introduction of LMS also gave heads and governors considerable freedom to develop creative approaches to the resourcing of special needs provision, and it is these approaches which emerged from our studies of 'innovative' schools.

The resourcing of special needs provision in the schools we studied was characterized by two inter-dependent features: a prioritization of special needs resources and a flexibility in resource management such that special needs and mainstream resources were, to a certain extent, interchangeable. Prioritization was, above all, a matter of principle and commitment. Although schools were under considerable pressure to economize wherever they could, heads and governors nonetheless found money to appoint special needs co-ordinators (or their equivalent), often in quite senior positions, to provide them with time on the timetable, to employ classroom assistants, to establish systems of in-class support, and so on. This prioritization and protection of resources seems to have been possible because special needs provision was not seen as some peripheral aspect of the school in competition with its 'real' work. Rather, as teachers variously put it, 'special needs is what this school is about' or 'special needs [is] part of the fabric of the school'.

This notion gives a clue to the second aspect of resource management. Because schools were seeing special needs as integral to the school's activities and because, as we saw in the previous section, they were developing a pedagogy which was appropriate for pupils with special needs by being appropriate for *all* pupils, they did not feel the need to draw sharp distinctions between special needs resources and the rest of the school's resources. There were many examples of this. It was common, for instance, for schools to use support teachers and classroom assistants to work, not simply with identified pupils with special needs, but with any child who needed help at a particular time. Similarly, the role of special needs co-ordinators was often reconstructed (as we shall see below) so that they had responsibilities which extended well beyond the identified special needs population and encompassed, for instance, very able children or, indeed, the whole pupil population. On the same principle, the resource centres which we described above were neither exclusively special needs nor exclusively mainstream resources. On the one hand, insofar as special needs teachers were involved in running them and they were used to deliver special needs support, it could be argued that they constituted a means of giving access to special needs resources for a wider pupil population. On the other hand, insofar as they made use of mainstream teachers, library and IT facilities and mainstream curriculum materials, it could equally be argued that they constituted a means of giving pupils with special needs access to a wider range of mainstream resources than might otherwise be the case. In fact, the schools which had resource centres tended to be untroubled by such arguments, seeing them simply as a resource for *all* pupils.

One final aspect of resource management is perhaps worth noting. Given that these schools tended to be concerned with the *development* of appropriately differentiated pedagogy, there was a tendency for resources to be viewed to a significant extent developmentally. That is, resources were not seen simply as a means of sustaining a particular form of provision, but as a means of promoting the *development* of provision. Heavy investment in resource centres, for instance, tended to be justified in terms of the catalytic effect those centres would have on teaching throughout the school; there were often systems of 'bidding' for resources internally as a means of encouraging teachers and departments to develop resource-worthy schemes; some element of resourcing was often withheld in order to support curriculum initiatives; and, above all, the special needs co-ordinator was often provided with time not simply to work directly with pupils, but to work with teachers to promote pedagogical developments.

Staff development
This leads directly on to the third characteristic of these schools. This again is expressed neatly by Wheal:

> . . . the school's staff development policy and the school's development plan are a vital part of our special needs provision. Because the thrust of staff development is to get teachers to manage a range of complex needs . . . ; because we are aiming, as a staff development issue, to make our provision effective for all students; because we are, as a school, constantly alert to each individual's different needs; because our notion of curriculum is essentially based on the student's *response* to the content rather than just on the content, we believe that we can dramatically reduce the percentage of students about whom teachers feel concern and the percentage of students and their parents concerned about their own progress. (Wheal, 1995, pp. 85–6)

We have seen how, given the aim of these schools to meet special needs through an appropriately differentiated pedagogy for *all* pupils, it is not possible or necessary to draw hard and fast distinctions between special needs and mainstream resources. However, the principal 'mainstream' resource is the teaching staff. The development of an appropriately differentiated pedagogy depends crucially on the development of the staff's pedagogical skills, and therefore staff development has to be a major plank of the school's approach to special needs.

To a certain extent, this is simply a continuation of the notion within the whole school approach that special needs teachers would 'give away' their skills to their subject and class teacher colleagues. However, there is an important difference. In many of the schools we studied, the pedagogical skills that were considered desirable were not necessarily typical special needs skills. The traditions of diagnostic assessment and individual programming were certainly in evidence, and special needs teachers were likely to take the lead in disseminating these techniques. However, development initiatives were equally likely to come from 'mainstream' sources such as the flexible learning initiative or the introduction of thinking skills, and the leaders of such initiatives might well be subject and class teachers rather than special needs teachers. Indeed, we came across cases where the special needs co-ordinators deliberately stood back from initiatives which they thought would be highly beneficial to pupils with special needs precisely so that they should be seen as mainstream initiatives of relevance to all teachers and all pupils.

The mode of staff development was also significant. The vision of the whole school approach – that skills should be 'given away' – however liberal and open it may appear, actually implies that special needs teachers have skills which their mainstream colleagues lack. It therefore depends on an assumed superiority and privileged position of the special needs teacher, at least when it comes to dealing with pupils with special needs. It is scarcely surprising, therefore, that many class and subject teachers balked at the notion of a 'partnership' in which they would be forever inferior! The situation within the emerging approach was somewhat different. The parity and interchangeability of special and mainstream pedagogies meant that they tended to be less concerned with notions of 'experts' and 'novices'. Again, Wheal captures the thrust of this new approach when he declares that, 'the most effective staff development occurs when teachers are helping one another to reflect on their practices' (1995, p. 87). It was common in these schools to find collaborative staff teams, problem-solving groups, peer support groups and team teaching not simply as forms of provision or planning, but as opportunities for staff development. Frequently, the role of special needs teachers and co-ordinators was not so much to lead these activities as to participate in them as equal partners, with an open acknowledgement that the existing pedagogical skills of class and subject teachers were as important to children with special needs as any specialist skills which special needs teachers might have. Indeed, many special needs teachers were somewhat reluctant to claim that they had any particular expertise.

Moreover, much staff development stemmed, as Wheal indicates, from current notions of 'reflection' (Schön, 1983/1991). Many development activities, therefore, did not consist of skills-instruction by one professional to another (though such sessions certainly still took place) so much as collaborative attempts to think through real classroom problems which admitted of no 'expert' solutions, and in which any progress demanded that all participants contribute different forms of expertise. An obvious example of this sort of approach, which we found in a number of schools, is Hanko's (1995) notion of a teacher support group in which a whole group of staff work with a particular teacher to help that teacher find solutions to some classroom problem – without any assumption that any one member of the group will have 'the' solution, or that any solution is valid which the class teacher him/herself cannot accept.

Collaborative working

The notion of 'partnership' was, as Gains (1980; Gains and McNicholas, 1979) and Bines (1986) point out, central to the whole school approach. However, we have already seen how, in respect of staff development, the collaborative tendencies of this new approach were subtly but significantly different from this. These tendencies, however, extended well beyond the boundaries of staff development. Because the approach was centred not on the importing of special teaching techniques into the mainstream, but on the development of a fundamentally differentiated pedagogy for all pupils, it was, in a more complete sense, a genuine 'whole school approach', calling on the skills of all teachers and encompassing the teaching of all pupils. It follows that its implementation required a high level of collaboration right across the school.

There are two examples of this which will serve to make the point. In primary schools, although the whole school approach sought to promote partnerships between class teachers and special needs teachers, it is doubtful whether it did much to promote collaboration *between* class teachers themselves. The new approach, however, was only ever likely to be effective if all class teachers worked in a co-ordinated way, and if their efforts to develop an appropriate pedagogy were supported by clear and coherent school-level policies and approaches. Moreover, the introduction of the National Curriculum as an entitlement for all pupils, regardless of their 'special needs' and, indeed, regardless of the interests and preferences of their class teacher, was equally dependent on such cross-school co-ordination. We commonly found in primary schools, therefore, a relatively high level of whole school planning and co-ordination on matters of curriculum and pedagogy. In some cases, this took the form of year or key stage teams who planned teaching jointly and who might well include a special needs teacher or co-ordinator as a full member. In other cases, it took the form of agreed strategies for approaching, for instance, reading difficulties or behavioural difficulties. In other cases again, it took the form of whole-staff planning groups, perhaps working on specific development plans for a limited time span, or perhaps as standing planning and decision-making bodies.

The organization of secondary schools – both in terms of separate subject departments and the tradition of separate special needs departments – meant that collaboration there took different forms. In particular, we noted an attempt to dismantle some of the boundaries which separated special needs and mainstream provision. Special needs co-ordinators, for instance, would often work to some sort of steering group made up of subject teachers, representing the interests of the school as a whole and acting as a channel of communication back and forth between the special needs co-ordinator (or equivalent) and the mainstream of the school. Co-ordinators would frequently operate as members of planning and development groups that were concerned with 'mainstream' issues, on the grounds that the mainstream-special distinction was redundant. Commonly, special needs teachers would be attached to subject departments and, indeed, in one school, such teachers were appointed jointly to both departments and were full members of each.

Perhaps most significant of all, separate special needs departments – a term we have used as a convenient short-hand in this chapter – were actually beginning to disappear. A wide range of arrangements was beginning to take their place, though they all shared the characteristic of being somewhat less separate from the rest of the school. Hence, in some schools, 'departments' became 'teams' seen as having a specific role but not quite a separate organizational existence. In other schools, the department merged in a larger support faculty whose remit extended well beyond special needs to the support of all students. In yet other schools, lone co-ordinators operated without a department, contributing to the development of appropriate pedagogy within subject areas, but studiously avoiding being seen as the embodiment of the school's special needs provision.

Managing change, managing roles

It is no accident that, in describing this new approach, we have frequently had occasion to talk of 'development'. There was a very strong sense in many schools that special needs could not be met simply by putting together a package of provision and teaching from an established repertoire. Indeed, if special needs were to be met by developing an appropriately differentiated pedagogy, then the clear implication was that those needs existed in the first place because existing pedagogy was inappropriate and undifferentiated. There was also a strong awareness in some schools of the limitations of the established orthodoxy of the whole school approach and an awareness of some of the segregatory tendencies which it embodied. Change which would move provision beyond these limitations thus became a priority for such schools.

Many aspects of the way change was promoted and managed have already been mentioned in describing other elements of the new approach. However, there are three that deserve further analysis. The first is that change was not simply structural – the substitution of one form of provision for another – but was, rather, an attempt to create what Pickup (1995) calls a 'thinking school'. She defines this attempt as follows:

> A 'thinking school' is one which is constantly searching to increase the effectiveness of the teaching and learning environment. Staff are involved, at different levels, in activities which reflect upon what is happening and then attempt to improve provision through the modification of practice. The Learning Support team are a flexible resource within a college which aspires to be a 'thinking school', and can assist in response to identified needs and help provide educational excellence. (p. 91)

Pickup, herself a co-ordinator, hints at a number of elements which we found in schools. First, a 'thinking school' is made up of 'reflective practitioners', teachers who are prepared to reflect upon their work in a Schönian sense, and for whom – as we saw above – such reflection constitutes a major form of professional development. Second, such a school develops a sense of 'what is happening'; that is, it has strategies for gathering data on the effects of practice on the pupil's learning. Such strategies might include quantitative data on pupil performance, or observational data derived from team-teaching situations, or reported data produced in the sorts of peer support groups described above. Third, special needs pupils and teachers play a central part in this process. On the one hand, the difficulties of pupils are an important indicator of limitations in existing pedagogy and provision. On the other hand, special needs teachers are an important resource both for gathering data and for enabling colleagues to change their practice.

A second important feature of change in these schools is the role played by the headteacher. We have already seen how the isolation of special needs co-ordinators from power and decision-making in schools was a major limitation and source of tension in the whole school approach. However, whereas the persistence of the view of special needs as something 'bolted onto' the school's central concerns may have made this inevitable in the whole school approach, the new approach seems to have made it equally inevitable that powerful decision-makers in the school – and, in particular, the head – would be centrally involved. Because the approach is based on the development of appropriate pedagogy for *all* pupils, it is inevitably at the centre of management's concerns. Indeed, not only did we find headteachers willingly taking the lead in this development, but we also found them viewing the reconstruction of the school's approach to special needs as a key strategy for bringing about the sort of changes they wanted to see to improve the quality of teaching and learning across the school as a whole. More than one head was openly using their co-ordinator as a sort of surrogate change agent, able to work closely with colleagues on the detail of practical teaching issues in a way that the head and other members of the school's management were themselves unable to do.

The third aspect of the management of change is, perhaps, the clearest and most tangible evidence we have of a genuinely 'new' approach, particularly in secondary schools. It will be evident from the references we have made hitherto that the role of the special needs co-ordinator in these schools was quite different from the traditional role of the 'remedial teacher' and significantly different from the role of the co-ordinator as it developed in the whole school approach. Indeed, these differences were often marked by the abandonment of the term 'special needs co-ordinator' in favour of such titles as 'learning support co-ordinator' or 'teaching and learning co-ordinator'.

The essence of this change was that co-ordinators were ceasing to be responsible simply for the learning of children with special needs, and were taking on wider responsibility for the promotion of appropriate pedagogy for *all* pupils. Again, Wheal (1995) defines this new role succinctly: 'My role is to work with curriculum areas, examining what they do and helping them create development agendas – agendas which are primarily concerned with the strategies, techniques and methods of catering effectively to all learners and by necessity therefore to all atypical learners' (p. 86). The rationale for this reconstructed role is implicit in Wheal's statement. On the one hand, the most effective (and ethical) way of responding to the needs of 'atypical' learners is to develop pedagogy that is appropriate for all learners – and therefore co-ordinators cannot avoid becoming involved in these wider developments. On the other hand, such 'atypical' learners – what Wheal calls 'pupils who challenge the curriculum' – are powerful test cases of the extent to which existing pedagogy genuinely is appropriate for all. It follows, therefore, that the co-ordinator's base in special needs makes him/her ideally placed to evaluate, challenge and develop existing pedagogy.

This pattern of appraisal, challenge and development frequently underpinned the way co-ordinators constructed their role. In some cases, this interpretation of the role was both formalized and explicit, with the co-ordinator operating as a quality assurance manager (see, for instance, Simpson, 1993). In other cases, it simply formed an implicit framework for the co-ordinator's interactions with colleagues, though many of the surface features of the role remained unchanged. However, these more traditional features – the assessment and teaching of identified children with special needs, the organization of support teaching and so on – frequently acquired a new flavour as co-ordinators increasingly used them as strategies for developing pedagogy across the school rather than simply as means of providing for individual children.

These changes were reflected in the positioning of the co-ordinator within the school's management hierarchy. A number of patterns emerged. In some cases, there was no formal hierarchical change, but the co-ordinator became involved in a number of managerial and cross-curricular issues – attending working parties, being consulted by senior management and so on. In other cases, the co-ordinator was a full member of the senior management team and had responsibilities which extended well beyond special needs as such. In other cases again, the role was divided between a special needs co-ordinator, who would carry out the more traditional aspects of special needs work, such as the direct teaching of identified pupils, and a senior manager who would co-ordinate the development of teaching and learning across the school as a whole and would line-manage the special needs teacher as part of this wider brief.

Even in primary schools, which lack the secondary phase's tradition of well-qualified co-ordinators in middle management positions, similar changes were in evidence. Where the school had a specialist unit for children with statements, the head of the unit might well operate in the sort of extended role we have just outlined. Where this was not the case, it was common to find the headteacher taking on the wider developmental role, but liaising very closely with the special needs co-ordinator as to how this might be done. However, as we pointed out in discussing teaching and learning, the development of differentiated pedagogy in primary schools tended to involve the formulation of specific strategies for responding to special needs rather than – as in secondary schools – the merging of those approaches with mainstream pedagogy. The widening of the co-ordinator's role, therefore, tended still to be concerned with special needs as such, but to focus on the development of school-wide strategies rather than on the direct teaching of identified children.

BEYOND THE WHOLE SCHOOL APPROACH?

Throughout this chapter, we have attempted to highlight some of the key differences as we see them between this 'new approach' and the whole school approach. One of the questions which was repeatedly put to us during our research, however, and which we ourselves raised on many occasions, was the extent to which this 'new approach' really *was* new, or was simply an extension of the whole school approach. The answer to this question is inevitably somewhat complex. First, it is probably fair to say that the schools we worked with could be located along a continuum in terms of the extent to which they articulated and embraced something that was clearly different from the whole school approach. At one end of that continuum were a few schools where there was a self-conscious effort to overcome the limitations of special needs provision as it had traditionally been understood and to develop something significantly different. It is the work of these schools – and especially of the even smaller group that have sought to articulate the features of and rationale for their approaches in the literature – that enables us to posit the coherent and distinctive model of provision that we have described above.

At the other end of the continuum, however, were schools which appeared to have no particular desire to develop an entirely new model of special needs provision, but which were simply extending the practices and assumptions of the whole school approach in small ways in response to local circumstances. And between the two ends of the continuum lie the majority of schools which were pursuing what we might call a 'reformist' agenda – pushing established practices beyond their initial scope, with some awareness of their inherent limitations, but without, necessarily, an intention of carrying out a wholesale reconstruction of special needs education in mainstream schools. The significance of these smaller-scale and less ambitious developments only becomes clear, we suggest, when they are seen in the light of the model being developed explicitly in other, more adventurous institutions.

It is probably most accurate to say, therefore, that what we identified was not so much a wholesale change of direction on the part of large numbers of mainstream schools, but rather a shift in the assumptions which had underpinned the whole school approach. In some schools, that shift was explicit and resulted in major changes in many – though not all – aspects of organization and practice; in other schools, it was more implicit and tentative, and it left the surface features of practice only marginally disturbed. In all schools, however, that shift can be seen as an inevitable consequence of the working out of the implications of the whole school approach by thoughtful practitioners, stimulated in particular by the new set of opportunities and challenges of the post-1988 situation. The attempt to 'merge' special and mainstream education which had been embodied in that approach had, as we have seen, failed to engage with the resistance of an unreconstructed and essential alien (from a special needs point of view) mainstream education system. As the limitations of that projected merger revealed themselves, therefore, it became apparent that any further attempt to realize the 'human values' of participation and equity – on which Sayer (1994/1987) claims the whole school approach was founded – would have to find ways of engaging with the mainstream and bringing about significant changes within it.

The 'new approach' can be seen as seeking to bring about precisely such changes. Certainly, it shared with the whole school approach a commitment to the values of participation and equity. It also shared some of the forms of provision which were characteristic of that approach – particularly in the less radical schools that we studied. However, in seeking to create a flexible pedagogy appropriate to *all* learners, to replace the notion of special needs with one of individual differences, and to create systems and structures which would realize these ambitious aims, the new approach was engaged in an endeavour which was essentially beyond the scope of the whole school approach as originally conceived. Equity and participation were to be achieved, not by maintaining pupils in an uncongenial environment and by 'bolting-on' supports and adaptations to an essentially unreconstructed mainstream, but by premising mainstream education itself on the notion of diversity. At one and the same time, therefore, the new approach was an attempt both to work out the *values* on which the whole school approach had been founded and to develop a significantly different rationale and set of practices through which to achieve their realization. Whether that attempt was – or could be – entirely successful is the question which we shall address in the next chapter.

NOTES

1. In 1991–2 one of the authors (Dyson) acted as consultant to an internal (and confidential) LEA review of the impact of LMS on special needs provision in its schools. The review found that, at a time of budgetary constraint in the LEA, special needs provision was being cut disproportionately to curriculum provision. However, in many schools these cuts were disguised by the tendency to redeploy special needs teachers into non-special needs work, rather than simply to make such teachers redundant.

—4—

The case of Downland

The previous chapter highlighted some of the key features of what we describe as the attempt to develop a response to special educational needs in mainstream schools that went 'beyond the whole school approach'. In this chapter we will focus on the extent to which these features were leading to an unproblematic resolution of the dilemmas which we identified in Chapter 1. To do this we will again make extensive use of our own research and in particular of material arising from a detailed study of one school. We have previously reported on some of the developments in this school, Downland, (Dyson *et al.*, 1994). In this chapter we will attempt to establish whether the approach to special education needs within this school was successfully resolving the dilemmas which we believe have characterized previous efforts at merging special and mainstream education.

Downland emerged, from our research, as the school which could best be regarded as having an approach to special education in mainstream schools that went beyond many of the established features of the whole school approach. It represented the most 'radical' attempt to transform the whole school approach in a conscious attempt to realize the values of equity and participation. We regarded Downland as having the clearest and most refined examples of systems and structures in place, which characterized what we believed might represent a 'new approach' to special education in mainstream schools. It appeared, on the surface, to be an interesting example of a school that was resolving many of the issues that we have previously instanced as symptomatic of the field of special education provision and practice.

The school had been formed from the recent merger of two single-sex schools creating a single comprehensive school serving the majority of secondary-aged pupils from the town. The process of merger had not been without its problems. It was made clear to us by many of the former staff from the girls' school that in their opinion it had not been a merger of equals but more of a take-over by the boys' school. We were certainly aware of these tensions in the school as they provided an interesting undercurrent in respect of special educational needs provision as we shall discuss below. At the time we conducted our research, the school was utilizing both sites, with the inevitable problems that such situations create. There were, however, ambitious plans to consolidate the provision utilizing funds from an endowment which had supported the boys' school. Despite these surface problems a number of key features of the school's response led us to the view that Downland represented a 'radical' alternative to traditional approaches to the whole school approach.

The school espoused a particularly strong values position based on a commitment to the participation of all its students in a full entitlement curriculum in which individual and collective achievement were celebrated. Full participation of all pupils was the distinguishing characteristic of the school's policy and was regarded as an essential component of a strategy through which a positive whole school ethos could be created in which all pupils would be able to realize their potential. In this respect the school could be regarded as seeking to realize inclusive values; though it should be noted that, unlike the inclusive schools we shall consider in the next chapter, Downland did not include in its population pupils with marked learning or physical difficulties who might otherwise have been placed in a special school.

Despite these limits, Downland had a number of distinctive features in respect of its attempt to realize its values which we believed made it distinctive at that time. The school had consciously adopted a language within the school which avoided, as far as possible, the traditional terminology of special education. There had been a deliberate attempt to purge the internal language of the school of discriminatory terms and the use of what was regarded as language which conveyed any negative images of groups or individuals. Instead a vocabulary based on potential and achievement was used to encourage a dialogue at all levels within the school which emphasized success, achievement and participation. Thus in place of the traditional notion of 'pupils with special educational needs' the school used instead the term 'children who challenge the curriculum'. In this way the school was concerned to convey the extent to which it regarded difficulties with learning as fundamentally a problem related to the nature of the curriculum rather than as characteristics of individual learners. The school was concerned to establish the principle that resolutions of learning difficulties should be seen in terms of the development of the curriculum and the approaches that were adopted to teaching and learning rather than through the creation of a separate system in which something 'special' was done for individual pupils. In this sense, when pupils were experiencing difficulties in accessing the curriculum they were regarded by the senior management as 'opportunities not threats' in that they acted as key indicators of the effectiveness of the quality of the teaching and learning that was taking place throughout the school, and the extent to which the curriculum had been sufficiently developed to accommodate a range of learning styles. A metaphor of 'energy' was thus encouraged to describe the relationship between teachers and students. Students were to be given headroom: 'they have to find their own levels' (teaching and learning co-ordinator). All pupils were seen as being imbued with an enormous potential which it was the task of the school to release. The headteacher, who had been instrumental in introducing this particular vocabulary, reinforced this view regarding pupils experiencing difficulties as 'not a problem but an opportunity' for the school; he was concerned that the discourse of the school reflected this view and that such pupils were not seen as 'threats' to an existing *status quo* but as the key indicators of the effectiveness of the school in 'unleashing' potential.

To reinforce the adoption of this powerful rhetoric, further attempts were made to challenge traditional conceptualizations of special needs. This was reflected in the way that the school sought to structure its response to those pupils who were 'challenging ' the curriculum. The school's teaching and learning policy document for example sought to convey an alternative view of how pupils should be viewed:

> there is not a distinct and identifiable group of pupils who always and exclusively have SEN ... and ... SEN only exists in contexts ... the classroom organization and delivery of the curriculum will have to be considered.

This view of special educational needs as a dynamic phenomenon which was located within the context of the classroom and the curriculum rather than within individual pupils was central to the way that the school sought to ensure entitlement and participation. Exclusionary forms of provision such as withdrawal were eschewed in favour of a dual approach of in-class support and curriculum development led by a charismatic co-ordinator of teaching and learning. This attempt to avoid any form of segregation was expressed thus: 'The policy of the school is that all educational needs are best met in mainstream classes' (Staff Handbook).

Instead of seeking to identify a group of SEN pupils, and to make them the subject of a distinctive system, all pupils were seen as having individual needs and a potential which was capable of being released within the context of the curriculum offered in the mainstream class-room. The principal vehicle for achieving this, the extensive support system, was not concerned, therefore, with supporting an identified group of pupils but with working with the whole class and the teacher. Class teachers were encouraged to experiment with different ways of working with support teachers, and support teachers, who were also all class teachers, were encouraged to see their role as offering advice, 'not on what is taught but ways in which it can be taught'. A member of staff involved in providing support described this process as one of 'trying to slide in ideas', whilst at the same time asking themselves: 'Does what I am observing help me improve my own teaching?' The process was regarded as one in which all staff were able to review and reflect on their *own* teaching as they observed and participated in the teaching of other staff. The overall goal of the support teachers was, therefore, to ensure that every pupil in the classroom was accessed to a full curriculum and that they achieved their full potential.

Support teachers also fulfilled other vital roles. They were able to attend meetings in departments which they supported, offering feedback on the quality of teaching and the extent of differentiation within lessons. They were also charged with providing the teaching and learning co-ordinator with feedback on the effectiveness of the school's approach to diversity. The teaching and learning co-ordinator was central to this process and his role was clearly different from that of many SENCOs. He had been appointed by the headteacher with whom he clearly shared a common philosophy in respect of how teaching and learning should be conducted. He had an extremely flex-ible role which enabled him to observe any aspect of the teaching and learning in the school as well as to marshal the support system which the school had established. This gave him a unique insight into the way the school's values were being realized. He became, as he was later described by the headteacher, the 'conscience of the school', hav-ing an overview of teaching and learning, able to identify any particular difficulties that were emerging either at the level of indi-vidual pupils, staff or departments and to provide feedback into the school's development programme.

Interestingly, the teaching and learning co-ordinator, who was a long-standing member of the staff, was not ingrained in the traditions of special education, having been a subject teacher before taking on this role, a background which perhaps freed him from some of the pre-conceptions which sustain many traditional conceptualizations of special education. He also had a clear view of his role as relating to the improvement of teaching and learning across the school rather than as being directed at the needs of a select group of pupils. He saw his role as one of development and change which involved the collection and dissemination of information from all areas of the school, reporting on successes and failures in attempting to realize the school's avowed values; this enabled him to design both whole school development activities as well as group or individual staff support. The process of staff development was regarded as integral to the realization of the values of the school, and an extensive staff development programme with a focus on improving access and achievement had been implemented by the headteacher immediately on his appointment.

It was in this context, therefore, that we identified Downland as the clearest example of a 'new approach' to special educational needs in mainstream schools, one which appeared to extend the standard systems and approaches of the whole school approach. If a new approach was to be successful in reconciling the issues and dilemmas which we believe underpin provision of special needs education in mainstream schools then we hoped that evidence of its success would be found in Downland. As we have suggested, our initial impressions were that there was indeed a reconstruction of provision and practice; that the values of participation and equity were being realized in the radical approach of this school.

Accordingly, we undertook a more detailed analysis of provision and practice to establish whether our initial impression was correct. Further data were collected through a series of interviews, and observations across most aspects of the school's functioning. Policy documentation was analysed and key architects of the policy of the school were tracked, observed and interviewed on a number of occasions. In this way we sought a deeper understanding of the school and the ways that it sought to achieve the realization of its values.

As our analysis of the data proceeded and our understanding of the school deepened, we became increasingly aware of certain factors which caused us to question the extent to which Downland was successful in its ambitious project. As we developed an understanding of how the school operated we were able to identify a number of trends and developments which suggested to us that the resolution which had apparently been achieved was not as stable as it at first appeared. We came to the conclusion that the apparent stability was temporary and that many of the issues we have referred to were in fact merely in a state of partial equilibrium, ready at any moment to re-emerge within this school. The school's avowed aim of realizing a powerfully articulated set of values was also being undermined by other developments within the wider educational field as well as because of certain internal tensions.

In particular it seemed to suggest that the problems experienced in

Downland related to a failure to take account of two key factors which make the provision of special needs education in mainstream schools so problematic. Firstly, we suggest there was a failure to develop, in conjunction with the change in language and views about teaching and learning, an actual technology within the school through which both the pedagogic, curricular and organizational problems of responding to diversity could be resolved. Secondly, we believe the school failed to appreciate the extent to which the changing socio-political climate was actually requiring schools to be able to demonstrate precisely the extent to which they were making 'special' provision for statemented and registered pupils. In our continuing analysis of Downland, therefore, we will focus on three main themes: the re-emergence of traditional notions of special education; the reproduction of traditional special needs structures; and the issues of inclusion and exclusion. We will take each of these in turn.

THE RE-EMERGENCE OF TRADITIONAL NOTIONS OF SPECIAL EDUCATION

The values position of this school was one based very firmly in notions of commonality, potential and success. It was, except for a small number of pupils attending special schools, the only comprehensive in a small town and therefore in a limited sense offering something akin to an 'inclusive' education. This view was articulated at every opportunity: within formal staff meetings; at the interface between the staff and the pupils; in discussions with parents; and at governors' meetings. It was used to convey to visitors, such as ourselves, both a view of the school and also the basis on which any dialogue should be conducted when discussing the school. Its emphasis was on the potential which resided in every individual and which could be 'unleashed' given appropriate circumstances. The culture of the school was premised around a positive and achievement-driven ethos which was expressed in all the operations of the school. Discipline problems, for example, were dealt with in terms of the degree to which particular pupil behaviours had failed to match this view of achievement, value and individual self-worth.

The issue for us was to establish the extent to which this rhetoric was not only shared by all the staff but actual realized at the level of the classroom. What became apparent as we considered this feature of the school was the extent to which this rhetoric was actually layered in terms of the rate of its absorption and use and the extent to which it actually impacted on practice. We became increasingly aware that the further one moved from senior and middle management the more obvious it was that this rhetoric lost its power. Initially this was obscured from us as many class teachers made a point of referring to the use of the particular language as a part of an institutional tradition – a tradition which they saw as in part a chore but which they were happy to endorse, as it formed such an important aspect of the way the school worked. As we undertook detailed classroom observation and gradually became more integrated into the school, it became obvious that the rhetoric was severely weakened at classroom level both in its use and much more importantly in the actual practices that were being utilized by the teachers. We found for instance that at a general level some teachers were struggling to implement the new vision. In many classrooms there was not the evidence of a systematic implementation of the principles of differentiation which were central to the realization of its inclusive values. The curriculum was in many cases still being delivered in a traditional way with those students experiencing most difficulty receiving varying degrees of support from either the class teacher or the support staff when they were present. These pupils, far from opening the window on the effectiveness of existing teaching and learning strategies, were in effect producing a growing resistance on the part of some staff, as was evidenced in a return to practices which were reminiscent of those associated with more traditional notions of special education.

We observed particular resistance at a number of specific levels. Firstly, there was resistance from some long-stay members of staff in particular departments who argued that their subject discipline required the maintenance of a traditional approach. This was evidenced by the pressure exerted on the senior management team (SMT) to reintroduce streaming in one of the core subjects of the National Curriculum, backed up by the claim that exams results would decline if mixed ability grouping was forced on the department. Secondly, there were some members of staff who pre-dated the headteacher, maintained an adherence to the old values of the previous regime and saw no justification in changing their practices. Finally, there was resistance from some members of the girls' school who made no secret of the fact that they felt the provision made in their former school, based on the withdrawal of small groups of pupils, provided a much more appropriate education for those with difficulties than the system on offer in Downland. They regarded the system at Downland as having much to commend it at the level of values and principles but as failing to deliver in practice and therefore being deleterious for a number of 'vulnerable' pupils.

In all of these cases we can see the existence of an alternative values position being argued and voices suggesting a return to a more traditional view of special needs education, suggesting that instead of the consensus which the SMT portrayed there was in fact considerable diversity of view within the staff group. This presented an obvious challenge to the SMT who depended on a consensus among the staff if their vision was to be fully realized. Their response was surprisingly traditional. When we presented our evidence of this resistance their reaction was in terms of the existence of certain 'unreconstituted' elements within the staff who, for a variety of reasons, were beyond redemption. It was suggested to us that this was just the residual resistance of a small minority who were unable to respond to the new challenges of the adoption of an approach based on equity and participation. We noted that those who had expressed resistance, especially those from the former girls' school, had been increasingly marginalized within the new school, occupying few positions of responsibility.

This ability to suppress or sideline resistance within the school was in contrast to the SMT's inability to deal with external challenges. Two examples illustrate this and reveal the extent to which the school's internal values system can be undermined by a hostile external environment and factors in the wider socio-political context. In Downland there were a number of pupils with statements of special educational needs, largely for specific learning difficulties. These statements had included reference to individual non-specialist support. This was at odds with the ethos of inclusion and non-withdrawal from the mainstream classroom. Initially, the response of the school had been to provide non-specialist support in the context of the classroom, but this had been challenged by the parents of the statemented pupils who demanded that the requirements of the statement were fulfilled. The response of the school was to set up an alternative system in which the statemented pupils were to become the responsibility of a former member of the girls' school and to receive the 'entitlement' of their statement through her specialist teaching.

Clearly, the school, forced by the pressure of parents and the existing legislation, had been obliged to modify its overall response. The solution was in effect to 'hive off' a small sub-group of pupils in an effort to retain the liberal values of the school for the overwhelming majority by leaving the existing system intact. This may well have been a genuine attempt by the school to maintain its participatory and inclusive principles whilst at the same time bowing to the inevitable pressure of parents who were supported by a statutory entitlement to something that was 'special'. However, it pointed to an interesting dilemma for the school. The system was based on individual potential and made no provision for needs that could not be met in the context of the ordinary class. When confronted by a need that was apparently demanding of something additional to that on offer in the ordinary class the school reverted to a very traditional 'special' response. We shall see in Chapter 5 how some of the schools have responded to similar dilemmas.

The second example relates to the impact of the *Code of Practice* on the school. The *Code* (see Chapter 7) requires schools to demonstrate in a number of formal ways that they are taking steps to identify, assess and respond to the 'special' needs of pupils that cannot be met in the mainstream class. The formality of the assessment and recording procedures of the *Code* and its requirement for differentiation of pupils with special needs from their peers, was in many ways counter to the principles of Downland and presented a significant dilemma for the school. At Downland the emphasis was on meeting individual needs and releasing potential for all pupils within the context provided by the mainstream classroom. This is an admirable notion but does not, as we have seen, address the issue of what happens when that potential proves difficult to release in a mainstream classroom or when it is challenged by parents. It was clear to us that in some classrooms the system was not meeting the individual 'needs' of many of the pupils, not just those with statements. As a result of the *Code*, the school would have to demonstrate that it was effectively responding to the 'needs' of these pupils. In subsequent interviews it was not surprising to find the teaching and learning co-ordinator expressing considerable ambivalence about the *Code* because of the extent to which it required the school to create a distinctive special needs system and structure in place of the embedded approach they had sought to reflect their values of participation and equity. For the teaching and learning co-ordinator this represented the very antithesis of the approach the school was wanting. He saw in the *Code* a resurrection of a deficit model, a view of special education which was concerned with the failure and inability of a pre-determined population of pupils to access an unreconstructed curriculum. He contrasted this view with the view of the school in which the focus was on individual pupils as learners with potential requiring teachers and schools to rethink concepts of 'ability, difficulty and curriculum'.

There is here, therefore, a clear and understandable dilemma: the attempt to maintain the values position of the school in the face of an external imperative for the adoption of a more traditional view of special education. It is not surprising therefore that the teaching and learning co-ordinator was equally critical about one of the major features of the *Code* which can be seen as reinforcing the separateness of special educational provision. For him the use of a staged process of assessment and identification was a further retrograde step. He saw stages as being linked with a return to a form of labelling which was contrary to the values of equity and participation that the school wished to develop. He believed that this would reproduce a reductionist view of students rather than reflect the metaphors of 'potential' and 'energy' with which the school wished its students to be viewed.

This again demonstrates the admirable consistency with the formal views of the school but clearly indicates the tensions that faced the school as it was forced to review its provision in the light of the *Code.* The response of the school is interesting and consistent with that adopted to deal with the problems generated by the statemented pupils. It was based on a dividing of responsibilities. A special educational needs co-ordinator was appointed taking responsibility for those pupils for whom the mainstream curriculum was insufficiently responsive to 'release their potential' whilst the teaching and learning co-ordinator maintained a development role striving to make the curriculum *more* responsive to individual need across the school. As the school was confronted by these various challenges it was increasingly obliged to re-introduce more traditional notions of special educational needs. In the next section we shall see how the attempt to achieve greater equality and participation was further compromised.

THE REPRODUCTION OF TRADITIONAL
SPECIAL NEEDS STRUCTURES

When reviewing the way in which Downland actually responded to pupils who 'challenged the curriculum' it is interesting to note the extent to which it continued to rely on a significant support system. A large number of staff were involved in this system, acting as the primary response mechanism of the school to the issue of difference. The teaching and learning co-ordinator may well have acted as the 'conscience' of the school and carried out reviews of practice in departments, identifying particular areas of need and development, but the face-to-face response to difference remained a traditional piece of the armoury from the 'whole school approach'. The existence of pupils who presented as different, regardless of the label ascribed to them, presupposes the existence of mechanisms for their identification and allocation of additional 'special' help or support. The rhetoric may have been that these support teachers were there to act in the general support of the curriculum or for a range of pupils in a class, but our experience was that they were used primarily to ensure that pre-identified children were nursed through a largely unreconstituted curriculum.

The existence of this gap between rhetoric and practice produced in

Downland, a reversion to and significant reliance on a traditional model of support teaching as the principal means through which this particular contradiction could be managed. By relying so heavily on supporting pupils who were experiencing difficulties with the curriculum, the school was, in effect, acknowledging in practice what it disavowed in public – the existence of a level of difference within its pupil population which it was unable to accommodate within its standard form of provision. In this way we would argue that in Downland, despite the rhetoric of equity and participation, what was often actually happening was the extensive use of the traditional techniques of the whole school approach and a tacit acknowledgement of special need as the basis of the response to children who 'challenged' the curriculum.

It is also significant to note the high number of children with statements relating to specific learning difficulty. This suggests to us yet a further example of the extent to which the response to diversity through classroom provision was perceived, by some at least, as failing to meet the needs of all the pupils. Even with a reconstituted view of individual difference and a significant level of support provided to class teachers, here was a further group of pupils whose characteristics were seen as requiring them to have access to external resources so that they could be accommodated within the standard curriculum of the school. The case of specific learning difficulties is of course complex and is one that we will return to later in this book (see Chapter 6). It is, however, interesting to reflect on the extent to which, in this school, the pupils with a specific learning difficulty and those who required classroom support because of more generalized learning difficulties were actually experiencing anything that was innovatory or in any other way significantly different from what they would have received in any other mainstream school. Certainly, they would not have been labelled in the same way and it may well have been that their contributions to the life of the school were in a context in which they were certain to receive a high and sustained level of praise. But in terms of their being able to access a curriculum that was more differentiated or engage in learning activities that were new or novel, the case remains unproven.

ISSUES OF INCLUSION AND EXCLUSION

An issue of growing concern nationally – the exclusion of pupils with behaviour problems – also impacted on the situation at Downland. The school was not unwilling to exclude pupils who did not live up to the high expectations that it set, or who were considered to damage the internal or external image and reputation of the school within the wider community. Indeed, the headteacher made it clear to us that he regarded the exclusion of non-conforming pupils as an appropriate response in order to establish the type of ethos and climate that he was seeking to establish. It would, of course, be unreasonable to assume that a headteacher should not retain the ultimate sanction of exclusion as a part of the repertoire of responses that a school has to deal with difficult pupils. However, it did appear to us that this was a school which was not having to deal with an over-representation of pupils who were likely to prove especially problematic. The rate of exclusion did, therefore, appear to us to be high, and not in the overall spirit of inclusion that the school espoused. Recent research on exclusion (Imich, 1994; Parfrey, 1994) points to the differential rates of exclusion that occurs between areas and individual schools. This suggests that it is within-school factors which may play the most significant part in accounting for this phenomenon. If this is the case, then a school as committed to inclusion as Downland is placed in a somewhat contradictory position in terms of the extent of the match between the rhetoric and the practice. The issue of the rate of exclusion, moreover, was not something that was concealed from us; for the school it was clear that those pupils who could not function successfully represented a threat to the integrity of the overall ethos of the school and had, therefore, to be excluded.

This is just one example of what we might refer to as the dilemma of inclusion and exclusion that characterized at least part of the culture of this school. Exclusion existed at other levels within the school. For example, we have already suggested that there was a tendency to stereotype those staff who were most resistant to the rhetoric of inclusion and most demanding in respect of their call for support in the classroom. It was clear to us that these staff were in effect an excluded minority insofar as they were characterized as the irredeemable and those unable to respond to the challenges of an inclusive approach. Many of these staff were formerly employed at the girls' school which became a part of the newly created Downland during the process of rationalization of secondary provision in the town. It was made clear to us that this was far from a merger of equals but essentially a takeover whereby the longer established and financially better endowed boys' school effectively subsumed the girls' school.

Any merger which involves the loss of identity of one of the partners is necessarily painful, the more so for those with a very strong sense of identity and attachment to what we can describe as the victim. In a situation which can be conceived as one where there are winners and losers, there may well have been a sense in which opposing camps were established as a means of maintaining some sense of that lost identity. What we found in Downland was that there had been a high rate of attrition of the former members of the girls' school staff, and that most of them had become stereotyped as 'the unreconstituted' members of the new school. As we untangled the process of the merger it became clear to us that not only had members of the girls' school been encouraged to leave but that there had also been a deliberate attempt to undermine the practices and systems which the former school had operated.This was confirmed by the few remaining staff including one who had become a member of the senior management team in the new school. It was suggested to us that the response to diversity as it was practised in the girls' school, although not having the high profile that it was accorded in Downland, and although relying very heavily on withdrawal and the nurturing of the most vulnerable in small groups, did in fact produce better outcomes for both the pupils and staff.

We were not able to check these assertions out in any rigorous sense, but they are interesting indicators yet again of what we might refer to as an exclusionary attitude within Downland. The existence of alternative perspectives was not tolerated and although the school focused on the development of the institution through the development of its staff, it was clear that only certain perspectives were likely to be tolerated as part of the process of that development. The exclusion of staff insofar as they were either encouraged to leave or in terms of their being marginalized within the school was a characteristic of the situation as we found it at Downland. The notion of the existence of dissonance as an adjunct to the process of development at either individual or institutional level was not, therefore, part of the rationale of the senior staff. Pupils were excluded if they could not or would not respond. Staff who were not 'one of us' were encouraged to leave; those that remained found themselves marginalized and often denied a voice within the school.

INNOVATION OR RENOVATION

In seeking to locate the developments in Downland into the wider context of this book we must stress that we are not seeking to undermine the serious effort that this particular school had made in seeking a new resolution of the dilemmas involved in attempting to realize the values of equity and participation. Nor are we suggesting that Downland was the only school taking this particular path or that it was the only site where these issues were emerging. In Chapter 5 we will make reference to other schools which operate with a similar rhetoric of participation and equity and where we have subsequently conducted extensive fieldwork. In these schools the same kinds of issues and dilemmas emerged. In striving to realize human values through these kinds of radical approaches it would appear that schools do not simply resolve the problem of how to respond to difference. What appears to happen is that they generate a new range of issues and dilemmas which continue to resonate as an agenda for debate. These issues and dilemmas have some common features and it is worth exploring them here.

It is clear that attempting to realize the values of equity and participation does not remove but increases pressures for schools. In particular there are pressures and issues for schools at an organizational level along the lines suggested by Skrtic (1991), and Ainscow (1991/1994). There are also pressures and issues for those teachers who are asked to take on board new ways of working; this presents a number of problems for those teachers in the way they view themselves as developing professionals. Writers such as Ainscow point to the likelihood that change within an institution is likely to produce casualties amongst the staff. It is certainly likely to produce resistance amongst those expected to realize it in practice, and this is perhaps why in the school effectiveness literature (Ainscow, 1994 etc.) there is an emphasis on the need for a clear lead from the senior management team. For those who remain 'unconverted', the senior management team are left with a range of options. Internal exclusion is one of these as we saw at Downland and elsewhere. This does, however, generate mixed messages for those who view exclusion of this nature as a part of a contradictory process within the school as a whole community. Furthermore, teachers charged with implementing change need to have the confidence that a range of support will be available to them as they begin to explore, implement and accept new approaches. In Downland, as elsewhere, the potential danger was that the rush to achieve change in the way that teaching and learning was undertaken exceeded the capability of the school to deliver the new materials, professional development and other support necessary for its implementation. Where this 'technology' is not immediately available there is always the potential for resistance and retrenchment to occur. Similarly, for those experiencing the most difficulty in implementing the new approaches there is the danger that they become the institutional scapegoats for the failure to achieve change.

What appears to happen in the struggle for greater participation and equity is that resistance is generated throughout the system. From within the mainstream itself, subject teachers, for example, faced with a range of competing demands, are understandably faced with a major readjustment of their pedagogy if they are to accommodate the values of equity and participation. Without a 'technology' to support them, they are inevitably confronted with complex pressures which not all will be able to assimilate. Furthermore as that 'technology' emerges it may well be that it demands of these teachers a change in their working practice which they are not willing to make, despite the impact this might have on realizing the liberal values to which they apparently subscribe. The effect of this may well be to increase rather than reduce the resistance within schools.

In this situation, it appears that even the most 'radical' schools may be forced to revert to some of the provision associated with more traditional special education values. Schools are increasingly forced to balance competing values and demands. They are required to compete in a market place and will inevitably adjust their systems and structures to the prevailing climate. Many of the changes in the external context have increased the 'voice' of parents, leaving schools and LEAs to attempt to balance what may well be a number of competing and conflicting views as to how schools should respond to the various pressures they face. As we will suggest in Chapter 8, the extent to which an individual school can reconcile competing parental 'voices' is open to conjecture, and that even LEA planning can be blown off course if there is significant parental opposition. A set of liberal values and its accompanying rhetoric of participation and equity may not be sufficient to counter the demands of well-organized pressure groups demanding 'special' treatment for *their* children.

We would reiterate, however, that the processes and systems that we found in the innovatory schools that we identified despite their difficulties in implementation are not to be regarded as simply temporary. In all the schools that we visited, the attempt to reconceptualize special needs education and to develop new systems and structures were often producing a dynamic and self-critical context in which new ideas were subject to constant scrutiny and adaptation. The schools and the majority of the staff were actively trying to work through the implications of viewing special needs as the result of an interactive process rather than simply operating some loose but convenient rhetoric of a 'whole school approach' which would have provided them with a legitimate reason for not attempting the very difficult task of breaking new ground in respect of pupils with special educational needs. Where we report in a critical light the implications of some of these attempts at rethinking, or highlight contradictions in rhetoric and practice, or point to contradictions between the degree of assimilation and practice, we do so as part of a process of reflection and analysis. Such an endeavour is intended to support the development of ideas and practice by providing an interpretation of developments in such a way that those charged with their actual implementation have an alternative perspective through which they might seek a further extension of their practice systems and structures.

Tensions and contradictions in these schools are indicative to us of the dilemmas inherent in attempting to resolve the fundamental problem that schools face in attempting to realize an agenda of liberal values. In attempting a response which might be regarded as more 'inclusive', these schools were seeking one particular resolution of this problem. The problems that we identified can be seen in relation to a number of levels. There are clearly those that revolve around the development of an 'effective' school. They relate to the development of an organizational culture and ethos through which the response to diversity is seen in terms of an indicator of individual and institutional effectiveness rather than as a characteristic of aberrant individual pupils. Also, there are problems that relate directly to the application of actual pedagogical practices in individual classrooms and in which individual teachers have to become fluent. This is an issue which, we contend, has not been given sufficient prominence within the inclusive schools movement.

Finally, there are those problems which relate to the broader context of education and to issues such as the appropriateness of a centrally defined curriculum for *all* pupils. In the absence of a fully developed and effective pedagogy through which this can be achieved by all teachers this will remain a fundamental tension and the source of continuing dilemmas for schools and teachers. Striking a balance between the notions of curricular entitlement and full inclusion will require a period of intense reflection before it is both fully understood by all involved and a pedagogy evolved through which it can become a practical reality. It is in this light, therefore, that developments in the innovatory schools should be seen.

ISSUES OF RESISTANCE IN THE DOWNLAND EXPERIENCE

Although this might appear a disappointing way of reporting on developments in this school, we believe it quite clearly demonstrates the inherent instability which exists within attempts to resolve the complex issues which underlay special education in mainstream schools. Resolutions of these issues based on a powerful articulation of a values position premised on the rhetoric of participation and equity may, therefore, be only temporary. We will suggest in the case of Downland we find an attempt to respond to diversity which engages with some of the dimensions of this complexity but ignores others. In particular we will point to the problem of resistance to the adoption of this approach at a number of levels. For example, one explanation of the failure of the rhetoric to be realized in practice could be in terms of the inevitable weakening of messages that takes place as they are transmitted throughout a complex organization. The evidence from Downland suggests that in attempting to realize this value position the proponents of the 'vision' failed to take account of the extent of the resistance they would meet from subject teachers. The extent to which staff could be 'converted' by a continued assertion of the 'correctness' of the vision was to misunderstand the nature of change within professional groups. In particular the SMT failed to appreciate the extent to which the adoption of a new approach to special educational needs depended on the active participation of subject staff who were expected to carry through this significant innovation. Downland represents an example of how, when there is a mismatch between institutional rhetoric and the availability of a suitable technology through which it can be delivered, resistance is likely to be experienced, frustrating the intended change. In the case of Downland where the rhetoric of participation and equity was articulated so forcefully, it is interesting to compare the extent to which the zeal of the senior management was replicated in those who were required to realize the vision on a practical basis. Those invested with promulgating the rhetoric maintained their enthusiasm and conviction; some of those required to deliver the new approach were clearly losing faith and returning to traditional classroom practices, seeing no benefit to them as class teachers in changing their practices in the absence of a better alternative though the new vision might be realized.

Staff development was central to the overall strategy within Downland, but much of it had focused on the recharging of the rhetoric in the expectation that the practice would follow the rhetoric. Although there had been some interesting work attempted in developing the curriculum, this was not universal throughout the school, and where gaps existed the message from the teaching and learning co-ordinator tended to stress the need for staff to find their own solutions to problems. Although congruent with the general vision of the school, this hardly inspired confidence in those staff who were used to a more 'traditional' teaching role. Calls for 'creative' solutions in the absence of a systematic and sustained commitment to developing the curriculum are unlikely to sustain an initiative. In Downland the understandable reluctance of some staff to replace carefully developed pedagogic repertoires for an only partially developed alternative remained as a major problem for the SMT and the teaching and learning co-ordinator as they attempted to realize their vision. The failure of this alternative to emerge contributed to the resistance of many of the staff.

Other commentators in this field offer a similar analysis. Ainscow (1991/1994), for example, writing about the creation of effective schools for all, suggests that the question of school improvement and development depends on more than the straightforward espousal of a particular rhetoric from the senior management. He identifies five widely acknowledged key conditions involved in the development of inclusive schools:

- Effective leadership spread through the school.
- Involvement of staff, students and community in school policies and decision-making.
- A commitment to collaborative planning.
- Attention to potential benefits of enquiry and reflection.
- A policy of staff development.

For Ainscow the key to the process of creating effective schools is staff development. He is concerned to ensure that the staff of a school see their own professional development as intimately linked to the over-all development of the school as a whole. This requires the development of a group of teachers who become skilled in the art of problem-solving. Without the capacity to respond to problems as they emerge *in situ*, rhetoric alone is not sufficient. For Ainscow (1995): 'the professional learning of teachers is central to the development of an inclusive policy, and the classroom is an important centre for teacher development as the training workshop' (p. 72).

The work of Skrtic (1991) can also be adduced to support this per-spective. For Skrtic the failure of schools to develop along inclusive lines is a function of the tendency of many institutions to develop into bureaucratic organizations. Drawing on a number of sources (Mintzberg, 1979/1983), Skrtic argues that there is a likelihood for schools to configure themselves as professional bureaucracies. This results in the emergence of organizational and professional structures which are designed to maintain an institutional homeostasis or inertia in the ways that it responds to client groups. For schools, this results in the establishment of principles and professional practices which are concerned to preserve existing and established notions of what constitutes 'good practice'. These boundaries, once established, become extended into standardized systems which are resistant to change. When confronted by atypical clients who are not easily assim-ilated into the existing organizational systems and practices, the response is usually one of rejection or exclusion.

For Skrtic this account helps to explain the development of exclusive schools. There is a clear tendency for schools to resist the challenge presented by non-standard clients; to react to such clients by a re-statement and endorsement of existing practices. Such a process can lead to the development of non-innovative approaches on the part of professionals, of a tendency for practices to revert to an acceptable and standardized norm, and the emergence of a culture that is exclusive and resistant to changes in the way it performs its basic routines. According to Skrtic what is needed to develop inclusivity in schools is: 'A fully open ended process – one that seeks a truly creative solution to each unique need – requires a problem-solving orientation premised on innovation rather than standardization' (Ainscow, 1991, p. 25).

This search for 'creative effort to find a novel solution . . . and . . . divergent thinking aimed at innovation' (Mintzberg, 1979, p. 436) was, we suggest, at the heart of the approach that was adopted in Downland. The role of the teaching and learning co-ordinator, someone deliberately chosen from a non-special needs background, was clearly an attempt to challenge from within, the existing notions of how the teaching and learning of these pupils could be approached to meet the inclusive criteria of the school. This represents in Skrtic's terms an attempt to create the basis on which a 'discursive coupling' could take place throughout the school in which novel solutions could emerge and be promulgated by the catalytic effect of a change agent and the ending of traditional structural arrangements for the response to the problems created by diversity. Whether as problem-solvers (Ainscow, 1995) or reflective thinkers (Skrtic), those at the 'sharp' end of delivery are seen as central to the development of alternative responses to diversity.

The rhetoric of 'reflection' is deeply enshrined in much of the writing on teacher/school development. It is, however, a problematic concept easier to describe than to establish and, therefore, not immune from criticism (Smyth, 1991). In Downland, despite the strong emphasis on professional and institutional development, there remained, at the level of the classroom teacher, a continuing gulf between the espoused institutional rhetoric and the actual practices in relation to pupils with special needs. When we presented our evidence of this gulf to the teaching and learning co-ordinator and the senior management team, it was significant to note how this resistance was interpreted in terms of individual culpability on the part of some teachers to reconstitute their practice rather than a failure on the part of the school to realize its aim through the development of an inadequate pedagogy, or the appropriate organizational structures. Locating the failure of *all* teachers to rise to the challenge of diversity as the result of the inadequacy of a small unreconstituted minority is one way of avoiding the issue of the adequacy of the available pedagogy. It highlights the extent to which, when an emphasis is placed on participation and equity, there is a significant risk of breakdown at the level at which this policy is realized, that is at the level of the classroom teacher. Unless there is an adequate and appropriate technology available to ensure that teachers have the confidence to adjust their methods and procedures to accommodate the new demands, there is the danger of significant resistance.

In much the same way there was resistance on the part of a section of the parents to the attempt to respond to diversity through an approach based on equity and participation. Parents who had struggled to achieve statements of special educational needs which specified individual support and tuition to meet specific difficulties were quick to challenge the situation in Downland when that individualized support was not forthcoming. This particular 'voice' expressed no interest in participation if that meant that *their* children were not receiving the additional 'special' support which the statement had recommended. The realization of equity for this group was a tangible system of individualized and specialist support delivered to individual pupils rather than a less tangible realization of a values position which offered little of concrete value other than placement within the mainstream classroom. Faced with this resistance the school reverted to a more conventional approach.

If resistance from parents constituted a local resistance then the final dimension of resistance that the school faced can be seen in relation to the national context. It is extremely difficult for a school to resist guidance issued at national level. For Downland the introduction of the *Code of Practice* represented the vehicle through which the resistance inside the school and from within the parent body could be given formal expression. It placed the school in a vulnerable position in respect of parents as it legitimized their demands for a 'special' and 'distinctive' provision for statemented pupils; it also allowed the voice of those staff who were calling for a more 'effective' provision for non-statemented special needs pupils to press for the systems and structures which the school had consciously attempted to eradicate. As much as the absence of the systems and structures was regarded as an expression of the commitment to equity and participation for the SMT, so it represented an omission for external scrutineers such as Ofsted which might have resulted in an adverse report. As we have indicated, the school was thus forced to reinvent vestiges of a traditional approach to the special education system to meet an external imperative which, in requiring schools to demonstrate the distinctiveness of their provision for special needs, actually ran counter to the attempts to achieve a greater equity and participation on the part of this school.

It is of course always easy to focus on aspects of a school's provision, and we could be accused of criticizing a school that was in the process of evolving its response to diversity at a time when external factors were requiring a greater uniformity and consistency of practice in respect of special educational needs. In making this analysis we are not concerned with undermining what Downland was trying to achieve; indeed we still regard the developments in this school as an important contribution to the response to special educational needs in mainstream schools. Our concern, however, is to raise questions about the implications implicit in attempting to achieve a certain values position in mainstream schools, and the extent to which the mere espousal of a powerful rhetoric is sufficient in its own right to realize these values. Our choice of Downland is grounded very much in the knowledge that as a school concerned about its own development, this analysis will be viewed as a contribution to the process of self-review and reflection on which it prided itself and on which it based its institutional development.

Integration and inclusion

Throughout the period which we have been considering, from the late 1970s to the present, a significant minority of children has continued to be educated, not in the mainstream schools where new 'approaches' to special needs provision were emerging, but in special schools and other specialized settings. Given the concern within these new approaches for questions of participation and equity, therefore, it is scarcely surprising that their emergence has been accompanied by similar concerns about the extent to which children with more marked difficulties and disabilities could and should be educated alongside their peers in mainstream schools. Such concerns have, as we shall see, centred around the notions of integration and, latterly, of 'inclusive education'.

To a significant extent, integration, inclusion and mainstream 'approaches' to special needs provision are simply different ways of addressing the same core issues. Certainly, for writers such as Dessent (1987), the development of whole school approaches is very much about finding means of reducing and removing the segregation of children into special schools. However, the issues around integration on the one hand and the development of mainstream approaches on the other are not entirely the same. Many schools have developed sophisticated responses to the 'special needs' of their pupils without ever having to address the educational needs of children with more severe difficulties, who were, as a result of LEA policy, placed in special settings. Indeed, the school we studied in the preceding chapter is a not untypical example of the emergence of a radical – indeed, avowedly 'inclusive' – response to special needs in a school which contained no pupils categorized as having moderate or severe learning difficulties, significant behaviour difficulties, physical disabilities or sensory impairments.

The interest in integration from the mid-1970s onwards, therefore, both reinterprets and extends the issues raised by special needs 'approaches' in mainstream schools. Moreover, it is arguable that the emergence of inclusion as an issue in recent years has posed a new set of challenges to those schools and has defined a new way of thinking about the relationship between mainstream schools and what we choose to call 'special educational needs'. In this chapter, therefore, we turn our attention to the ways in which the 'human values' of equity and participation have been played out in respect of attempts to promote integration and inclusion.

THE EMERGENCE OF INTEGRATION

As special education developed in the first three-quarters of the twentieth century, there seems to have been no great faith that the majority of children in special schools would be sufficiently transformed by their educational experiences to allow them to be returned to mainstream schools. On the contrary, as we saw in Chapter 1, the concern was that there were many children already in mainstream schools who could scarcely cope with the standard curriculum and pedagogy to be found there, and who were seen to be in need of some form of special education themselves. Not surprisingly, therefore, far less attention was placed on transferring *children* from special to mainstream schools than on transferring *special education* in the form of special classes and remedial teaching.

The reasons why this situation should have changed are many and complex. Vislie (1995), for instance, suggests that a period of economic expansion was accompanied by a liberalization of values and an increased concern with issues of equity in many Western democracies – reflected in the UK, for example, in the growth of comprehensive schooling. Moreover, a steady stream of research began to raise questions about the effectiveness of special education in enabling children to learn and the breadth of the educational experience which it was able to offer (see Galloway and Goodwin, 1987, for a useful review of this research). Finally, the examples of other national systems – the Scandinavian countries, Italy, the USA – began to suggest that special schooling could, to a greater or lesser extent, be dismantled without disastrous consequences either for its pupils or for mainstream schools. When these national experiments began to be replicated in the UK in a few schools and LEAs, it looked as though the tide was set fair for a massive increase in integration.

The Warnock Report (DES, 1978) and the subsequent 1981 Education Act appeared to be the enabling devices that would serve as the trigger for this anticipated increase. Although the latter gave no stronger commitment to integration than had been given in previous legislation (such as the 1976 Education Act), it did abolish the old ascertainment procedures which had effectively restricted legally-protected special provision to special schools. Instead, the section 5 assessment procedures and introduction of 'statements' of special need enabled such provision to be made and protected wherever the child was placed – including in mainstream schools. Moreover, by giving official recognition to the term 'special educational needs' and by abolishing the old categories of handicap, it gave a strong indication that the rigid boundaries between 'types' of children with learning difficulties and disabilities and between them and all other children were to be lowered, if not completely removed.

In the period since the 1981 Act most, if not all, LEAs have reorganized their special school provision (many more than once) in ways which are derived to a greater or lesser extent from the principles of the Warnock Report. Across the country, special schools have sought to develop closer ties with mainstream schools, or have disappeared to be replaced by units attached to mainstream schools – many of which have themselves become more flexible 'support bases', or have dissolved themselves entirely into ordinary classes. Similarly, it is unusual now to come across a mainstream school which does not have a number of children with statements in its population and which does not educate children who in earlier times would probably have been placed in a special school.

However, these changes in the surface structures and practices of integration give a somewhat misleading picture. A series of studies of placement statistics (Swann, 1985/1988; Norwich, 1994) have revealed a somewhat complex situation. There has certainly been a high level of activity in relation to integration, with LEAs busily rearranging their patterns of provision and statementing. Moreover, there may have been changes in respect of certain sub-groups within the special needs population – with some groups becoming more fully integrated at the same time as segregated provision for other groups increases. However, there is no convincing evidence of a substantial overall increase in levels of integration between 1981 and the present.

This process of activity without real change may be somewhat more intelligible when we look at a specific example. Like many metropolitan authorities, 'Northborough'[1] had developed by the time of the 1981 Act a substantial special school sector, comprising a full panoply of day and residential schools for children who were regarded, in the pre-Warnock terminology, as educationally moderately or severely sub-normal, maladjusted, physically handicapped and so on. It was no accident that the city had more special schools than comprehensive schools, for instance, since such extensive provision was widely regarded, before the rhetoric of integration became dominant, as a mark of an LEA's commitment to meeting the needs of *all* its pupils.

In the period immediately following the Warnock Report, Northborough made no significant changes in the overall structure of its provision, though a series of small-scale developments took place: special schools began to be described using the new terminology; children with statements began to appear in mainstream schools; and various integration projects sprang up around the city, often on the initiative of particular schools and teachers. One particularly significant change that did take place across the system as a whole was that the population of a number of special schools began to shrink. The rolls of the city's moderate learning difficulties schools, for instance, shrank by some 15 per cent between 1980 and 1985, and those of its schools for children with physical difficulties shrank by nearly 40 per cent. To a certain extent, this was due to the enhanced flexibility which the 1981 Act created for meeting children's special needs in mainstream schools and thus avoiding referral to special education in the first place. However, it was also due to an overall decline in the numbers of children of school age in the city which saw the closure and merger of a number of mainstream schools at this time.

The difficulties which this created for the city were compounded by the fact that it already had surplus capacity within its special school sector. By 1985, only just over 900 of its 1300-plus special schools places were actually filled. When, therefore, Northborough decided to reorganize its special schools, the motives were inevitably mixed. The proposals were couched in a rhetoric of integration that was, no doubt, sincere: barriers *between* types of special school were to be broken down in order to integrate the old categories of handicap within 'generic' special schools, and the special schools themselves were to form partnerships with mainstream schools in order to explore the possibilities of outreach and integration. However, the merger and closure of schools in the special sector would also serve exactly the same purpose as equivalent moves in the mainstream sector – the removal of surplus places, the reduction of the number of buildings to be maintained, and the creation of larger, more economical schools.

The reorganization that eventually took place reflected these ambiguities. Special schools were closed and special school places reduced. However, special schooling was by no means abolished. Two large 'generic' special schools were created at secondary level, for instance, catering between them for children with moderate learning difficulties, severe learning difficulties, profound and multiple learning difficulties, autism and emotional and behavioural difficulties. Although these schools eventually began to develop the sort of integration partnerships which the original plan had envisaged, this was only after the partnerships which mainstream schools had had with their predecessors had been disturbed, if not destroyed, by the process of reorganization. Strangely, in view of the national trend and the rhetoric of integration within the reorganization plans, the school for children with physical disabilities was left untouched. Whether because the cost of adapting mainstream schools would have been too great, or because the school, as a regional facility, was an income-generator for the LEA, or because of a fear of possible parental resistance, children with any significant level of physical disability continued to have no alternative to special schooling. Moreover, the reorganization actually created not only a new special school, but a new *type* of special school – a college for young people aged 14+, offering a largely vocational curriculum, and recruiting its population not only from those already in special schools, but also from disaffected pupils in the mainstream.

Whatever the rights and wrongs of Northborough's reorganization, it starkly illuminates the statistical analyses of Swann and others. Whatever there was in these changes that was likely to promote integration, there were other tendencies that were just as likely to promote segregation. Moreover, integration initiatives remained substantially the responsibility of individual headteachers who could choose to be more or less proactive in this respect. Integrated facilities as such (units, support bases, satellite classes and so on) were, by and large, not mandated by reorganization. Not surprisingly, therefore, after an initial dip following reorganization, the proportion of children placed in special schools began to climb again so that by the early 1990s it was approaching the pre-reorganization level and by 1996 Northborough had established itself in the top ten of 'segregating' LEAs in the country.

Moreover, the process is currently being replicated once again. Since reorganization, numbers of pupils in the city's schools – and therefore in its special schools – have continued to decline, mergers and closures in the mainstream sector have continued, and the city, in common with other LEAs, has been under significant financial pressure from central government. It has now decided to undertake a second reorganization of its special schools, this time closing schools and reducing capacity significantly. Once again, an upturn in integration is a distinct possibility, and this time there is a clear intention to create integrated facilities in mainstream schools. Once again, however, there is to be no total abolition of special schooling: six special schools will remain, catering for some 400-plus children (about 60 per cent of the 1991 figures), and even the vocational college looks set to remain open, albeit in a somewhat modified form. Moreover, although a marked increase in mainstream placement is proposed, much of this is in the form of unit provision rather than placement in mainstream classes as such; a further 200-plus children will be educated in such provision. In other words, although there will be some move away from special *schooling*, even in this relatively radical reorganization there will be no significant move away from special *placement* as such.

THE LIMITS OF INTEGRATION

What is striking about the Northborough experience – an experience, we suggest, that has been replicated in LEAs across the country – is the way in which major reorganizations of special education have failed to result in anything that might reasonably be called an integrated system of provision. The reasons are, perhaps, not too difficult to discern:

- It is evident that special education policy in Northborough has not been driven by integration alone. Whatever commitment there may or may not have been to integration as a principle on which policy should be based, more pragmatic considerations have clearly played at least as big a part. The most obvious of these has been the need to reduce surplus special school places and hence to manage tightly-constrained resources more efficiently. However, other, less overt, considerations may also have been at work: a reluctance to stress mainstream schools by moving too quickly to integration; the need to make provision where mainstream schools felt they could not accommodate particular pupils; a lack of resources to make physical adaptations to school buildings or to engage in the whole-sale training of mainstream teachers; a concern about the views of the parents of children originally placed in special schools (the 1985 proposals were accompanied by a hefty programme of parental consultation and by considerable parental anxiety) – and so on.
- It is equally not evident that such commitment to integration as there may have been in Northborough has been unequivocal and over-riding. Both reorganizations, far from sweeping segregated special education away, have established a place for special schools and units. If anything, they have been more concerned with refurbishing special provision – creating larger special schools, establishing new types of special school, and redistributing the special school population – than with creating integrated provision.
- This preoccupation with reorganizing the special sector has meant that neither reorganization has sought to address the nature of *mainstream* provision in order to create ordinary schools and classrooms

in which a wider diversity of children might be appropriately educated. Although both the 1985 and 1996 proposals involved, to a greater or lesser extent, the relocation of some special provision and pupils into mainstream schools, neither set out to achieve any significant restructuring of mainstream schooling as such, or any redefinition of teaching roles, or any reskilling of mainstream teachers.

There are, of course, examples of LEAs which have addressed the question of integration much more comprehensively and effectively than Northborough. For every Northborough, there is a Devon or Cumbria or Oxfordshire where levels of integrated provision and commitment to the principles of integration are palpably higher. However, we suggest that Northborough illustrates an ambivalence at the heart of moves towards integration over the past two decades – an ambivalence which goes to the heart of the way in which integration has been understood in the UK.

This ambivalence is perhaps most clearly seen in the governmental and quasi-governmental pronouncements of this period. Although the promotion of integration has been an avowed goal of government policy since at least the 1976 Education Act, such pronouncements have invariably stopped short of an *unequivocal* advocacy of integration as a goal either for all pupils 'with special needs' or for any particular group. The formulation of the Warnock Report, taken up in the 1981 Act and echoed again in the 1993 Act, is both typical and illuminating in this respect. Warnock makes it clear that integration is no absolute aim by entering two important caveats. First, even where 'integration' is seen as desirable, it is defined in such a way as to legitimate the continuation of a high level of segregation. Integration is seen to take the form of a sort of continuum – from locational integration (placing children 'with special needs' physically into mainstream schools), through social integration (some degree of social – but not educational – interaction between children 'with special needs' and their mainstream peers) to functional integration (some unspecified level of participation in common learning activities and experiences). There is no expectation that every pupil 'with special needs' will be functionally integrated, but rather that children will be integrated in the manner and to the extent that is appropriate to their particular 'needs' and circumstances.

Second, Warnock repeats the formula of the 1976 Education Act to the effect that the desirability of integration in any particular case is dependent on meeting the three conditions of 'practicability, efficiency and cost' (7.49). As Warnock interprets these three nebulous conditions, they emerge as: the capacity of the integrated placement for meeting the child's 'special needs'; the compatibility of that placement with the effective education of the mainstream peers amongst whom the child was to be placed; and the use of LEA resources in a cost-efficient and cost-effective manner. Warnock adds that the 'paramount aim' of these three conditions 'is to ensure a high quality of special educational provision' (7.49). In other words, the concern to integrate children 'with special educational needs' is simply one of a number of concerns that have to be taken into account in making placement decisions. Moreover, the *over-riding* consideration is not integrated placement but the delivery of special educational provision. Integration, however desirable, is thus not a radical *alternative* to special educational provision, but is, rather, a means of delivering that provision in a somewhat less segregated setting.

It is, we suspect, this priority accorded to special educational provision which creates the ambivalence within the integration movement and sets insuperable limits to its achievements. So long as this priority remains, integration will inevitably be halted wherever and whenever it is seen to conflict with the delivery of special educational provision. A lack of resources, the challenges posed by a particular child's or group's difficulties, resistance from mainstream teachers and schools, the inadequacies of skill and pedagogy in mainstream classrooms – any or all of these can and do constitute good enough reasons to curtail attempts at integration.

Moreover, the preoccupation with special educational provision means that integration has tended to be interpreted simply as the *relocation* of the provision made by special schools into mainstream schools and classrooms. Northborough's 1996 proposals are thus entirely typical in their assumption that integration requires the creation of 'units' in ordinary schools which can operate as mini-special schools. By the same token, Warnock's continuum of integration is nothing more or less than a sliding scale to indicate how deeply particular forms of special educational provision can be located within the mainstream setting. The corollary of this notion of relocation, of course, is that mainstream schools and classrooms tend to be seen simply as the 'hosts' of special educational provision rather than as an integral part of it. It is evident in Warnock, in the Northborough reorganizations and, we suggest, in attempts at integration across the country, that the nature of mainstream schooling is taken largely for granted, and that serious and fundamental attempts to restructure mainstream education as part of the integration process are few and far between.

It is, perhaps, worth drawing attention to one further source of ambivalence and limitation in attempts at integration in the UK. Writing in the mid-1980s, Tomlinson (1982/1985) argued that special education was likely to remain resistant to all attacks from outside, and indeed to continue to expand because it was the product of the vested interests of the professionals working within it. Although this 'vested interests' account of special education has been criticized for being somewhat simplistic (Copeland, 1993), it is certainly the case that integration, at any rate, is a highly *professionalized* arena. Although, therefore, placement in mainstream settings alongside non-disabled peers has tended to be taken as something to which children 'with special needs' have some sort of entitlement, decisions as to the feasibility of such placement have been assumed to require the exercise of professional judgement. If, then, such children have rights in respect of integration, they are rights which are mediated by professionals' concerns for the management of resources, the maintenance of the education system as a whole, the quality of provision for other children than the individual in question – and so on. It is no accident, therefore, that the decision-making procedures established by the 1981 Act give the final say about placement to LEA administrators acting on the advice of professionals rather than to parents (let alone children), and that parents have, in practice, found it very difficult to get their voices heard within these processes (Armstrong, 1995; Sandow *et al.*, 1987).

It is not difficult to see parallels between the course of the integration movement and the course of the whole school approach which we outlined in Chapter 2. In both cases, we see an essentially liberal movement – embodying Sayer's (1994/1987) 'human values' – which has brought about some reconstruction of how special education is conceptualized and delivered. In both cases, that reconceptualization has involved an attempt to bring special education into a closer relationship with mainstream education. And in both cases, that attempt has been limited by the absence of any means or will to engage in a radical reconstruction of the education system as a whole or, indeed, of the wider socio-economic system within which education is located. We saw how, in the case of the whole school approach, a growing awareness of these limitations contributed to the emergence of a more radical alternative which attempted just such a reconstruction. Something similar is, we suggest, happening in respect of integration; a new and radical conceptualization of the relationship between the education of children 'with special educational needs' and the nature of mainstream schools is taking shape under the aegis of the inclusive schools movement. It is to this that we now wish to turn.

INCLUSION: A RADICAL ALTERNATIVE TO INTEGRATION?

At the time of writing, both the strength and the coherence of the inclusive education movement are somewhat difficult to assess. In the United States, notions of inclusion are being heavily promoted by particular lobby groups (Fuchs and Fuchs, 1994) and are beginning to play a significant part in guiding policy in states and districts. Similarly, in Britain, the growing interest in inclusion is reflected by, amongst other things, the advocacy of inclusive education by senior figures in the 'traditional' special needs field (Mittler, 1995; Wedell, 1995), whilst at least one authority has begun to develop and implement a policy on inclusion as opposed to integration (Corbett, 1994). Certainly, there is a widespread interest on the part of academics and researchers across the world who see inclusion as a potentially radical alternative to the somewhat faltering approach which has been characteristic of integration (Ainscow, 1994; Clark, Dyson and Millward, 1995; O'Hanlon, 1995; Ainscow and Sebba, 1996).

On the other hand, the terminology of inclusion is by no means common among educators in the UK, nor is it at all clear that it has common meaning across national boundaries (Booth, 1995). In many cases, particularly in the American literature, 'inclusion' seems to be used simply as a more fashionable alternative to 'integration' – a problem which is recognized by the increasing use of the term 'full inclusion' as a means of signalling that something different and more radical than 'mere' integration is intended. Part of the difficulty undoubtedly is that the *outcomes* of both 'full' inclusion and 'full' integration would appear to be the same – that is, that children are educated alongside their peers in mainstream schools, regardless of their 'special needs'. However, within the inclusive education movement it is possible to detect ways of approaching this common outcome which are quite different from those which have informed the integration movement. This is perhaps most vividly illustrated by the so-called Salamanca Declaration (UNESCO, 1994).

In 1994, representatives of eighty-eight national governments and twenty-five international organizations concerned with education met in Salamanca under the auspices of UNESCO and the Spanish government. The Statement which they adopted sets out the rationale for inclusive education in the clearest possible terms, and is worth quoting at length:

We believe and proclaim that:
- every child has a fundamental right to education, and must be given the opportunity to achieve and maintain an acceptable level of learning;
- every child has unique characteristics, interests, abilities and learning needs;
- educational systems should be designed and educational programmes implemented to take into account the wide diversity of these characteristics and needs;
- those with special educational needs must have access to regular schools who should accommodate them within a child-centred pedagogy capable of meeting these needs;
- regular schools with this inclusive orientation are the most effective means of combating discriminatory attitudes, creating welcoming communities, building an inclusive society, and achieving education for all; moreover, they provide an effective education to the majority of children and improve the efficiency and ultimately the cost-effectiveness of the entire educational system. (Salamanca Statement, para. 2)

The Statement is supported by a *Draft Framework for Action on Special Needs Education* which spells out in some detail the sorts of policies which national governments will need to adopt in order to realize these principles and is, if anything, even more forceful in its commitment to inclusion:

The guiding principle that informs this **Framework** is that schools should accommodate **all children** regardless of their physical, intellectual, social, emotional, linguistic or other conditions. This should include disabled and gifted children, street and working children, children from remote or nomadic populations, children from linguistic, ethnic or cultural minorities and children from other disadvantaged or marginalized areas or groups. . . . Schools have to find ways of successfully educating all children, including those who have serious disadvantages. There is an emerging consensus that children and youth with special educational needs should be included in the educational arrangements made for the majority of children. This has led to the concept of the inclusive school. The challenge confronting the inclusive school is that of developing a child-centred pedagogy capable of successfully educating all children, including those who have serious disadvantages. The merit of such schools is not only that they are capable of providing quality education to all children; their establishment is a crucial step in helping to change discriminatory attitudes, in creating welcoming communities and in developing an inclusive society. (Para. 3; emphases in original)

We suggest that this Statement has two features which make it something other than a restatement of the aims of integration. First, and most important, it is couched in terms of human rights; indeed, the preamble to the Statement invokes both the 1948 Universal Declaration of Human Rights and the 1993 UN Standard Rules on Equalization of Opportunities for Persons with Disabilities (UN, 1993). Such deployment of the language of rights is, of course, not new within special needs education (Roaf and Bines, 1989). However, within the UK at least, integration has rarely if ever been seen as *predominantly* an issue of rights – and certainly not by policy-makers at national level. On the contrary, as we have seen, integration has largely been conceptualized in terms of changing and enhancing the nature of special educational provision. If there has been a rights component within the rationale for integration, then it has tended to be a rather weak one, since whatever right to integration there might be could easily be over-ridden by considerations to do with the quality of education both for the individual child, for his/her peers and for all other children in the LEA.

The Salamanca Statement, on the other hand, is unequivocal in asserting inclusion as a right – and, moreover, as a right which appears to take precedence over those other considerations. One immediate consequence of this is apparent in the Statement itself. Throughout its history in the UK at least, integration has been promoted almost exclusively on the assumption that it was a more appropriate form of provision for some groups and individuals than for others; if some were to be placed in mainstream classrooms alongside their peers, others were to be restricted to 'social' or 'locational' integration – or, indeed, to remain in their special schools. Integration, in other words, has rarely been seen as a *universal* aim.

The reason for this, we suggest, is not simply arbitrary decisions of innate prejudice on the part of policy-makers. So long as integration is judged in terms of its feasibility, effectiveness and efficiency, then it is inevitable that there will be some groups for whom it is less feasible, effective and efficient than others, and for whom segregated provision will be seen as a preferable option. It is no accident, for instance, that in our Northborough example, children with sensory impairment, physical disability and moderate learning difficulties are, under the 1996 proposals, to be integrated, whilst children with severe learning difficulties and emotional and behavioural difficulties are to remain in special settings.

However, reconstructing integration as inclusion, and seeing it as a *right*, means that *no* group can be denied this right. Questions of feasibility, effectiveness and efficiency may be real and important, but they cannot be allowed to over-ride the rights of individuals. For this reason, the Salamanca Statement addresses the right to inclusion of all children who are denied full participation in the educational experiences enjoyed by their peers. In practice, this means that the inclusion movement tends to have placed particular emphasis on the provision made for those groups who have traditionally been less integrated than others – notably, those children whose intellectual and physical disabilities have traditionally been held to call for segregated provision.

There are further implications which flow from such a rights-based approach. First, whereas integration has been a predominantly *educational* aim, inclusion is both educational and more broadly *social* in its scope. Integration has tended, as we have suggested, to be seen primarily as a means of enhancing the quality of educational experiences for children with special needs; inclusion, however, is a right, and as such does not stop when the young adult moves out of the education system. Hence, the Salamanca Statement sees the creation of inclusive schools merely as part of the creation of an inclusive society, and offers justifications for such schools that are at least as much social as they are educational. For similar reasons, many writers on and advocates of inclusion make little distinction between the issues of inclusive education and the issues which are addressed by the wider disability rights movement (Oliver, 1990; Barton and Oliver, 1992; Barton and Landman, 1993; Barton, 1994; Ballard, 1996). Moreover, both inclusion and disability issues tend to be seen as a sub-set of the issues surrounding all forms of the routine and structural denial of human rights, so that common cause can be made between inclusive schoolers, disability rights activists, and others in the women's, ethnic minority rights and gay and lesbian rights movements. It is for this reason, for instance, that Keith Ballard, a prominent advocate of inclusive education in New Zealand, sees the issue of the exclusion of children with disabilities from mainstream schools as one and the same as the exclusion of Maori from mainstream New Zealand society (Ballard, 1994/1995). As Bidder (in Corbett, 1996) tellingly puts it:

During the twentieth century we have witnessed the successive liberation paths of women, black peoples, and gays and lesbians. Disabled people have been left behind, and amongst disabled people, mental health system survivors and people with special needs (who embrace all cultures, classes, races and disabilities) are the

most oppressed – often denied the most basic civil rights. Disabled
activists and artists – often the same individuals – are articulating
powerful messages: demanding access in the widest sense, civil lib-
erties, and the right to control their own lives. (p. ix)

The process of advocacy which Bidder – himself disabled – outlines
here is itself significant: it is the disabled activists and artists themselves, he asserts, who are advocates for the rights of disabled people.
This emphasis on self-advocacy, on allowing the 'voice' of disabled
people to be heard, is central both to the wider disability rights movement and to inclusive education (Garner and Sandow, 1995). In both
cases there is an attempt either to enable disabled people and children
'with special needs' to speak for themselves or for able-bodied writers
to allow themselves to be used as mouthpieces for those authentic
voices (Oliver, 1992a and b; Barton, 1994; Clough and Barton, 1995).
Any claim by non-disabled academics and researchers to speak on
behalf of disabled people is thus dismissed, as Oliver puts it, as 'yet
one more example of people with abilities attempting to speak author-
itatively about us' (1992b, p. 20).

This is no accident. Integration, judged as a strategy for enhancing
the quality of special educational provision, demands, as we have
seen, the exercise of *professional* judgement to determine its feasibility,
efficacy and efficiency. Not surprisingly, therefore, both the literature
on integration and the decision-making process leading to integration
have traditionally been dominated by the professional voice. Indeed,
the 'clients' of integration seem to be largely disqualified by their 'special needs' and their status as children from speaking on these matters.
Inclusion, on the other hand, is a human right and, in common with
other human rights, the only reliable judges of the extent to which that
right is being realized are the individuals and groups to whom it per-
tains. Indeed, in a reverse of the situation in respect of integration, it is
the professionals – who, in claiming to speak on behalf of children
with special needs have signally failed to realize the right of inclusion
– whose voices now have to be, if not silenced, then at least quietened
so that their 'clients' may be heard (Oliver, 1992a and b).

THE LIMITS OF INCLUSION

When seen in the context of the historical development which we have
traced in this book, the inclusive schools movement marks both an
extension of and a rupture with the trends which have dominated
special needs education over the past three decades. It is an extension
of those trends in being based on the same 'human' values of partici-

pation in common institutions and experiences that marked the whole school approach, the comprehensive movement, the flourishing of mixed-ability teaching, and so on. In essence, the basic model of the 'inclusive school' is identical with that of a fully comprehensive school. However, it marks a rupture with these earlier movements in transforming the 'human values' of participation from being the ultimate *goals* of concerned professionals into the immediate *rights* of excluded children and young people. Inclusive schooling is thus not – as the integration movement assumed – something which has to wait upon the ability of professional educators to resolve questions of feasibility, effectiveness and efficiency, or which is bounded by the capacity of mainstream schools to respond to children with marked impairments. On the contrary, the development of truly inclusive schools constitutes a moral imperative which professionals are obliged to find ways of obeying.

Such a position gives the advocates of inclusion considerable moral authority. However, it also raises three crucial questions to do with the *limits* of inclusion:

- To what extent are schools proving capable in practice of 'including' the full range of student diversity – and what does inclusion mean in these cases?
- What sorts of changes would be necessary if schools were to become fully inclusive, and how feasible, likely and possible are those changes?
- What theoretical limits might there be to inclusion, in the sense of points at which the move towards inclusion comes into conflict with other, equally important, rights and values, or, indeed, becomes self-contradictory?

These questions are far from straightforward to answer. In the first place, the language of education is notoriously slippery when it is used across national boundaries (Booth, 1995), and there is good evidence that 'inclusion' means very different things in different sites within the same national context (Baker and Zigmond, 1995). Even in the familiar English context, being 'included' in a primary school or in a secondary school are likely to be very different processes in terms of the child's experience, the implications for teachers and the systems and structures that are required to facilitate the process. Second, inclusion is a relatively young movement (particularly in the UK) and is distinguished from integration in terms of its politico-ethical stance rather than its outcomes in observable provision. It is scarcely surprising, therefore, if there are relatively few examples available of what can unequivocally be characterized as 'inclusion' (Booth, 1996). Finally, the inclusive schools literature is far richer in critique, advocacy and exhortation than it is in evaluation. Relatively few studies exist which analyse the claims of particular practices to be inclusive, examine the implications of those analyses for practice elsewhere, and interrogate critically the assumptions of the inclusive schools movement in the light of particular cases. Moreover, even where such studies exist, there is a danger that they are premised on rearguard actions in defence of the *status quo* rather than on a disciplined inquiry into the possibilities and limitations of inclusion.

Nonetheless, some useful indications are beginning to emerge in the UK and beyond of what inclusion looks like in practice. In a series of studies, Ware (1995), for instance, reports very different outcomes of attempts to promote inclusion in different schools. Whilst some teachers in some sites transform their practices to the point where they have a genuine claim to being regarded as inclusive, other teachers in other sites display all the characteristics of conservatism and resistance that characterized many responses to the whole school approach. The experience for children in this latter group's classrooms is therefore one of 'locational' inclusion, but certainly not one of participation. Ware's conclusion, interestingly, is not that inclusion is non-viable, but that its promotion requires changes of a breadth and at a depth that are greater than is commonly supposed – a point to which we shall shortly return.

From a UK perspective, Vlachou and Barton (1994) similarly point out that moves towards inclusion are frequently resisted by teachers, and that the promotion of inclusion is dependent on ways being found of enabling change in teachers' attitudes, values and practices. Booth (1995/1996) likewise reports a series of small-scale studies which highlight the complexity lying beneath the surface of apparent examples of inclusion. The mere presence of a group of previously- or traditionally-excluded pupils in a school tends to conceal a whole host of ways in which not only those pupils but a range of other individuals and groups are excluded from full participation in shared learning and social experiences. Rather than 'inclusive schools' and 'non-inclusive schools', defined in terms of certain clearly-identified characteristics, therefore, Booth suggests that there are *processes* of inclusion and exclusion at work in *all* schools. It is only by engaging with these subtle and complex processes that inclusion can be promoted

Similarly, Zigmond and Baker (1995/1996) report one of the few substantial evaluative studies of inclusion-in-action – and their findings do not make comfortable reading. Reviewing their case studies of a number of 'inclusive' classrooms and schools, they comment,

. . . we believe that students with L[earning] D[isabilities] in these models of inclusive education were getting a very good *general* education. They were being taught enthusiastically, not grudgingly, by general education teachers. Special education teachers, in the roles of co-ordinator, co-planner, and co-teacher, were making it possible for these general education teachers to feel comfortable about the educational tasks with which they were confronted, and for students with LD to feel comfortable about functioning in a general education setting. Accommodations that were made were generally implemented for the entire class. . . . (Baker and Zigmond, 1995, p. 175)

However, these observations are somewhat double-edged, for Zigmond and Baker are not at all convinced that what they saw amounted to provision that was responsive to the individual characteristics of the children who were 'included':

We saw very little 'specially designed instruction' delivered uniquely to a student with LD. We saw almost no specific, directed, individualized, intensive, remedial instruction of students who were clearly deficient academically and struggling with the schoolwork they were being given. We heard no philosophizing about what special education was or should be, only pragmatic talk about helping all students manage the general education curriculum and providing extra help to anyone who needed it. If special education once meant a unique curriculum for a child with a disability, careful monitoring of student progress, instruction based on assessment data, or advocacy for an individual student's unique needs, it no longer held those meanings in these schools. (Baker and Zigmond, 1995, p. 178)

There are, of course, difficulties in interpreting this analysis, not only for a UK readership where notions of curriculum and special need are significantly different, but also because of Zigmond and Baker's unwillingness to let go of the traditional values of 'special education' as the yardstick against which all other forms of provision should be measured. As one commentator on their work has observed, concepts such as 'needs', 'disability' and 'special education' are highly problematical and admit of a wide range of definitions beyond those that Zigmond and Baker employ (McLaughlin, 1995).

However, our own work, as part of one of the studies reported by Booth (1996), has raised similar concerns in respect of inclusion in an English context. This is an ongoing case study of an urban secondary school which 'includes' students categorized as having severe learning difficulties and where we are beginning to find a pattern very similar to that reported by Zigmond and Baker (Ainscow, Booth and Dyson, 1995). By and large, the teachers in the school embrace the notion of including pupils with learning difficulties enthusiastically and in a committed manner. Little doubt is expressed about the social benefits of this form of provision, and teachers, students and parents all report a range of positive outcomes. In some lessons, moreover, pupils with marked difficulties are successfully involved in activities alongside and, in some cases, in collaboration with their peers.

However, the overall picture is not entirely rosy. Where students with learning difficulties share activities with their peers, the same questions could be asked as in the Zigmond and Baker study – questions, that is, about the appropriateness of those activities to individuals and the quality of the resultant learning experiences. An even greater concern, however, is the extent to which the most positive features of classroom practice fail to appear across the school as a whole. For the most part, students with learning difficulties are present in lessons which follow a standardized and undifferentiated format. Where the activities within the lesson are beyond the capabilities of the students, classroom assistants intervene to help them through their tasks or devise amended tasks for them. Such interventions enable students to maintain the superficial appearance of participation, but the resultant activities are frequently so far removed from the teacher's original intention as to be of dubious value. Hence, when the rest of the class write in their books, the classroom assistant writes 'on behalf of' the student for whom s/he 'is responsible'; when the rest of the class listens to the teacher's exposition, the classroom assistant offers his/her student a watered-down 'translation'; when the rest of the class design and make something, the classroom assistant designs and makes 'on behalf of' her/his student. Indeed, we observed one lesson in which a student with learning difficulties successfully completed the lesson whilst being at home ill; the classroom assistant, of course, attended and completed the lesson for him!

There are further similarities. Zigmond and Baker report that in their case study schools, forms of segregated provision ('pull-out programs') were reinvented to respond to the apparent student needs which classroom provision seemed unable to meet (Baker and Zigmond, 1995). In our study too, a whole series of support bases, special classes, and withdrawal lessons had grown up as alternatives to the classroom. Zigmond and Baker report how the role of the special educators had become diffuse and how they were spread thinly across the school (Baker and Zigmond, 1995). We too found a special needs co-ordinator uncertain of her role, unable to divide her time between pupils with statements and non-statemented pupils with equal difficulties, and therefore reliant on a small army of untrained classroom assistants who were themselves proving too costly for the school to maintain.

Such findings, however depressing, are scarcely surprising. If we are right in suggesting that inclusive schooling seeks to take forward the project of participation and hence the 'merging' of mainstream and special education which has characterized developments in this area in recent decades, then we should expect that it will encounter the same difficulties and setbacks. Simply renaming that project 'inclusion' and seeking to encompass a greater diversity of students will do nothing to overcome the limitations of much classroom practice or the resistance of some teachers and schools; indeed, it may make those problems worse.

Findings such as those we have just discussed certainly cast doubt on the feasibility of inclusion as an effective (however defined) and widespread form of provision *given the current condition of many schools*. However, we already know a good deal about the limitations of schools in respect of their existing populations; what is more important, therefore, is that the problems encountered by attempts at inclusion tell us something about *what needs to be changed* if the aims of inclusion are ever to be realized (Sapon-Shevin, 1996). Zigmond and Baker make a telling observation in this respect. The inclusion movement, they argue, has allowed itself to become preoccupied with the concept of 'place' – the place, that is, in which children with special needs are to be educated:

> Place is not the critical element in defining special education: theoretically, relentless, intensive, alternative educational opportunities could be made available in any venue of a school. But in practice, or at least in the practice of schooling that we have observed, place *does* set parameters on what can be accomplished. Within the ecology of the general education classroom, where the learning and social interactions of dozens of students must be orchestrated, the *how* of instruction (materials, instructions, structure) could be tinkered with, but the *what* of instruction (curriculum, pacing) was less amenable to change. Valuing place over all else leads one to accept the mainstream curriculum (however it is reformed) as immutable and defines the goal of special education as access. Putting place in its place – as only one element to be considered within the broader context of what needs to be taught, at what level of intensity, with what materials and strategies, at what pace, and in what place –

leads one to challenge the meaningfulness of the mainstream curriculum for all students and to define the goals of special education as individual achievement. (Zigmond and Baker, 1995, pp. 246–7)

It will be evident that Zigmond and Baker adopt a position of concerned scepticism towards inclusive schooling. Their conclusion, therefore, that when place and curriculum conflict, it is place which should give way, is entirely in accord with this position. However, even ardent advocates of inclusion are apt to emphasize the powerful link between these two key factors in inclusion (see, for instance, Stainback and Stainback, 1992). Moreover, although much of the debate on inclusive curricula focuses on ways in which existing mainstream curricula can be adapted to meet a range of learning needs (e.g. Udvari-Solner and Thousand, 1995), much of it also calls for fundamental changes beyond the level of 'delivery' – changes, that is, in content (Oliver, 1992b), in curriculum structure (Sapon-Shevin, 1996), in the context and process of learning (Thousand, Villa and Nevin, 1994), or in the model of learning upon which curriculum is based (Ware, 1995).

In the same way, a number of advocates of inclusion have seen the current structure of schools as a major obstacle to inclusion. Commentators in both the USA and UK (Skrtic, 1991; Villa *et al.*, 1992; Ainscow, 1994) for instance, have argued that the typical organization of schools physically into isolated classroom 'cells' and organizationally into hierarchically-ordered functions (classroom teachers, subject departments, managers, pastoral staff and so on) is a major factor in their inability to respond to children who do not 'fit in' to a standard pattern of characteristics. If schools are to become inclusive, they argue, they must be radically restructured into much more flexible and collaborative organizations in which teachers can pool their experience and expertise in order to devise new responses to 'atypical' children.

Other writers (Fulcher, 1989; Slee, 1995/1996) have drawn attention to the powerful forces both within and beyond the education system which bolster an anti-inclusive education system as part of an anti-inclusive society. Barton (1995), for instance, responds to the concept of 'education for all' – the theme of the 1995 International Special Education Congress – by drawing attention to one of these wider political issues: 'a fundamental barrier to the realization of education for all' he argues, 'is the growing emergence and implementation of policies and practices informed by a market ideology' (p. 156). However, in pursuing his arguments, Barton succeeds in encapsulating the relationship between inclusive education and the wider changes that it entails:

It is essential that the demand for inclusive education does not result in a critique of special schooling which becomes an end in itself. We are not advocating that these developments are merely in terms of the existing conditions and relations in mainstream schools. They too will need to change and there are certain features that are unacceptable, including the plant, organization, ethos, pedagogy and curriculum. It will demand the transfer of resources, careful planning and continual monitoring. We are not advocating a dumping practice into existing provision. (pp. 157–8)

He continues,

If we are to see the fundamental changes required in order for us to realize a truly inclusive society, then it will necessarily involve us addressing questions of politics and power.

What we are ultimately concerned with when we allude to the issue of education for all is determining what constitutes the 'good society': how is it to be achieved and what is the role of education in this task? (p. 159)

For commentators such as Barton, the practical difficulties of developing high-quality provision for children with special needs constitute major challenges. However, whereas the tendency within the integration movement may have been to ascribe such difficulties to the problematic characteristics of pupils, and hence to set limits to the level of integration that would be attempted, advocates of inclusion are much more likely to use these difficulties to illuminate the features of the education and social systems which demand to be changed. The scope and complexity of these changes may be daunting, but that is not the same as saying that they are impossible or ought not to be attempted. However, they do beg the third of our questions – that is, whether the proposed changes are not just difficult to achieve but impossible and/or undesirable, either because they are inherently self-contradictory or because they conflict with other principles and values which are as important as the principle of inclusion. It is to this question that we now wish to turn.

Certainly, Zigmond and Baker (1995) believe that their findings point to a fundamental conflict of principles. Whether or not one accepts their benchmarking of provision against a particular definition of 'special education', they are able to identify a contradiction between the principles of individually-customized education and participation in common educational experiences. Hence, 'an emphasis on access to the mainstream curriculum may be in conflict with a commitment to access to the most effective and appropriate educational experiences' (p. 247). One of the commentators on their case studies, Michael Gerber (1995), sets this conflict in an historical perspective by reinterpreting the origins of special education:

> Special education was the beginning of inclusion, not exclusion, and it has always had the same goal. Establishment of special day classes at the turn of the century was an attempt to make being at school worthwhile for students whose differences precluded their receiving adequate instruction in general classrooms. It was the beginning of a century-long effort to transform mere access to schooling into meaningful opportunity to learn. (p. 185)

Underpinning this development, he argues, was a need to resolve a fundamental dilemma:

> Teachers lobbied for special day classes when they recognized an inherent conflict between the social *goal* of universal public education and the *fact* of individual differences. For a century, this conflict and the conflict in social ideas and values it provokes have been in the forefront of every attempt to reform and restructure public schooling.
>
> Limitations in instructional methods, teachers' knowledge, other available resources, and organizational as well as physical structure continue to militate against definitive solutions to these conflicts. Rather, a range of choices emerges and tends to re-emerge, each facilitating some but not all goals. Individual differences first yield to modal needs. Then modal needs yield to individual differences. To date there has been no solution that does not necessitate a trade-off of equally desirable ends. (p. 185)

Although Gerber sees the difficulty in resolving this conflict as being, in part at least, determined by the limitations of currently-available resources and expertise, he also points to an underlying 'problem of teaching *all* versus teaching *each*' (p. 185) which may not be soluble simply through the provision of greater resources. Rather, such an intractable problem constitutes a fundamental 'dilemma of schooling' (Berlak and Berlak, 1981) which is endemic in the structure of any mass education system. Such dilemmas constantly recur in the study of an English secondary school referred to above. A science teacher, for instance, recounted the experience of having his lesson observed by an enthusiast for inclusive education:

. . . she came to see one of my lessons, and she was enthusing about isn't it lovely, we were doing circuit boards, circuits, bulbs, batteries, etc., and she was saying isn't it lovely that these SLD children can do this sort of thing, and sure, I felt comfortable about the lesson when she was there, it was a happy occasion, and when I did have this support member of staff who was excellent. And I felt good about that, yes. But when you look at the whole picture, you sometimes wonder really what service we're providing for them when their ability to grasp the concepts is so, well, it's so hard for them really. I mean, for example, as you know, we're filling in individual education plans, and for some, one child in year 8 for a module, I've written down simply that they know the things that run off electricity. Now, when you think of the amount of time, three lessons a week, a module lasts six weeks, that that person is in the science room, and that is the only realistic expectation, that they understand that some things use horsepower, call it what you will, electricity, to make things work, is just. . . . So, you know, I've talked obviously with the special needs department about that, and they say, it's the social element in that. I appreciate that that is very very important, but does it justify the resources that are being used, and the way that they are being used when there is so little gain in terms of science education, which is what I'm interested in. There is the social element, but that isn't my prime role, responsibility. (26. 9. 95)

All the trade-offs that Gerber talks about are present here: participation in common learning experiences versus appropriate teaching, cognitive gain versus social gain, a good 'general' education versus a good 'special' education. There is no doubt that the negative consequences of such trade-offs can be lessened by the sort of radical restructuring which advocates of inclusive education call for. However, insofar as such trade-offs arise out of fundamental dilemmas of schooling, they can never be entirely resolved. The question therefore is whether there is, in principle at least, a way of teaching about electricity – or organizing a science curriculum, or, indeed, the curriculum as a whole – which makes possible learning experiences that are equally meaningful and appropriate to children with vastly different learning characteristics. If not, then some trade-off has to be made between the principle of inclusion and the principle of 'appropriate' education.

A similar set of dilemmas presents itself in relation to the concept of 'voice' as it tends to be used within the inclusive education movement. As we have seen, the promotion of inclusive education is frequently seen to be dependent on allowing the 'voices' of currently excluded groups to be heard. The difficulty is that, unless all 'voices' say the same thing, any action in response to these voices means that some have to be heard above others. If different excluded groups want different outcomes, or if different individuals want to pursue paths that are different from those of the majority of their groups, then some process of arbitration between these different demands is necessary. However, arbitration inevitably means privileging the voice of the arbitrators over those who are arbitrated amongst; either that, or any semblance of arbitration gives way to a naked power struggle between different 'voices'.

This is by no means merely a theoretical point. As we shall see in Chapter 6, at least one group in the UK context – the so-called 'dyslexia lobby' – has succeeded in making its voice heard above many other groups. What it wants, however, is not the development of inclusive schooling and an equitable distribution of power and resource amongst the currently-excluded; rather, it seeks the re-establishment of a rather traditional form of 'special' education and appears reasonably content to capture whatever resources it can from other groups in order to fund this project. In the USA, some believe that a similar capture of the high ground has occurred within the inclusion movement itself. As Fuchs and Fuchs (1994) report, lobbies acting on behalf of children with severe learning difficulties have succeeded in making their voices heard at the level of both national and state policy. However, their voice is not the voice of all groups, and their advocacy of inclusion is not recognized by other groups representing children 'with special needs'. Basing the development of educational policy on an attempt to let the voices of the excluded be heard is one thing; but deciding which voices should be heard and how the different actions demanded by those voices should be turned into coherent policy is, it would appear, quite another.

INCLUSIVE EDUCATION: A FINAL ANSWER?

Looking back at the Salamanca Statement (UNESCO, 1994), we can, perhaps, detect a certain naiveté in respect of the prospects for inclusive education. Inclusive schools, the statement asserts,

> . . . are the most effective means of combating discriminatory attitudes, creating welcoming communities, building an inclusive society, and achieving education for all; moreover, they provide an effective education to the majority of children and improve the efficiency and ultimately the cost-effectiveness of the entire educational system. (Para. 2)

It is no small matter for schools to become, at one and the same time, inclusive of all pupils, effective for all pupils, cost-effective and effective in creating a different social order! We can say with some confidence both that large numbers of schools currently fail to live up to these high ideals (despite their best efforts) and that the realization of these aims might demand far-reaching educational and social reforms as a *prior condition* rather than as an outcome. Moreover, we can at least raise the question as to whether there are not theoretical limits to the project of inclusion, in the sense that it ultimately comes into conflict with other 'human values' which we might wish to realize, and that this conflict calls for difficult trade-offs between competing goals.

Viewed from this perspective, inclusive education may well not constitute a final answer in the attempt to 'merge' special and mainstream education. It is, rather, the latest in a succession of attempts to understand and realize the 'human values' which informed the whole school approach, the work of 'innovatory schools' and even the integration movement itself. In common with these other attempts, it faces enormous practical difficulties and, even if these can be overcome, may leave unresolved some fundamental dilemmas in education for diversity. However, unlike the whole school approach and unlike the integration movement, it does have some sense of the widespread reforms that any such merger would demand in terms of classroom practice, school organization and curriculum development. Moreover, unlike the 'innovatory' schools we examined in Chapter 3, it also has a sense that reforms in schooling have to be located within a much broader socio-political agenda, while the notion of 'voice', however problematic and unsatisfactory it may be, at least constitutes an attempt by inclusive education to develop a means of driving such an agenda forward.

This increasing awareness of the socio-political context of special needs education is, we suggest, particularly relevant at the current time. As Barton (1995) points out, the nature and possibilities of inclusive education are intimately bound up with the political realities of right-wing ideology which have resulted in the creation of an educational market place. Thus far in our study, however, we have dealt with such realities only in passing, focusing instead on a relatively unbroken thread of developments driven by a liberal agenda that has its origins in post-war expansion and optimism rather than in the political turbulence of recent times. The next three chapters, in contrast, encounter these external realities head-on as we turn to developments that are heavily determined by the political reforms of recent years.

NOTES

1. Northborough is used here as the fictional name for an actual industrial city in the north of England. Evidence on Northborough's special needs provision is drawn from a series of policy papers and evaluation reports produced between 1985 and 1996. Since Northborough is presented as 'typical' of developments (or, more accurately, failures of development) in special needs provision in this period, we have opted to preserve its anonymity.

—6——————————————

Specific learning difficulties: back to the future?

THE EMERGENCE OF SPECIFIC LEARNING DIFFICULTIES

Specific learning difficulties now constitute a major feature of special needs education in ordinary schools. The British Dyslexia Association estimates that some 10 per cent of all children experience such difficulties (BDA, 1995a); 'dyslexia' cases appear to figure prominently in the work of the Special Needs Tribunal (BDA, 1995b); there is evidence that special needs resources are being increasingly 'captured' on behalf of children with specific learning difficulties (Riddell, Brown and Duffield, 1994a and b; Gross, 1996); and our own surveys of school provision (Dyson and Skidmore, 1994; Dyson and Wood, 1994; Clark *et al.*, 1995; Dyson, 1995) suggest that it is by no means uncommon for specific learning difficulties to be the single largest category of special need in a significant number of schools – particularly where the more traditional categories (such as mild and moderate learning and behaviour difficulties) are somewhat under-represented.

This has not always been the case. As we shall see, specific learning difficulties were long regarded as affecting only a very small proportion of children for whom provision was, in any case, to be made largely beyond the ordinary school. The relatively recent and sudden expansion of specific learning difficulties provision, then, is a significant phenomenon in the field of special needs education currently – and one which calls for explanation.

SPECIFIC LEARNING DIFFICULTIES AND REMEDIAL EDUCATION

Although the numbers of children regarded as having specific learning difficulties would appear to have expanded recently, the category itself has a relatively lengthy history. Specific learning difficulties, dyslexia, word-blindness and a whole host of more or less equivalent terms have been in circulation from at least the time of Cyril Burt (Reid, 1977). 'Dyslexia' itself was recognized in legislation as early as the Chronically Sick and Disabled Person's Act, 1970 and 'specific reading difficulties' were the subject of a full government report as early as 1972 (The Tizard Report (DES, 1972)). However, these early perspectives were characterized by three features:

- Specific learning difficulties tended to be regarded as present only in children experiencing severe problems, most typically in learning to read and spell; the Warnock Report (DES, 1978), for instance, sees such children as characterized by 'severe and long-term difficulties in reading, writing and spelling' (11.48), as opposed to other children who simply require 'remedial teaching in these areas'.
- The number of such children was regarded as being small; Tizard (1972) for instance, speaks of 'the small group of children whose reading (and perhaps writing, spelling and number) abilities are significantly below the standards which their abilities in other spheres would lead one to expect' (Intro. para. 9), whilst Bullock (DES, 1975) sees children with limited intellectual ability and emotional factors as the major sufferers from reading difficulty, with specific difficulties accounting for a 'smaller group of children' (18.5).
- There was some doubt (and controversy) about the aetiology of specific difficulties, and therefore about the extent to which this group could effectively be differentiated from the larger group of children with 'non-specific' difficulties. As Tizard comments, 'We take the view that . . . there is really a continuum spanning the whole range of reading abilities from those of the most fluent readers to those with the most severe difficulties . . . we are highly sceptical of the view that a syndrome of "developmental dyslexia" with a specific underlying cause and specific symptoms has been identified'. (1972. Intro. paras 8–9)

Given the typical forms of special needs provision in ordinary schools during this period, it is not too difficult to understand why these views should have become dominant. As we have seen in earlier chapters, provision at this time very often took the form of remedial teaching. Such teaching, of course, concentrated heavily on problems in literacy, seeking to diagnose those problems that were 'specific' to individual children and to devise appropriate programmes to remediate those difficulties. It appeared to be, in short, a form of provision which was ready made for responding to specific difficulties. The controversies about the aetiology of specific learning difficulties were therefore, as the Tizard Report (1972) pointed out, somewhat irrelevant for teachers:

> There is general agreement among teachers, psychologists and neurologists – whatever their views on etiology – that the best way of dealing with specific reading difficulties is through appropriate remedial education. It is, of course, always necessary, as part of the remedial process, to make an assessment of a pupil's reading skills and an examination of the functions that underlie them – visual and auditory perception, association processes, language development and visuomotor skills such as handwriting; . . . The needs of children with specific reading difficulties are, in our view, most profitably considered as part of the wider problem of reading backwardness of all kinds. . . . (para. 10)

By the same token, although it might be of interest to 'psychologists and neurologists' to differentiate children with specific difficulties from those with more general difficulties, for schools and teachers such differentiation had no practical implications. Only when the specific difficulties became severe and 'treatment' exceeded the competence and resources of the school's remedial teacher was it, as the Bullock Report (DES 1975, 18.18) argued, necessary to make that distinction and refer the child with specific difficulties to a remedial clinic for more intensive teaching.

SPECIFIC LEARNING DIFFICULTIES AND THE WHOLE SCHOOL APPROACH

The advent of the whole school approach, of course, changed this situation in three major respects. First, its concerns with participation and access led it to identify as its client group the majority special needs population in ordinary schools – that is, those 'slow learners' who were experiencing difficulty in many aspects of their school work. It is no accident, therefore, that specific learning difficulties scarcely rate a mention in key documents of the whole school approach such as the Scottish HMI progress report (SED, 1978), Gains' and McNicholas' (1979) 'Guidelines for the Future' or Dessent's (1987) *Making the Ordinary School Special*. Second, the whole school approach shifted the emphasis of special needs provision away from a direct intervention in children's learning – and, in particular, literacy – difficulties. Instead, the dominant concerns, as we have seen, came to be first with 'remedial education across the curriculum' and then with access to a common (national) curriculum. Gains and McNicholas

(1979) were thus typical in arguing: 'Remedial education is not confined to basic subjects. Clearly children can learn their 3Rs as effectively through the study of general topics as they can through an analysis of specific weaknesses and the teaching of these in isolation' (pp. 185–6).

Third, and following from this, the whole school approach implied a shift of resources away from individualized remedial interventions. In particular, if, as both National Association for Remedial Education guidelines (Gains and McNicholas, 1979) and Scottish HMI (SED, 1978) suggested, remedial teachers were to become consultants and change agents, working across the curriculum, spending significant amounts of time with teachers rather than with children, and encountering children with special needs in classroom support rather than individual or small-group situations, then inevitably they would have less time available for traditional withdrawal activities.

Such changes undoubtedly made a great deal of sense if it was assumed that children's difficulties were global, extended across the whole curriculum and, perhaps, were not susceptible to remedial treatment. In such cases, children's educational entitlements could only be delivered if an appropriately differentiated pedagogy were developed, giving them access to a curriculum from which they would otherwise be largely excluded. However, despite the controversies which had traditionally surrounded the concepts of dyslexia and specific difficulties, there was nonetheless a widespread consensus that there were some children about whom such assumptions could not safely be made. These children's difficulties patently did *not* extend across the whole curriculum but were specific to one or more aspects of literacy acquisition. Their access to an entitlement curriculum was denied not by lack of differentiation (indeed, they might be achieving very highly in some curriculum areas) so much as by their untreated difficulties. Moreover, whilst it might be impossible to remediate global difficulties extending across a wide range of areas of functioning, it was not unreasonable to suppose it might be possible to remediate, alleviate or circumvent difficulties which were much more limited in their scope.

This situation was compounded by the very vagueness and contested nature of the definitions of 'dyslexia' and its alternatives. As we have seen, Tizard, Bullock and others at the time were reluctant to accept the idea that the difficulties experienced by children who supposedly 'had dyslexia' were any different *in kind* from the difficulties experienced by large numbers of other children whose reading was 'retarded'. As Tizard makes clear, the widespread availability of remedial teaching meant that the use of such a highly problematic term served no practical purpose, since the response in schools would be the same whatever term was used. However, the erosion of remedial provision in favour of the whole school approach effectively turned this argument on its head. The shrinkage of remedial tuition meant that the use of the term 'dyslexia' (or some alternative) became an important means of indicating a group of children whose needs were not likely to be met simply through differentiation and in-class support.

Moreover, Tizard's arguments for a continuum of difficulties could also be turned on their head: if so-called dyslexics are like many other children with reading difficulties, then many other children with reading difficulties must in some sense be dyslexic, or have dyslexic-type difficulties. It is common nowadays, for instance, for specific learning difficulties to be defined, in the *Code of Practice*'s (DFE, 1994a) terms as 'significant difficulties in reading, writing, spelling or manipulating number, which are not typical of [the child's] general level of performance' (3.60). Such definitions neatly avoid the controversy over the extent to which dyslexia is a distinctive condition with a single underlying cause. However, they open the floodgates: *any* child who has *any* weakness in literacy or numeracy has, according to such definitions, 'specific learning difficulties'. There are, after all, no criteria for determining when those difficulties become 'significant', since even the smallest weakness can be significant for a child who has (or whose parents have) high aspirations. It follows, moreover, that the remedial tuition which was for long seen as the appropriate provision for the small group of 'dyslexics' must also, in some updated form, be appropriate for this much larger group.

The emergence of specific learning difficulties, therefore, constitutes a sort of counter-movement to the whole school approach. It is, in effect, a reassertion of the traditional values of special education – values, for instance, of individually appropriate remedial intervention – in the face of a widespread attempt to 'merge' special and mainstream education. As such, it is not dissimilar to the sort of reassertion which we saw commentators such as Zigmond and Baker (Baker and Zigmond, 1995; Zigmond and Baker, 1995) in Chapter 5 making in the face of inclusive education, or individual teachers making at Downland School in Chapter 4. The 'human values' of equity and participation on which much development in special needs education has been premised over the last two decades and more are, it would appear, by no means either unproblematic or consensual.

SPECIFIC LEARNING DIFFICULTIES, PARENTS AND PROFESSIONALS

What has given the emergence of specific learning difficulties even greater impetus is that the groups for whom it has become a major concern have never been part of whatever consensus was established around the whole school approach. One such group comprises the psychologists and medics who were involved in the 'dyslexia' field from the very first, and whose professional interests in intervention and cure have little in common with the concerns of many educators for curriculum access and participation. Tomlinson (1982/1985) argues that these professions have had a powerful determining influence on the nature of special education, seeing its maintenance and extension as a means of consolidating and legitimating their own professional status. Certainly, they have tended to dominate thinking about specific learning difficulties to the extent that a substantial majority of research and writing in the field is conducted within a psycho-medical perspective (Dyson and Skidmore, 1996). Nor is this simply an intellectual hegemony; psychologists employed by, for instance, the Dyslexia Institute, appear to play a key role in helping parents secure resources and provision for their 'dyslexic' children, often in the face of opposition from professional educators and educational administrators. Similarly, it is not unheard of for schools to report that they are having to face a demand for additional resources for a pupil because the family GP has 'diagnosed' him/her as 'dyslexic'.

This alliance between parents, psychologists and medics is significant, for parents are another group from outside the educational consensus who have played a significant part in the emergence of specific learning difficulties. Regardless of the debates over the aetiology of specific learning difficulties or the most appropriate form of intervention, there is an obvious attraction for parents in psycho-medical explanations of their children's difficulties. If, in the words of the British Dyslexia Association, specific learning difficulties are 'constitutional in origin' (Crisfield and Smythe, 1993), p. 8) and can be explained in terms of psycho-linguistic, sensory or neurological impairments, then no blame attaches either to the child or to his/her family for the child's problems at school. Indeed, teachers frequently testify to the relief experienced by families when a diagnosis of specific learning difficulties is offered for the child's previously inexplicable failures (Dyson and Skidmore, 1994; Dyson, 1995). Moreover, such a diagnosis, thanks to the intensive research of recent years, brings with it the prospect of 'scientifically-proven' intervention and treatment and offers a platform from which to argue for special provision and additional resources.

To this is added a further factor which increases the power of parents. Throughout the 1980s and 1990s, there has been both a rhetoric of parental rights and a series of national policy initiatives designed to enable parents to exercise those rights. The representation of parents on governing bodies, the accountability of schools to parents via annual meetings, the publication of inspection reports, examination results and other performance indicators, and, above all, the introduction of open enrolment, have all combined to create a situation in which schools ignore the views of parents at their peril. Within the field of special needs education in particular, the legal and quasi-legal rights of parents have been considerably extended. The limited (but nonetheless significant) provision in the 1981 Education Act for parents to make representations about their children's needs has been followed by a *Code of Practice* which effectively mandates the involvement of parents at every step of the assessment and provision process, together with a legal recourse to special needs tribunals should they be dissatisfied with outcomes for their children.

It is, of course, in the nature of such rights that some parents will be better equipped than others to take advantage of them. Exercising rights in the context of a complex education system demands motivation, determination, knowledge and, in some cases, access to advice, legal representation and financial resources. Since specific learning difficulties, as a 'constitutional' impairment, are not associated with socio-economic status in the way that many 'special needs' are, it is only to be expected that many parents of children 'with specific learning difficulties' will be articulate and economically – and socially – well resourced. It is therefore not surprising that they have been quick to organize themselves into powerful groups which have been remarkably successful in lobbying policy-makers, fighting for provision through the courts, and exerting pressure on schools (Riddell, Brown and Duffield, 1994a and b). In other words, it is not necessary to posit an 'epidemic' of specific learning difficulties among children to explain the category's sudden expansion – simply to look at the resources and interests of those children's parents.

Whereas, therefore, the developments in special needs education which we have examined so far in this book – the whole school approach, the approach of 'innovatory' schools, the integration movement and even, to some extent, the inclusive education movement – have been driven in large part by professional educationalists, the emergence of specific learning difficulties has been driven much more from outside the education community. If the adherence of the 'dyslexia lobby' to a psycho-medical model of learning difficulties has sometimes led them to demand individualized and even segregated remedial provision, we should not be surprised. Such provision is a transparent way of responding to the overt needs of the identified individual children with whom they are concerned; it is a way of ensuring that those children are provided with additional resources to meet their needs; and it ensures that those resources, once allocated, are not spirited away to support some nebulous 'whole school approach' or to make the school in some mysterious way more 'effective for all'.

THE EMERGENCE OF SPECIFIC LEARNING DIFFICULTIES AND THE DILEMMAS FACING ORDINARY SCHOOLS

As specific learning difficulties have emerged as an issue throughout the 1980s and 1990s, so mainstream schools have increasingly been faced with a series of dilemmas about the nature of their special needs provision. Having been encouraged by their LEA advisers, by national government and by academics to adopt a whole school approach, and having, in some cases, begun to develop that approach even further along the lines of participation and equity, they suddenly find themselves confronted by demands from an entirely different quarter and premised on entirely different notions. For many schools, the level of these demands appears to have been so low that they have, thus far, successfully been able to ignore them (Dyson and Wood, 1994). A few schools have taken a principled stance against the more segregatory demands of the 'dyslexia lobby' and have attempted to preserve a 'pure' form of a participatory approach to special needs; some of these have had their fingers burned as court rulings or reverses in LEA policy have forced them to abandon their purist positions.

This still leaves, however, a large number of schools where a specific learning difficulties population has emerged relatively rapidly in the context of well-established whole school approaches. Such schools have been faced with a series of apparently irresolvable dilemmas:

1. Curriculum access versus remedial intervention
The whole school approach emphasizes curriculum access as the overriding concern of provision, and seeks to operationalize this through in-class support and differentiation. However, specific learning difficulties provision seems to be premised on the more traditional notions of remedial education; that is, the direct intervention in children's difficulties through specialized programmes and specialist teaching,

often taking place not only outside the mainstream classroom, but also outside the common curriculum.

A wide range of dyslexia/specific learning difficulties teaching resources is now available. Large numbers of them, however, presuppose a detailed diagnosis of individual literacy and pre-literacy difficulties (e.g. the *Aston Index* (Newton and Thomson, 1982)), followed by the prescription of an individualized programme which focuses narrowly on the highly structured teaching of a somewhat narrow range of (usually phonic) skills and knowledge (e.g. *Alpha to Omega* (Hornsby and Shear, 1975); Augur and Briggs, 1992). It is not at all clear how such programmes can be delivered in mainstream classrooms through the provision of in-class support; the pre-requisite seems to be a withdrawal situation with a specialist teacher. Indeed, some of the interventions are scarcely educational at all. Certain interventions such as the provision of tinted glasses (Irlen, 1991) or training the child in a series of physical exercises (the so-called educational kinesiology (Dennison and Hargrove, 1985)) are less to do with the delivery of a 'broad and balanced' National Curriculum than the application of quasi-medical techniques in an educational context.

2. Specialist teaching versus SEN co-ordination
The whole school approach requires the special needs co-ordinator to operate, in part at least, as a change agent and consultant. The sorts of interventions we have just described, however, seem to require special needs teachers who are specially trained and who work directly with children on an individual or small-group basis. The dilemma for schools, therefore, is not simply how they reconcile these interventions with a common curriculum, but how the special needs teacher finds time both to work in the mainstream of the school and to operate in a more traditional remedial role.

3. Resourcing specific learning difficulties versus resourcing special needs
If the BDA is correct in suggesting that one in ten children has specific learning difficulties, then schools face a massive resourcing dilemma. Most schools would argue that they are inadequately resourced to respond effectively to more traditional forms of special needs, let alone to a newly-identified population. Moreover, the sort of individualized interventions described above are likely to be more resource-intensive than the curricular approach to general learning difficulties. Furthermore, if LEAs have established patterns of resourcing to respond to traditional forms of special need, then two further problems are likely to ensue. First, some schools are likely to find themselves with low levels of special needs resourcing historically, but

with a large newly-identified specific learning difficulties population. Second, schools with more 'traditional' populations are likely to find their resources being diverted towards these other schools. The whole situation is, of course, compounded by the ability of the specific learning difficulties lobby, in all its forms, to pressure LEAs and schools to develop specific learning difficulties provision.

In effect, these dilemmas amount to a thoroughgoing problematization of the whole school approach and, in particular, of its capacity to respond to special needs other than those for which it had been established. Clearly, one option for schools – particularly those in which the whole school approach has not taken root – is to revert to earlier remedial forms of provision, though this path is itself made problematical by the advent of a statutory National Curriculum. Other schools, however, have embraced the whole school approach whole-heartedly and, indeed, may have been moving in some of the more radical directions outlined in previous chapters. The impact of specific learning difficulties on these schools is particularly interesting since it promises to test the robustness and to expose the limitations of the whole school approach. It is to the responses of such schools that we now wish to turn.

THE RESEARCH STUDIES

In order to explore schools' responses to the challenges of specific learning difficulties, we have undertaken a series of studies of 'test-case' schools. These are schools which have well-established whole school approaches, which are committed therefore to notions of curriculum access, differentiation and in-class support, but where the emergence of a significant population of pupils with specific learning difficulties has compelled the school to rethink and reconstruct that approach. Although such processes have doubtless occurred in primary schools, the inevitable dependence of schools in this phase on local authority provision reduces their flexibility to carry out major reconstructions. We have deliberately focused, therefore, on developments in secondary schools, through four investigations:

- A survey by questionnaire and follow-up visit, of provision in twenty-seven secondary schools in Scotland, nominated by their regions as having both well-developed approaches to specific learning difficulties and well-developed whole school ('Learning Support' in the Scottish terminology) approaches.
- A parallel questionnaire survey of fourteen secondary schools in

English LEAs. Both of these surveys were published in Dyson and Skidmore (1994).
- A collaborative cost-benefit evaluation of specific learning difficulties provision in four secondary schools in the former Cleveland LEA (Dyson, 1995).
- A questionnaire survey of specific learning difficulties provision in all the middle and high schools in one LEA (Dyson and Wood, 1994).

Taken together, these investigations probably constitute the most comprehensive database we have on developments in secondary schools' provision for specific learning difficulties, particularly when set alongside the work undertaken by Riddell and colleagues from Stirling University (Riddell *et al.*, 1992) and the limited number of accounts of provision which are now beginning to appear in the literature (e.g. Reid, 1994; Brown, 1996).

The emerging model
Rather than setting out the findings of each study in detail, what we propose to do is to describe a common model which we believe underpins provision across many of the schools we investigated. This model is like the emerging model of special needs provision described in Chapter 3, in that its implementation in detail varies considerably from school to school. Moreover, by no means all the schools which seem to base their provision upon it are able or willing to articulate the model fully or analyse its founding assumptions in great depth. They had arrived at their current form of provision through a mixture of historical accident, pragmatic decision-making and professional judgement rather than by building that provision on a carefully worked-out blueprint. The model, therefore, has had to be *inferred* from schools' practice and teachers' accounts of that practice. Nonetheless, it does offer a means of accounting for the forms of provision we found as coherent responses to specific learning difficulties. Moreover, it makes it possible to contrast those responses both with the whole school approach and with the subsequent developments of that approach which we discussed in Chapter 3. The model is represented diagrammatically in Figure 6.1 (page 116).

Schools' responses to specific learning difficulties can, we suggest, be understood at three levels. At the surface level, they comprise a set of activities and forms of provision which constitute what schools *do* about specific learning difficulties. Underpinning these is a set of underlying aims which give coherence to what the school does and constitute the *rationale* for provision. And this itself is underpinned by

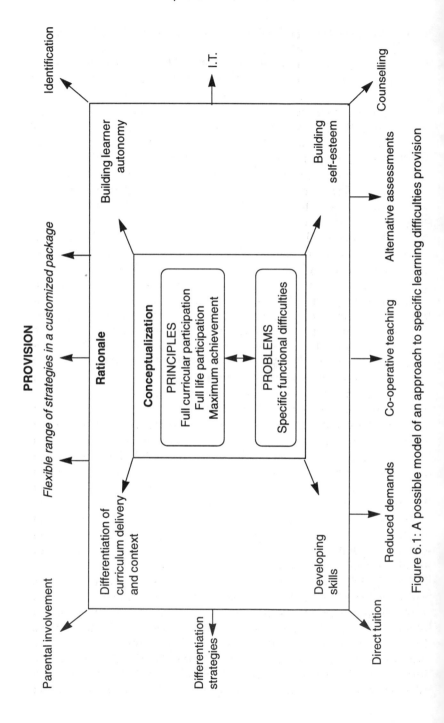

Figure 6.1: A possible model of an approach to specific learning difficulties provision

a set of assumptions about what specific learning difficulties 'are' – a *conceptualization* on which the school's response is based.

As we have seen, there has long been a debate about the extent to which 'dyslexia' can be seen as a distinct 'condition' or rather as part of a wider continuum comprising all forms of reading difficulty. However, neither position within this debate has strayed far away from the notion that the child's difficulties are to be understood in terms of his/her deficits or weaknesses, and that such deficits and weaknesses need to be diagnosed and, so far as possible, remedied. Not surprisingly, the dominance of psychologists and medics in the field has led to a *conceptualization* of specific learning difficulties in terms of deficit and weakness, and to a *rationale* for provision which is essentially remedial and curative.

However, in the schools we studied, we detected something subtly – but importantly – different. Although the teachers we interviewed did not reject outright the more psycho-medically-oriented definitions of specific learning difficulties, they were, as one teacher put it, 'not greatly impressed by theories'. They tended to accept that children with specific learning difficulties had a 'jagged profile' in their attainments, along the lines of the definition proposed by the *Code of Practice*. However, this acceptance was set within the context of a continuing commitment to the values of participation and equity which informed the whole school approach. The significance of discrepancies in attainment, therefore, was not so much that they indicated a deep-seated neurological or psycho-educational malfunction, but that they interfered with the child's entitlement to participate in a common curriculum, to experience educational achievement and ultimately to enjoy a fulfilling adult life. As one school put it, 'there is a discrepancy between what a pupil can do and understand and what he/she can show he/she can do and understand', with the consequence that his/her achievement and participation might be limited. In the words of one teacher: 'It became clear by observation and HMI reports that certain obviously intelligent pupils were being failed by a system that constantly judged them on a single criterion at which they were bound to fail, i.e. written performance.'

The significance of this subtle shift becomes more evident in the rationale to which it gives rise. If specific learning difficulties are seen simply in terms of deficits and weaknesses – whether constitutional or otherwise – then the rationale for provision is obviously to intervene in order to remedy such weaknesses. However, where the concern is with the realization of entitlements and of full participation, then *any* intervention is justified which might ensure that realization. In other words if, as the teacher above indicates, the system is failing the child, then intervention might well be in 'the system' rather than in the individual.

The following two statements are typical of the sorts of rationales which the schools we studied gave for their provision:

> Our rationale is: to provide access to the mainstream curriculum; improvement in basic skills; appropriate means of circumventing specific learning difficulties in order to enable pupils to achieve their maximum potential and, where appropriate, access to further and higher education; and to raise self-esteem and confidence.

Or again:

> We hope that pupils are able to show what they are capable of, despite their specific difficulties. We hope to give them a range of coping strategies and a sense that they are valued as individuals, and can achieve without undue frustration. We want them to take full part in the life and work of the class and the school.

The concern within these rationales is not so much with how children's difficulties can be remediated as with how children can circumvent their difficulties, or learn to cope in the mainstream despite them, with how they can be helped to participate in a common curriculum, and with how this can help them achieve their maximum potential.

In particular, they indicate four broad aims which provision should fulfil:

- *Differentiation*. If pupils are to participate in a common curriculum *despite* their difficulties, then that curriculum has to be delivered in ways which are differentiated to take account of those difficulties.
- *Building self-esteem*. If pupils are to achieve their potential in education and in adult life, they need to see and value themselves as potential learners and potential achievers. They should be helped, therefore, to move beyond the negative views of themselves which an exclusive focus on their difficulties might create.
- *Building learner autonomy*. If pupils are to participate in a common curriculum without massive (and ultimately disabling) levels of support, then they need to learn how to function autonomously, drawing on their strengths and finding ways round their weaknesses.
- *Developing skills*. If pupils are weak in certain skill areas, then some attempt might be made to address those weaknesses directly. However, whereas more traditional approaches to specific learning

difficulties saw such attempts as the central aim of provision, these schools saw them as having to take place alongside the three other aims of provision. They do not, therefore, form the basis for a full-blown return to 'remedial' education.

This four-fold rationale directly informed provision in the schools we studied. Much of what we actually saw in those schools was drawn from the repertoire of the whole school approach and/or remedial education, though with one or two additions. What made these schools distinctive, however, was the way in which these strategies – familiar and otherwise – were deployed. This deployment had four characteristics:

Eclecticism
Because the aim of provision is to enable the child to function effectively in the full curriculum, schools tended, in the words of one teacher, to 'try anything!'; that is, to draw on any resource or strategy which might be helpful in achieving this aim. Tried and trusted remedial and support techniques were, as we have indicated, prominent; however, other, more distinctive forms of provision were also in evidence: some of the psycho-medical interventions advocated in the specific learning difficulties literature, programmes of counselling as means of developing pupils' self-esteem, programmes of thinking skills and problem-solving aimed at developing learner autonomy, the provision of lap-top computers, spell-checkers and other IT aids for the same purpose – and so on.

Pragmatism
Significantly, in a field which is frequently characterized by ideological conflict, the schools in our studies tended to select the particular techniques and forms of provision they wished to use on a pragmatic basis. Being 'not greatly impressed by theories', the criterion for using a particular technique was not whether it conforms to some theory about the aetiology and treatment of specific learning difficulties as such, but whether it is of immediate use in enabling a particular child to function effectively in the curriculum. As one teacher commented when asked to justify her use of Educational Kinesiology: 'It works with some pupils. It doesn't always show results. . . . For me it's another tool.'

The same principle can be seen at work in the attitude teachers took towards withdrawal. The use of withdrawal – with its capacity to deliver individual instruction, but often only at the cost of moving the child outside the mainstream curriculum – has, of course, been a battleground between remedial education and whole school approaches. By and large, however, the teachers who participated in our research subscribed to neither of these positions, seeing with-drawal as simply one more technique which might – or might not, depending on individual circumstances – be helpful in furthering the aim of effective functioning in the full curriculum. Thinking pragmat-ically, teachers made it clear that the furtherance of this aim justified some compromise on questions of participation and access: 'Pupils have an entitlement to access the curriculum but they do not have to be physically in the classroom at all times.' Or, as another teacher put it, 'It all depends on the balance of advantage for the child.'

Customization
This notion of a 'balance of advantage' that is different for different children led one teacher to assert that '. . . we wouldn't do the same thing with two pupils', and another that '. . . the provision for any pupil is determined by need not "label".'

A characteristic of the way these schools deployed their repertoire of strategies, therefore, was that they tended to put together cus-tomized 'packages' that differed somewhat from pupil to pupil. Some pupils would be withdrawn, others would not; some would receive counselling, others would not; some would be provided with lap-top computers, others would not – and so on. Moreover, an important con-sideration in assembling these packages was the child's own wishes; if a pupil was happy with in-class support, for instance, make it avail-able, but 'It is a central tenet that if the youngster doesn't want support, don't give them it. . . .' In other words, provision was deter-mined not simply by what the child was believed to 'need' but also by what s/he *wants*.

The emerging model: a resolution of dilemmas
How far, then, does this model go towards resolving the dilemmas outlined above? There is certainly an argument that all these schools were doing is hurriedly shoring up a beleaguered whole school approach with opportunistically-chosen elements of remedial educa-tion in order to placate a vociferous parental lobby. Our 'model', in this case, is nothing more than a *post hoc* rationalization of a somewhat messy and incoherent picture.

However, this is only part of the truth. There were, for instance, ele-ments in these schools' responses that are not to be found in the standard repertoire of either remedial education or the whole school approach. The commitment to lifetime participation and achieve-ment, the emphasis on building self-esteem and autonomy, and the direct teaching of thinking skills or the provision of supportive IT on demand are cases in point. Moreover, the responses being developed by these schools did indeed seem to be coherent, rational and based on a distinct and distinctive conceptualization of specific learning difficulties. They added up, in other words, to a coherent *model* and, furthermore, a model which seems to go some way towards resolving the three principal dilemmas which the schools faced:

1 It reconciles *curriculum access* with *remedial intervention*. Whereas each of these had, traditionally, been seen as justified in quite different terms, the model sees them both as contributing to the same overarching aim of realizing children's entitlements, participation and achievements. They thus constitute different pathways to the same end rather than totally contradictory approaches.
2 It reconciles *specialist teaching* with *SEN co-ordination* by reconstructing the special needs teacher's role as that of a *co-ordinator* of a package of provision for each individual child. It may well be that different packages include different elements of direct tuition or of development and consultancy work with other members of staff. However, it is the need to construct these customized packages which gives coherence to the role and determines how its different aspects might be balanced.
3 It reconciles the *resourcing of specific learning difficulties* with the *resourcing of special needs*. The approach adopted to specific learning difficulties is individualized, to be sure – but it is not necessarily resource-intensive. Some children will require minimum intervention; others will draw only upon the existing repertoire of strategies (such as in-class support) that are already available under the whole school approach; and in every case, the intention to develop pupil autonomy should mean that they become less, not more, dependent on support. Moreover, the availability of a coherent model which clearly responds to the individual needs of children while maintaining them to a large extent in mainstream lessons, is a powerful means of reassuring anxious parents that they do not necessarily have to press for ever more individualized and ever more expensive forms of provision.

What these schools effectively accomplished through this resolution was the discovery of a way of maintaining the 'human values' of the whole school approach in the face of imperatives that were based on very different values and assumptions. Their responses to specific learning difficulties are thus testimony both to the resilience of those values and to the tenacity and creativity of (at least) some members of the teaching profession in their defence. Indeed, it may be legitimate to view these responses less as last-ditch defences of the whole school approach than as attempts to drive that approach forward beyond the limitations that were inevitably appearing in it a decade and a half after its first formulation. If the 'innovatory' schools of Chapter 3 were trying to overcome the tendency for the whole school approach to replicate segregatory forms of provision and its failure to tackle the inadequacies of mainstream education, then the schools we have investigated here can, perhaps, be seen as attempting to refine the whole school approach's somewhat crude conceptualization of individual differences. In a very real sense, their work answers the concerns of Zigmond and Baker (Baker and Zigmond, 1995; Zigmond and Baker, 1995) that forms of provision based on participation in common experiences might be fundamentally irreconcilable with the traditional concerns of 'special' education with individualized interventions to meet particular learning needs. For this reason, if for no other, their approaches to specific learning difficulties deserve attention.

However, their resolution of the dilemmas was, by their own accounts, only partial. In all schools, some stresses and strains were being felt, and in some schools these were quite acute. In particular, the emphasis on individualized packages of strategies was proving to be overly resource-intensive and many schools were concerned about the sustainability of the model in the longer term, particularly if school funding was any further constrained. Moreover, a number of schools were finding that the level of demand was escalating quite markedly – partly because of the activities of parental organizations, partly because the school acted as a magnet for pupils with specific learning difficulties once it had developed a credible approach, and partly because the ambiguities in the definition of specific learning difficulties meant that almost any child could be so categorized. In the words of one teacher, 'The more you look, the more you find.'

These problems were exacerbated even further where the schools experienced significant levels of demand in other forms of special need. By and large, the schools we worked with – and indeed most schools we have encountered which have a significant specific learning difficulties population – had pupil populations where the level of other learning and behaviour difficulties was relatively low. However, where other demands did exist to any significant extent, schools were finding their resources stretched to the limit. They ended up making trade-offs between provision for different groups of pupils, lamenting that, as one teacher put it, 'hard decisions have to be made' or, in the words of another, that 'It's balancing one set of needs against another.' Where such balancing acts became necessary, of course, all the dilemmas which surround the emergence of specific learning difficulties began to reassert themselves. The model of provision described here, therefore, appears to depend for its sustainability on a delicate balance between levels of demand in respect of specific learning difficulties, levels of demand in respect of other forms of special need, and the availability of resources. These levels, of course, are not controlled by teachers and schools so much as by parents, lobby groups and politicians. Its resolution of dilemmas, in other words, is a resolution that depends crucially on the wider social, political and economic context.

Unfortunately, the indications from special needs education elsewhere in the English-speaking world are not good. In recent decades, for instance, the USA has seen a sudden mushrooming of the population of children categorized as 'learning disabled (LD)' (Sleeter, 1986; Coles, 1987; Walberg, 1993), whilst both the USA and Australia have witnessed the emergence and growth of the 'Attention Deficit (Hyperactivity) Disorder (ADHD)' category (Reid, Maag and Vasa, 1993; Slee, 1996). Both LD and ADHD are themselves, like specific learning difficulties, rooted in an essentially psycho-medical perspective on special needs. Like specific learning difficulties, they tend to be seen as originating in some form of neurological or psycho-educational dysfunction and as calling for some form of psychological or medical intervention; indeed, ADHD is commonly treated through the administration of drugs. Moreover, as commentators have pointed out, 'new' categories of disability such as these tend to be accepted – and indeed promoted – by articulate parents seeking explanations of their children's difficulties in schooling which would on the one hand be non-stigmatizing and, on the other hand, secure additional resources and specialist intervention (Susman, 1994; Cooper and Ideus, 1995; Slee, 1996).

These similarities are troubling on two counts. First, the history of both ADHD and LD is one of unchecked expansion and of the diversion of resources into these categories from other forms of special needs provision. Second, there is already evidence that ADHD is taking root in the UK (Cooper and Ideus, 1995). In other words, not only is specific learning difficulties likely to expand as a category, but it may well be joined by other 'new' categories of special need. There is, therefore, a 'nightmare scenario' which might face the education system in years to come. At its worst, this would involve a context in which levels of demand from traditional forms of special need remained high, resources within the education system remained under constraint, the level of demand from specific learning difficulties rose, and other categories of special need arose alongside it.

Under such circumstances, not only the model we have described, but the approaches to special needs in mainstream schools which have developed over many years, would become unsustainable. Short of a massive (and improbable) injection of funds, the only way to resource the new categories of special need would be to divert resources from the traditional categories of need – that is, in particular, from the large groups of children with general learning difficulties and emotional and behavioural difficulties. Such a move would indeed spell the end of the whole school approach and the final severing of links between special needs education in ordinary schools and its traditional client population.

What is significant is that the avoidance of such a scenario is not exclusively – indeed, not predominantly – in the hands of the community of professional educators who have been instrumental in promoting the whole school approach and its later variants. Regardless of how schools organize themselves or how skilful teachers become, there is little they can do alone about the overall resourcing of education, the extent to which the education system is driven by the agendas of certain parents, or the way in which such parents conceptualize their children's difficulties and needs. These are clearly broader political and social issues, and the fate of the 'human values' which have informed special needs education in recent decades may ultimately depend on the ability of the advocates of those values to engage with this wider arena.

The crucial nature of this engagement becomes even more apparent as we turn to examine the impact of the major government intervention in special needs education in mainstream schools: the *Code of Practice*.

The *Code of Practice*

Many of the developments that we have examined so far in this book have been focused on an attempt in one way or another to 'merge' special and mainstream education. Such an attempt, as we have seen, has much to commend it as a mean of realizing the 'human' values of equity, participation and access to common educational experiences. However, in the last chapter we saw how such values are by no means universally shared, and how certain groups outside the broad 'educational consensus' around these values may have somewhat different priorities which lead them to advocate more traditional and separate forms of special needs provision.

In this chapter we turn our attention to a further irruption into that consensus: the *Code of Practice* (DFE, 1994a). The *Code* is arguably the single most important government intervention in special needs education since the 1981 Education Act, and an intervention which seems set to provide the framework for special needs provision for many years to come. Certainly, it surrounds itself with a rhetoric of equity and participation which is entirely in line with the developments we have been exploring. It declares, for instance, that:

> children with special educational needs require the greatest possible access to a broad and balanced curriculum, including the National Curriculum. (Para. 1.2)

and that

> the needs of most pupils will be met in the mainstream, and without a statutory assessment or statement of special educational needs. Children with special educational needs, including children with statements of special educational needs, should, where appropriate and taking into account the wishes of their parents, be educated alongside their peers in mainstream schools. (Para. 1.2)

Despite these fine words, however, we will suggest that the actual *impact* of the *Code* is ambiguous, for while the rhetoric points towards participation, the procedures and practices it establishes are likely to point towards something very different.

THE CONTEXT OF THE *CODE*

An understanding of the context within which the *Code* was introduced – a context largely created by the Education Reform Act of 1988 – is important if we are to appreciate the *Code*'s significance. As we saw in Chapter 3, although the Act had little to say directly about special needs education, its provisions had major implications in that field. We argued there that these implications were complex but that some schools, at least, saw the 1988 Act as an opportunity to extend their existing whole school approaches by developing new responses to the diversity of their pupil populations. However, by no means all schools saw the Act in this way. For many, the 1988 'reforms' did not so much invite creative experimentation as generate overwhelming constraints and imperatives which threatened to undermine whatever commitment to special needs education they had previously been able to maintain. These threats, moreover, stemmed from precisely the same source as the opportunities which were perceived by our 'innovative' schools – from the introduction of a National Curriculum and the changes in the governance of schools.

A traditional response to 'special needs' had been, even within the whole school approach, to develop 'modified' or 'alternative ' curricula – based on different content, utilizing different teaching styles and, quite possibly, founded on different theories of learning from those underpinning the curriculum followed by the majority of pupils (see, for instance, Ainscow and Tweddle, 1979; Brennan, 1979). However, the newly-introduced National Curriculum was, as we saw in Chapter 3, an unequivocally *mainstream* curriculum. Its organization in terms of subject-disciplines (even at primary level), the hierarchical ordering of knowledge and skills within those subjects through a system of 'attainment targets', the compulsory nature of each of those disciplines for all children, the introduction of regular assessment, increasingly based on pencil-and-paper tests, the prescription of teaching programmes common to all pupils, the expectation that pupils would be placed on the age-appropriate 'programme of study', regardless, for the most part, of attainment – all added up to a curricular approach that looked remarkably like a somewhat traditional version of the secondary school curriculum with its associated final examinations. Despite guidance (NCC, 1989a and b) which emphasized the flexibility of interpretation possible within this framework, therefore, the framework itself was one that was essentially alien to a substantial tradition of curriculum development within special needs education.

Moreover, the prescriptive, mandatory and all-encompassing nature of the National Curriculum removed much of the room for manoeuvre which schools had previously enjoyed in respect of their 'special needs' populations. It was not simply that the new curriculum appeared intimidatingly 'academic', but that it also effectively outlawed any form of provision other than itself. What had previously been standard special needs practices – alternative curricula for older 'non-examination' pupils (e.g. LAPP), regular withdrawal from certain subject areas, the provision of alternative courses to, or in, Modern Foreign Languages, and the development of a wide range of other 'modified' or 'adapted' versions of the mainstream curriculum subjects – were either explicitly banned or made extremely difficult to sustain. Suddenly, schools were confronted with the prospect of having to engage their most problematic pupils in an extensive and tightly-prescribed curriculum which appeared on the face of it to be alien to their learning characteristics and interests. The guidance that was issued at national level was that teachers should learn to 'differentiate' the curriculum (NCC, 1989b; HMI, 1990/1992). However, whilst that guidance seemed reasonable enough, it never quite reached the level of detail which would enable teachers to implement it without difficulties, and the notion of differentiation itself came to seem somewhat problematical (see Chapter 2).

In addition to the National Curriculum, however, the 1988 Act also marked, as we saw in Chapter 3, the culmination of a series of changes to the governance of education throughout the 1980s which had far-reaching implications for special needs provision. Two of these changes are particularly significant from our point of view. First, as a result of the 1988 Act, schools were given increasing autonomy from LEAs, and LEAs, in turn, found their ability to control schools much diminished. This was achieved in part by increasing the power of governing bodies and reducing LEA dominance thereof, partly by giving schools control of their own budgets – thereby, of course, reducing the funds available to LEAs – and partly by enabling schools to 'opt out' of LEA control if governors and parents so wished. Second, a quasi-market was created in education by offering parents the prospect of choosing their children's school and providing them with information on the quality of education provided in each school through a process of regular and published inspections and through the publication of 'league tables' showing the performance of each school on key indicators such as examination results.

Once again, these changes did not address special needs issues directly. Indeed, the mechanisms for delegating budgets to special schools and delegating funds for pupils with statements did not follow until some time after the 1988 Act. However, such major changes could scarcely fail to affect special needs provision, in ways that proved to be somewhat complex. In terms of the resourcing of special needs provision, for instance, the mechanism for delegating school budgets made it possible for LEAs to include weightings designed to take account of the size of a school's special needs population. However, the extent of these weightings was ultimately controlled by central government, and there was no guarantee that schools in the most socially- and economically-deprived areas would necessarily be resourced as favourably as they formerly might have been. Moreover, the special needs element in the budget could not be hypothecated, so that there was no means of ensuring that it would be spent on special needs provision.

Similarly, in terms of schools' accountability for their special needs provision, the system of four-yearly school inspection introduced by the 1988 Act in one sense did constitute a tighter form of regulation than anything that had existed before. However, the accountability that it created was not to the LEA as such: inspections were carried out by a national body (Ofsted) in accordance with a nationally- rather than locally-determined framework, and the findings of those inspections were made available to the public rather than solely to the LEA. Together with the other changes in governance, the consequence was that the accountability of schools to the LEA – which had never been total – was now significantly weakened. If schools chose to reduce the level of their special needs provision, or return to streaming, or otherwise move away from what might be local policy, there was little the LEA could effectively do beyond persuasion and cajolery. This was particularly damaging where LEAs felt the need to impose a special needs policy that was unpopular with some of their schools. It was not unknown, for instance, for LEAs to be unable to complete a reorganization of special education because ordinary schools refused to allow special schools to be closed and pupils with special needs to be relocated into the mainstream. Indeed, schools possessed the ultimate sanction against the LEA of threatening to 'opt out' of LEA control entirely. Certainly, in one LEA where the authors worked closely with schools, this sanction was used by a number of schools which were dissatisfied, amongst other things, with LEA special needs policy – and we simply do not know how many LEAs exerted a form of self-censorship which led them to steer clear of controversial policy moves.

Perhaps most significant of all, however, was the 1988 Act's introduction of a quasi-market (Barton, 1995; Bines, 1995; Bowers, 1995). From being part of a locally-organized service, meeting the needs of an entire community, schools suddenly found themselves operating as small businesses, focusing first and foremost on their own survival and eager – even desperate – to attract new customers in the form of children and their parents. Since the funding a school received was tied directly to the number of pupils it was able to enrol, and since parents could, in principle at least, select the school of their choice, it was clearly imperative for schools to make themselves as attractive as possible to those parents who were most able and most likely to exercise their right to choose. Although the processes of market economics are complex, it is clear that many schools interpreted this situation as meaning that they had to make themselves attractive to parents who would judge a school primarily by the examination performance of its pupils and by its reputation for high academic standards (Bowe *et al.*, 1992; Ball, 1993). For such schools, special needs provision would inevitably be a lower priority, since there was little point in diverting money, personnel and energy into an aspect of provision which would scarcely show in the league tables and would be of little interest to the majority of parents. Indeed, there might actually be a disincentive to developing special needs provision in that the presence of a large special needs population or a reputation as a 'special needs school' might be positively unattractive to some parents (Ofsted, 1996). Certainly, our own work in schools at the time revealed considerable ambivalence amongst headteachers on these issues.

The situation which faced schools following the 1988 Act, then, was one which was none too auspicious for the maintenance of a high level or high quality of special needs provision. On the one hand, they were under pressure to 'deliver' an apparently inappropriate curriculum to problematic pupils with little room for manoeuvre, and on the other hand they were under pressure to pay attention to priorities other than special needs. There was, therefore, a real danger that pupils with special needs would be marginalized and rejected by many ordinary schools in a system which seemed heavily skewed in favour of more able and more advantaged pupils and their parents. Indeed, there is some evidence that this is precisely what began to happen. Some schools began to reduce their staffing for special needs or began to divert their specialist teachers into non-special needs-related teaching[1] ; the level of support provided by LEA special needs support services began to decline (Garner *et al.*, 1990; Bangs, 1993; Copeland *et al.*, 1993); the rate of referral for statementing, of statementing itself and of special school placement began to rise (Swann, 1992; Lunt and Evans, 1994); the number of pupils (including those with statements) excluded by schools began to grow markedly (Stirling, 1992; Imich, 1994); and the move towards integrated provision for pupils with statements, always (as we saw in Chapter 5) hesitant, became very slow indeed (Lunt and Evans, 1994).

This situation led to expressions of anxiety from a wide range of commentators on special needs education (Wedell, 1988; Russell, 1990; Copeland, 1991; Swann, 1992). What the post-1988 situation revealed was that schools' commitment in the preceding decade to principles of participation and equity, however genuine that commitment may have been at a personal level, had depended heavily on a particular configuration of external circumstances. The inherent flexibility in a non-prescribed curriculum, the dominance in school governance of LEAs accountable to the entire community, the guarantee to schools of stable – even increasing – levels of support and resource if they pursued 'educationally desirable' policies – all made it possible for schools to develop liberal and inclusive approaches to special needs education at minimal cost to themselves. The 1988 Act, however, reversed this situation at a stroke. What Vincent *et al.* (1994), call 'the traditional benevolent humanitarianism of special education professionals' began to sit somewhat uneasily with the need to ride free-market forces. Suddenly, the pursuit of such 'humanitarian' policies carried significant penalties for schools, and although the commitment to 'human values' may have been every bit as strong, the costs to schools of realizing those values in practice increased enormously.

Concern about this state of affairs was not restricted to the professional special needs community. Special needs provision is both a resource-intensive and a politically-sensitive matter: insofar as the 1988 Act led schools to marginalize pupils with special needs and reduce the extent and quality of their special needs provision, the government was likely to incur the wrath of powerful special needs lobby groups (see, for instance, Davie, 1994); insofar as it led schools to reject such pupils and refer them for statementing, it was likely to put pressure on the already stretched resources of LEAs and lead to an upward spiral of demand for more favourable resourcing of the system; and insofar as it led schools to exclude pupils, it raised the spectre of large numbers of problematic children roaming the streets of towns and cities which had already witnessed (in the popular imagination at least) an increase in crime and in social disorder.

Not surprisingly, therefore, the government saw fit to act – and to act quickly. That action took, in the first instance, the form of two Audit Commission/HMI reports (Audit Commission and HMI, 1992a and b) which sought to diagnose the ills of the special education system and to offer some guidance of particular relevance to LEAs. There were, they concluded, certain endemic problems in the situation: definitions of special needs were vague and unoperationalized; boundaries between the responsibilities of schools and LEAs were unclear; LEAs had few incentives to follow the prescriptions of the Warnock Report (DES, 1978) in terms of the prompt statementing of pupils in need or the promotion of integration; and large amounts of funding continued to be tied up in partly empty special schools rather than released to resource provision in mainstream schools. The overall implication was that a great deal of clarification was needed in the field of special needs so that resources could be deployed effectively and different levels of the system could be made to discharge their responsibilities without a constant upward pressure on those resources.

The draft *Code of Practice* (DFE, 1993) followed hard on the heels of these reports. Senior figures within the special needs community, who had previously expressed considerable anxiety about the direction in which the system was moving, now welcomed the *Code* – albeit with some reservations – as a means of protecting the interests of vulnerable children. Wedell (1993), for instance, asked, 'Does the draft code promote the basic principles of special needs education?' and answered his own question in the following way:

> Most people's answer to [this] question is likely to be 'Yes'. On its very first page, the Code's 'fundamental principles' refer to the continuum of need and provision, entitlement to the broad curriculum including the National Curriculum, the right to be educated in the mainstream as far as possible, the importance of identifying and meeting needs early, and the crucial place of the views of parents and of those with special needs themselves. (p. 119)

Russell (1994) similarly accepted the government's contention that the *Code* would 'promote good practice and . . . benefit children' (p. 48), seeing it as the basis for 'a more dynamic, interactive and consumer-sensitive approach to special educational needs' (p. 52). There is certainly much in the *Code*, both in its draft and final versions, to support a reading of it as a document which consolidates established good practice, protects the entitlements of pupils with special needs, and defends the humane principles of special needs education. However, our account of the context within which the *Code* arose suggests another reading may be possible. Whatever else it may be, the *Code* is also a piece of government *regulation* aimed at holding together a system fraught with tensions and, in particular, at exerting a downward pressure on resource demands by enforcing the responsibilities of schools and LEAs within existing resource constraints.

Even a cursory glance at the *Code* reveals its regulatory nature. Following the briefest of sections on 'Fundamental principles', the *Code* embarks on a delineation of 'good practice' which is far more detailed than anything previously attempted. The 1981 Act had certainly laid down detailed procedures for the assessment of that minority of pupils 'with special needs' who might be regarded as in need of statementing. However, the *Code* extends this detailed prescription to *all* pupils giving their teachers 'cause for concern' – in other words (accepting the Warnock Report estimates) from something in the region of 2 per cent to something nearer 20 per cent of the school population. Moreover, unlike the 1981 Act, it is not simply the assessment procedures which are specified. Under the heading of 'Criteria for deciding to make a statutory assessment', the *Code* also specifies the defining characteristics of what amount to categories of special need, the levels of 'difficulties' which constitute a *prima facie* case for statutory assessment, and the sorts of provision which schools might routinely be expected to make for children who fall into these categories.

Although, therefore, the *Code* itself does not form part of statute, and although there are exhortations both within the *Code* and in the dissemination activities organized by DFE that it should be interpreted with a degree of flexibility, the fact remains that the *Code* defines for schools their special needs population and the sort of provision they are to make for that population. Such a move is, of course, essential if the provision made by schools is to be regulated. However, it effectively reverses the trend which we noted in Chapter 3 to blur the distinction between 'special' and 'ordinary' needs, or, indeed, to replace the language of special needs with one of individual differences. In this sense at least, it strengthens the tension between special and mainstream education.

Moreover, it is clear that if schools' definitions and provisions fall outside those mandated by the *Code*, LEAs are placed in a strong position (as Dyer (1995) acknowledges) to decline to provide extra resources to the school through the statementing procedure. In this way, the *Code* provides LEAs – and thus central government – with a means of capping the spiralling demand for special needs resources by requiring schools to make provision for certain groups of pupils in specified forms from within their existing budgets. This extension of regulation and capping does not stop at the level of the school, but extends down through the school hierarchy to the level of the class teacher.

The *Code* introduces a staged model of assessment and provision which begins with the class teacher, moves on to the class teacher working with the special educational needs co-ordinator (SENCO) and then to the class teacher and SENCO working with external agencies such as psychological services and LEA special needs support services (para. 2.61 ff). The 'good practice' reading of these requirements is that they constitute a mechanism for ensuring that pupils' 'special needs' are adequately identified, assessed and met, ensuring that all members of the school staff play their part in this process. However, the alternative reading is that they constitute a mechanism for *compelling* class teachers to make certain specified forms of provision from within their existing resources before calling upon the SENCO, and for requiring the SENCO to co-ordinate more sophisticated forms of provision before calling upon external agencies. Although many SENCOs may be currently somewhat reticent about using their new-found power, the potential for them to move from a pleading and persuading to a controlling and requiring relationship with colleagues is certainly inherent in the *Code* (Dyson, 1995; Dyson and Gains, 1995).

A further, crucial part of this mechanism is the introduction of individual education plans (IEPs). Again, the rhetoric within the *Code* and among its supporters is that IEPs offer a means of planning appropriate provision for individual pupils across the whole curriculum. However, IEPs also offer a means whereby those who have the power to formulate them – which means SENCOs, with at least parental acquiescence and quite possibly responding to parental demands – can put pressure on those who have to realize them in practice – which is likely to mean class teachers – to teach particular children in particular ways. In the same way, therefore, as the *Code* as a whole offers a means whereby central government can intervene in the provision made by schools, so the IEP offers a means whereby the SENCO can intervene in the work of the class teacher. Moreover, the IEP also offers the opportunity – seized eagerly in some cases – for the LEA and its service personnel to use its ability to specify appropriate formats and content in order to increase its own control over classroom practice.

The mention of parental involvement highlights another aspect of the regulatory mechanisms within the *Code*. The version of parental partnership has, of course, been part of the rhetoric of special education since the Warnock Report (DES, 1978). However, the notion of 'parents as partners' so forcefully advocated by Warnock is essentially an apolitical one:

> It [the parent-professional relationship] is a partnership, and ideally an equal one. For although we tend to dwell upon the dependence

of many parents on professional support, we are well aware that professional help cannot be wholly effective – if at all so – unless it builds upon the parents' own understanding of their children's needs and upon the parents' capacity to be involved. Thus we see the relationship as a dialogue between parents and helpers working in partnership. . . . Parents can be effective partners only if professionals take notice of what they say and of how they express their needs, and treat their contribution as intrinsically important. Even where parents are unable to contribute a great deal themselves, at any rate to start with, their child's welfare will depend on the extent to which they understand and can apply the measures recommended by professionals and can help to monitor their effects. Parents will often be able to point to an aspect that the professional has overlooked or has insufficiently considered. (9.6)

Although such passages as this present parents as partners in the provision of special education, the overwhelming impression is that they are partners only in the sense of supplying professionals with additional information and implementing professional recommendations as effectively as possible. There is no indication that parents are expected to share other professional roles – notably the roles of strategy-formulation and policy-making. Not surprisingly, therefore, the processes of assessment of need, placement and the determination of provision remain firmly in the hands of professionals; the most parents can expect is to contribute 'advice' on these matters and express 'preferences'. Not surprisingly also, we know that parents have in practice found it difficult to break into the charmed professional circle in special needs education (Armstrong, 1995; Sandow *et al.*, 1987).

Although the *Code* repeats the views of Warnock almost *verbatim*, its provisions make it clear that parents are seen as serving a very different function from that of 'partners' in the making of provision. Whereas, for instance, Warnock had provided for the statutory involvement of parents only in respect of the minority of children with statements, the *Code* extends this involvement throughout the assessment and provision stages – that is, to some 20 per cent of the pupil population. Suddenly, the response which mainstream schools make to the learning needs of a large minority of their pupils is no longer their private, 'professional' business. Moreover, this involvement has a statutory flavour insofar as schools are required to 'have regard' to the *Code* and are inspected on the basis of the extent to which they implement its recommendations. Furthermore, the creation of the special needs tribunal in the 1993 Education Act means that parents have a right of redress against the decisions and actions of the school and

LEA. This mechanism builds, of course, on the legal processes which, as we saw in the previous chapter, some parental groups had already become extremely adept at using.

When all of this is set in the context of increased parental involvement in educational governance generally and, particularly, of the introduction of parental choice of schools, a somewhat different role for parents emerges from that envisioned by Warnock. The *Code*, as Russell (1994) rightly points out, forms the basis for a system of special needs provision that is 'consumer-sensitive', implying a system which is, to some extent at least, 'consumer-driven'. Parents are no longer the compliant 'partners' of professional experts in a consensually-defined endeavour, but are the consumers (on behalf of their children) of special needs provision. As such, they have rights to be consulted and listened to throughout the process of provision, and have the legal right to challenge professional decision-making. Schools are no longer simply accountable to their professional consciences and to the LEA, but also to the parents of individual children with special needs, who can be expected to monitor carefully the school's provision for their child. In this way, parents become part of the mechanism for regulating the work of schools.

We saw in the previous chapter, of course, that parents cannot necessarily be expected to share the values and assumptions of professional educators and that different groups of parents will exercise their rights to involvement differentially. Although, therefore, schools (and indeed LEAs) may continue to hold to principles of participation and access, and may see themselves as acting, as Dessent (1987) suggests, to provide 'positive discrimination' towards the most vulnerable members of their communities, there is no guarantee that the parents to whom they are accountable for individual decisions will see things in the same way. Already there is growing evidence in our own work with schools that, in the context created by the *Code*, schools are increasingly shaping their provision to fit the perceived and expressed priorities of those members of their parent bodies who are most articulate and involved. In effect, this may mean diverting resources away from developing the quality of teaching and learning for a wide range of pupils and towards providing a clearly identifiable level of recognizably 'special' education to individual children in the form of withdrawal, in-class support.

REGULATION AND INDIVIDUALIZATION

This emerging impact of parental involvement leads directly into the subtle ways in which the *Code* is beginning to reshape the nature of special needs provision in mainstream schools. As we have seen in previous chapters, the trend in such provision had been very much towards notions of access and participation. Although schools had sought to be responsive to individual differences, they had increasingly sought to do this by developing flexible pedagogy and strategies for *all* their pupils. The notion of separate 'special' pedagogy and provision for some pupils rather than others had thus come to seem unduly constraining and segregatory.

However, one consequence of this 'embedded' approach to special needs is that it becomes extremely difficult to monitor provision. This is true in a number of respects. First, it becomes exceedingly difficult to trace the resourcing of special needs provision. A new resources centre, or a work-card scheme for the Maths department, or an overall reduction in class sizes can all be argued convincingly to be either part of the school's special needs resources or a diversion of resources away from special needs. The designation of a teaching and learning co-ordinator on a senior post can similarly be seen as a substantial investment in special needs education or as a cheap alternative to appointing a teacher with specific special needs responsibilities. The problem becomes much more acute when one attempts to trace the resourcing of individual pupils 'with special needs'. If a particular pupil is placed in a class with a teacher who has undergone extensive training in differentiation, with a set of expensive commercially-produced materials and access to IT, and with a support teacher who works flexibly with any pupil in difficulties, then what proportion, precisely, of these resources can be regarded as dedicated to that particular child?

Second, it becomes difficult to define the nature of special needs provision and monitor its quality. Is special needs provision *only* that which is provided by specialist staff working directly with nominated pupils? Or is it everything which the school does in respect of those pupils – and if so, how does it differ from whatever the school does for all of its pupils? Moreover, if the nature of provision is so uncertain, then how is its quality to be monitored? Should one look at the specific interventions with individual pupils or at the overall quality of everything the school does?

This in turn leads to a third difficulty. If it is not possible to disentangle special needs provision as such from everything the school does, then it is also impossible to assess the effectiveness of that provision. If the attainments of pupils 'with special needs' rise, then this may indeed be directly due to the activities of the school's special needs teachers. Alternatively, it may be indirectly due to those activities, if they have been successful in energizing their colleagues to teach more effectively. But equally, it may not be due to their work at all, but to some quite unrelated factor – the appointment of good teachers elsewhere in the school, or a particularly successful INSET programme, or the reorganization of the school's grouping system.

Finally, the 'embedding' of provision leads, as we have seen, to a blurring of the distinction between pupils 'with special needs' and all other pupils. Even if the complex questions of monitoring and resourcing described above could be resolved, it is not at all clear which pupils should be so monitored and resourced. Positions grounded in the notion of individual differences – such as the assertion that no pupils have special needs or, alternatively, all pupils have special needs because each is different from every other – may be attractive ethically and philosophically, but they make it impossible to determine who should receive 'additional' provision, or what level of resourcing is necessary to ensure that all pupils' needs are met, or which pupils' progress should be monitored to determine if special needs provision is effective.

None of these matters becomes a serious issue so long as pupils with special needs seem to do well and levels of resource seem to be adequate. However, as soon as resources become constrained and/or pupils 'with special needs' begin to experience impoverished educational experiences, then the impossibility of monitoring provision becomes a crucial issue. Headteachers under pressure find it – as they did post-1988 – all too easy to divert resources away from special needs, arguing that everything the school does is part of its special needs provision; changes in the quality of provision become almost undetectable; and any decline in attainment is attributable to a whole host of extraneous factors. The corollary of this is that it becomes increasingly difficult to counter claims from schools that additional resources are essential if particularly problematic children are to be educated effectively. There is simply no means of knowing whether a school is using its existing resources effectively or what level of resourcing is appropriate for given pupil populations, or whether some children really are beyond the capacity of the school to educate.

In order, therefore, to monitor, regulate and fund special needs provision, it is necessary to recast that provision into some form which is *susceptible* of monitoring, regulation and funding: it has to become something which is identifiable and quantifiable rather than something which is so 'embedded' that it is indistinguishable from everything else in schools. In particular, special needs education needs to comprise an identifiable and defined population, with clearly articulated needs for specific forms of provision, which are themselves formulated in ways which can be costed and whose impact can be measured.

This, of course, is precisely what the *Code of Practice* attempts. It defines the special needs population in terms of identifiable characteristics; it specifies the sort of provision which each quasi-category of special needs demands; it lays down detailed procedures for formulating the specific forms of provision which particular individuals 'need'; and it institutes processes of assessment which monitor the effectiveness of that provision and allow any adjustments to be calculated. These processes, however, require a particular form of individualization. At stage 1 of the assessment and provision procedures, this involves the class teacher in identifying those pupils within the class who are not progressing sufficiently within the provision made for the class as a whole and formulating an individual plan for these pupils. At each successive stage, two things happen: first, the individual plan is made more formal and more specific, initially as an IEP and then as a statement of special need; second, additional resources are called upon both in the formulation and the implementation of the plan – first the SENCO, then external agencies, then other resources provided by the LEA. This is a very different form of individualization from that which many of the 'innovatory' schools described in Chapter 3 were attempting. It is emphatically *not* about the development of a learning environment which is sufficiently flexible and responsive to take account of individual differences without recourse to special measures and additional resources. On the contrary, it is a means of identifying precisely those measures which are to be taken *over and above* standard provision for all pupils, and of calculating precisely what resources are needed to service them *over and above* the resources provided for all.

THE IMPACT OF THE *CODE*: EARLY INDICATIONS

At the time of writing, schools are only just beginning to come to terms with the implementation of the *Code of Practice*, and we lack detailed studies of its impact on practice in mainstream schools. Nonetheless, our own work (Dyson, 1996; Dyson, Lin and Millward, *in press*) and that of others (Bines and Loxley, 1995; Evans *et al.*, 1995; NASUWT, 1995; Lewis *et al.*, 1996; Ofsted, 1996) is beginning to highlight a number of broad trends which seem to confirm the reading of the *Code* offered above.

First, it is evident that the *Code* is subtly changing the work of the special needs co-ordinator. Whereas our own earlier studies (Dyson, 1992/1993; Clark *et al.*, 1995) detected a broadening out of the SENCO role (see Chapter 3), a large number of SENCOs are now reporting that their activities are increasingly dominated by the *Code*'s requirements in respect of pupils 'with special educational needs'. In particular, they are being diverted away from the attempt to address questions of equity and participation by developing the quality of teaching and learning for all. Instead, they find themselves overwhelmed by the need to maintain and manage a bureaucratic system of individual identification, assessment and provision. As Evans *et al.* (1995) put it,

> The procedural aspects of the Code of Practice, particularly in secondary schools, seem to have created cultures of organization within schools, within which concern for curriculum and access across the curriculum [are] temporarily de-emphasized. We would infer . . . this from the narratives of SEN co-ordinators since these are characterized by the vocabulary of support rather than the grammar of curriculum access. (5.22)

This tendency is reinforced by the impact of IEPs in particular. Although IEPs apparently offer an opportunity for SENCOs and class teachers to work together in developing responsive classroom provision, the reality is somewhat different. Many SENCOs find that the time for such collaboration is simply not available, and, even where it is, the willingness on the part of class teachers to involve themselves may be lacking. One SENCO, for instance, reported to us that her school had no children placed at stage 1 of the *Code*'s procedures; as soon as class teachers identified a child as having difficulties, they insisted the child be placed at stage 2 so that he or she became the SENCO's responsibility. Although this may be an extreme case, we have found many schools in which IEPs are effectively teaching plans for the withdrawal teacher rather than plans for access to and participation in the curriculum as a whole.

It is not surprising, therefore, that the content of IEPs is following a path that was previously followed by individual planning in the USA (Goodman and Bond, 1993). The IEPs we have seen – particularly in primary schools – have focused almost exclusively on setting targets in the areas of literacy and behaviour, to the exclusion of the rest of the curriculum. Moreover, those targets tend to have been devised on the basis of a quasi-objectives model; SENCOs, often working to advice from the LEA (and, in particular, from educational psychologists), have attempted to construct targets that are 'SMART' (small, manageable, attainable, realistic) and which in consequence are somewhat limited in their range and ambition. Such targets are, of course, easy to specify, to teach and to monitor but their net effect may well be to narrow the curriculum for pupils and to reduce the range of teaching strategies and learning experiences that are available to them.

There are indications that the *Code* is beginning to have a similarly narrowing effect on definitions of special educational needs. Since the management of the new bureaucratic processes involves SENCOs and class teachers alike in onerous paperwork and meetings, there is an in-built incentive for schools to avoid identifying and 'registering' pupils wherever possible. Certainly, a number of SENCOs have reported to us that their class teacher colleagues tend to disguise the numbers of pupils in their classes whom they regard as having special needs, whilst they themselves decline to 'register' pupils if they can see no immediate benefit from so doing. In some cases, of course, such benefits are available; in particular, if the LEA operates an 'audit' model of resourcing, so that registered pupils release resources to the school, or if there is a realistic prospect of a 'registered' pupil ultimately being made the subject of a statement, then the work involved in registering is offset by the prospect of additional funding.

What this emerging evidence suggests is scarcely remarkable: since the *Code* (despite its protestations) essentially sets out to regulate schools, schools are inevitably beginning to behave as though they are being regulated. The commitment of individuals within them to principles of access and participation – to Sayer's (1994/1987) 'human values' and Vincent *et al.*'s (1994) 'benevolent humanitarianism' – may be as great as ever. It is certainly the case that, to the extent that the *Code* is itself founded on these values, such individuals find that it supports and protects their efforts; the early studies all indicate a welcome from professionals for the avowed *principles* of the *Code*. However, insofar as the *Code* seeks to turn special needs provision into something which can be regulated – which necessarily means something that can be separated out and monitored – it is inevitably changing the nature of schools' special needs approaches. In particular it is, to a greater or lesser extent, reversing the trend towards 'merging' special and mainstream education, since it is virtually impossible to regulate one form of provision which has embedded itself deeply within another.

This situation inevitably creates tensions for those schools which are most fully committed to principles of access and participation. Wheal (1995), for instance, describes a school which explicitly rejects the language, values and systems of traditional special needs education, and which has developed a teaching and learning co-ordinator role as an alternative means of responding to individual differences. However, it is also a school which, in response to the *Code*, has created a SENCO post founded on somewhat traditional notions of identification, diagnosis and intervention. As Wheal admits,

I am ambivalent about the Code of Practice. I don't like its bland acceptance of the dominant orthodoxy that knowledge exists outside the knower, that knowledge is hierarchically ordered and that there is a minimum level and rate of progress that students must reach to achieve normality. The 20 per cent who don't make that normality are then defined as 'special' and as in need of some kind of support or remediation. . . . On the other hand, I do like the individual education plans (IEPs). I like them because they are student centred, because they demand increased individuation of the curriculum and because evaluating their successes will help classroom teachers reflect on their own practice. (1995, p. 85)

However, Wheal's ambivalence also points towards some of the positive findings from our own work. Although SENCOs feel their work is being distorted by the *Code*, they, like Wheal, are at the same time finding ways of using its provisions in support of the values and approaches to which they are committed. Some SENCOs, for instance, have told us of the enhanced status which the *Code* has brought, not so much for themselves personally as for special needs education within their schools; like Wheal, they have begun to explore how IEPs can be used to broaden, rather than narrow, class teachers' perceptions; they have extended the involvement of colleagues in special needs issues by establishing SEN teams within the school to share the bureaucratic burden, or by devolving responsibility for managing the *Code*'s procedures to mainstream teachers within the school; they have begun to build a consensus around the school's approach to special needs by devising explicit criteria for each of the *Code*'s stages and by formulating strategies to be used at each stage. Such creative and principled responses do not, they report, entirely overcome the tensions generated by the *Code*, but they do indicate that we are likely to witness an interplay between the regulatory and, to a large extent, conservative tendencies of the *Code* on the one hand, and the continued commitment, on the other hand, of some teachers and schools to principles of access and participation.

THE *CODE* IN PERSPECTIVE

It is, perhaps, a little early to place the *Code* entirely in perspective. The interplay to which we alluded above has only just begun and it is, in any case, by no means impossible that the *Code*, or the guidance surrounding it, will be modified by DFEE and/or by LEAs as the process of implementation continues. Nonetheless, if we step back from the detail of the *Code*'s provisions and of schools' responses, and focus instead on the historical process of which it forms a part, some aspects of its significance begin to be clear.

It is evident, in particular, that 'benevolent humanitarianism' is a fragile plant. Despite the hegemony which principles of equity and participation enjoyed over special needs developments over many years, it is impossible to deny that those principles began to shake, if not crumble, in the face of the new pressures on schools following the 1988 Act. Moreover, although government policy – or, more properly, government's benevolent neutrality – may have played a significant part in maintaining that original hegemony, it also played a major part in destabilizing it. It is also evident that the *Code* is only partially based on those principles and most certainly does not mark a return to the pre-1988 situation. It is, as Bowers (1995) indicates, part of a whole range of strategies for regulating the newly-created educational market place rather than any retreat from market principles

Above all, it is evident that developments within special needs education are by no means entirely self-generating. Certainly, the *Code* itself focuses exclusively on special needs education, and certain members of the special needs 'community' undoubtedly played a major part in shaping its provisions (Davie, 1994). However, seen from a longer perspective, the *Code* is a response that was necessitated by an Education Reform Act which had little to say about special needs, which seems to have been formulated without much regard for, or understanding of, its implication for special needs education, and which was, for the most part, drawn up without much involvement of the professional special needs community. If ever those of us who work in the special needs field were under the illusion that the nature of that work was in our own hands, that illusion should now be well and truly shattered.

NOTES

1 Shortly after the 1988 Act, we worked on an internal LEA survey of the impact of LMS on special needs provision in mainstream schools. Although there had been much anxiety in the professional special needs community about the possibility of special needs teachers' being made redundant, we found the actual impact to be much subtler. Schools by and large retained their existing special needs staff and still described them publicly as such, but actually redirected their activities so that they undertook a much greater proportion of mainstream teaching. This, of course, had the effect of making the actual seepage of resource away from special needs provision following the 1988 Act somewhat difficult to detect.

The changing role of the LEA in the management of SEN provision

INTRODUCTION

In previous chapters we have concentrated exclusively on developments in mainstream schools and classrooms. In this chapter we are going to focus on the role of the LEA in the support and development of special needs education. Inevitably we will revisit some of the issues covered before in relation to schools but in this chapter we will analyse them from the perspective of the governance of special educational needs. We have already described (see Chapter 6) how the emergence of specific learning difficulties has placed new demands on the nature of specialist peripatetic support in many LEAs. Similarly, the *Code of Practice* (see Chapter 7) places a number of responsibilities on LEAs, including the co-ordination of assessment and the provision of specialist services to meet the needs of those pupils with more complex needs. It is also clear that challenges to LEA statementing decisions through the recently established tribunal system may undermine the overall special needs strategy by adversely affecting budgetary planning. Similarly, parental appeals to local independent committees over exclusions, an area of growing concern, are also likely to bring into focus the nature of the relationship between LEAs and schools over provision for special educational needs. All these are issues which have implications for the management and deployment of special education resources by LEAs. However, these potentially increased responsibilities have arisen at a time when significant changes in the relationship between local and central government have taken place.

The overall effect of these changes has been to significantly reduce the extent to which local government can control locally based services. The impact of these changes for education have been to increase the autonomy of individual schools in a number of key areas making it increasingly difficult for LEAs to exercise the degree of control that many had come to expect in the planning of provision and the management of resources at a local level. This presents particular difficulties in the field of special educational needs when the policy context as we have indicated is premised on a progressive merging of the mainstream and special education sectors. It is clear, therefore, that in the context of this book issues relating to the governance of special educational needs are of considerable significance in understanding policy and practice within schools. Given the potentially conflictual nature of many of these issues many LEAs are in the process of rethinking their role in the governance of special education. The development of effective systems of governance at local level will be instrumental in avoiding conflict and in realizing the current policy imperatives.

Although never a major issue within the literature, the issue of the governance of special education has, in the light of the issues identified above, become much more central to the interest of writers from a number of perspectives (Millward and Skidmore, 1995; Housden, 1993/1994; Robinson, 1994; Kramer, 1993 etc.). This interest reflects the significant changes brought about by the 1988 and 1993 Education Acts. The impact of these changes has been profound (Maclure, 1989; Audit Commission, 1992a and b, 1994) leading to the questioning by some of the continuing need for a role for local education authorities as their powers have increasingly been whittled away. The situation has, however, not always been so conflicted and it is possible to identify distinct phases in the evolution of the governance of special needs education.

SEGREGATION AND STABILITY

For example, according to Housden (1994) the period between the 1944 and 1981 Education Acts can be regarded as the 'sleep of the centuries'. It was a period in which he suggests the absence of leadership from central government and ambivalence of intent on the part of some LEAs produced an overall consolidation in respect of the delineation of role and responsibilities. Given the scale of changes introduced by the 1944 Act such a phase is, perhaps, both inevitable, and understandable. That is not to say that this resulted in a bland uniformity. Quoting Green and Steedman (1993), Housden (*op. cit.*) describes the evolution of an education system which was uneven, not only in terms of its provision for the student population as a whole, but which was also geared to the interests of an academic elite, selecting out high attainers, 'rather than encouraging the aspirations of the broad majority' (Green and Steedman, 1993). For LEAs the 1944 Act created a framework of stability in which they were able to discharge their responsibilities. In special education this stability was based on a system of segregation within which LEAs had the relatively simple task of identifying special educational needs according to the newly defined categories and developing an appropriate level of provision in the form of schools and services. In mainstream education the tripartite structure resulted in an essentially self-regulating system within which the LEA was left with a loose monitoring role.

The subsequent expansion of the special education sector, reported on by amongst others Ford *et al.* (1982) is thus understandable in terms of the LEAs assiduously fulfilling their statutory obligations. With a clear brief and little ambiguity over their role the LEAs were able to deliver a structure of special education which could be developed with little or no reference to what was happening in the mainstream sector. Indeed, the existence of a segregated special education system could be seen as a logical extension of the segregation that existed within the mainstream sector.

It is interesting to note, however, that in a period when the role of the LEA was essentially one of the development of fixed resources in the form of schools and services, that provision was not uniform. Housden (1993) suggests that there was inconsistency within and between LEAs as to how that provision was actually made, and the overall lack of regulation by central government in this period was responsible for the disparities that existed across the country. It was noted also (Ford *et al.*, 1982) that there were particular anomalies over the relative levels of provision for the categories of ESN(M) and Maladjustment. These latter two categories are significant in that they represent the most significant populations in special educational needs in mainstream schools.

That is not to say that in this period there were no attempts to bridge the divide between the special and the mainstream systems. Some experimentation did take place in this period as for example in the special units established by some LEAs to rationalize provision and achieve limited opportunities for integration of pupils with sensory impairments (DES, 1967/1968). Substantially, however, the system was marked by stability. For the LEA there was no imperative to engage in overtly interventionary strategies in its mainstream schools. Its monitoring role was supplemented by that of HMI, and in special education its role was predominantly that of ensuring an adequate level of provision in the form of special schools to meet its obligations under the 1944 Act.

Whilst the ordinary and special systems remained separate there was, therefore, no ambiguity over the role of the LEA. The special and mainstream education services were managed largely as separate entities with clear demarcation between the professional support teams that the LEAs maintained. Issues of resourcing the expansion of the special education sector were not significant as the macro economic climate enabled LEAs to meet the increasing numbers that were being assessed and referred. The policy of segregation created a clarity of role and at the same time a clear objective in the form of increasing provision which most LEAs were proud to develop.

This stability was, however, to be threatened by two developments. First, the systematic and rapid dismantling of the tripartite system in favour of comprehensive schools in the late 1960s; and, second, the advocacy of greater 'integration' through the means of the whole school approach following the Warnock Report. The outcome of these actions were to bring a new urgency and purpose to the role of the LEA. As we have seen this early attempt to merge special and mainstream education (see Chapter 2) was problematic. The whole school approach demanded a more active role on the part of the LEA. It required intervention in the mainstream school in ways that had not been attempted before.

INTEGRATION THROUGH CONTROL

If the period up to 1981 was characterized by sleep, then the following decade is best described as one of intensive restlessness on the part of the LEAs, provoked by what we have described in Chapter 2 as the increasing attempt to merge the mainstream and special sectors. The response of the LEAs to the challenge of attempting to merge the two systems was interesting; it relied on a number of assumptions. Firstly, it usually took the form of a systematic enhancement of the central resources and services that were available in an attempt to influence policy within schools and classrooms. For example, often for the first time, Advisers with particular responsibility for special needs in the mainstream school were appointed; the Schools Psychological Services were expanded as a direct consequence of the statementing process, and LEA peripatetic services were rapidly expanded to offer schools and teachers 'support' in identifying and responding to the needs of pupils as well as preparing the ground for 'integration'. In conjunction with this, additional staff were often appointed, especially in secondary schools, to act as the conduit through which these externally available resources could be funnelled into schools. According to Dessent (1987) this can be regarded as a classic, resource-led attempt by LEAs to implement policy through centralized direction.

Secondly, it made the assumption that schools would respond to the lure of a traditional carrot-and-stick approach. A combination of 'traditional loyalty' to the LEA and enhanced resources were felt to be sufficient to bring about the changes necessary to achieve this merger of the two systems. It was not seen as necessary at the time to actually question the extent to which the existing practices in mainstream schools were conducive to a greater merger of the two systems. This led many LEAs to assume that all that was required was to replicate the existing systems of traditional special education within mainstream schools through a policy of enhanced resourcing, and they would be able to create a context in which a continuum of provision would emerge, and the two systems would develop as a seamless whole.

As we described in Chapter 2 this early skirmish with the merging of the two systems experienced some considerable difficulties. In analysing this failure we have identified the existence of a number of 'tensions and conflicts' (Clark *et al.*, 1990; Dyson *et al.*, 1994; Dyson *et al.*, 1991) in the implementation of the whole school approach. In particular we identified a 'fundamental contradiction in the idea of developing complex organizations such as mainstream schools by centralized direction' (Clark *et al.*, 1990, pp. 280–1), and the dangers of focusing on 'the structure of provision' as the means of achieving change. For us the dilemma faced by an LEA in attempting to merge two previously separate systems lies, therefore, at a number of levels. Fundamentally, it requires an understanding of the complexity of organizational structure residing at the level of individual schools and the scope that there is for misunderstanding, subversion, resistance and non-compliance with central initiatives (Fullan, 1991). As we have previously stated: 'This problem is, we would suggest particularly acute in the field of special needs where the values, beliefs and presuppositions of teachers and administrators – the "paradigms" upon which they operate – are deeply implicated in both policy and practice' (Dyson and Millward, 1996).

What happened, as we saw in Chapter 2, was that little actual merging took place, with the mainstream schools reluctant to transform themselves along a special education model preserving their traditional approaches and assuming that special education in a mainstream context was simply a locational exercise which could be accommodated without any need for changes in structures, systems or practices.

That the LEAs did not seek to engage with the more complex issues of institutional change and development, teacher values, beliefs and presuppositions, may reflect their uncertainty as to how such changes might be achieved or a misplaced confidence in the extent to which the systems and approaches they were seeking to import were likely to become accepted in the mainstream context. That it faced stubborn resistance is not, therefore, altogether surprising. This stage of the development in the governance of special needs education is significant in that it highlights the extent of difficulties likely to be experienced in any attempt to realize a policy imperative within the context of mainstream schools when that policy requires a fundamental shift in pedagogic practices: it parallels the problems we identified at individual school level in Chapter 4. However, in our analysis of developments towards the end of this period (Clark *et al.*, 1990), we indicated that some LEAs were already exploring new ways of managing special needs provision especially as it related to mainstream schools. We referred to developments in Oxfordshire and Cleveland and to the views of CEOs such as Madden (1989) that collegiality and nurturing would have to form the basis of a new relationship if LEAs were to realize policy ambitions in comprehensive schools. It would, of course, be unfair to point solely to the difficulties experienced by LEAs in this attempt to deliver the implications of the Warnock Report and the 1981 Act. An alternative view of this period would be that the LEAs were never given sufficient time to achieve this continuum of provision before they were overwhelmed by a deluge of legislation from the end of the 1980s which significantly reduced their ability to direct what was happening in mainstream schools.

By the time of the 1988 Act there were a number of concerns about the overall effectiveness of special education. Different levels of provision between LEAs suggested a lack of consistency and an element of chance as to the provision which children and their parents might expect. Variations between LEAs in the level of placement in segregated schooling reinforced this view, leading some (e.g. Collet, 1988) to the view that policy depended simply on the existence of places in special provision rather than any objective notion of need. With the implementation of the 1988 Act, the issue of the governance of special education was given a further twist as LEAs were restricted in their capacity to direct change centrally and were to be faced by schools with much greater autonomy in a number of key respects. This autonomy would impinge on the ability of LEAs to achieve the merger of the two systems which had been given an additional impetus by the 1988 Act.

It is in this context that for some commentators the post-1988 Act era was regarded as marking the effective beginning of the end of the active role for the LEA in the governance of education. For Housden (1993), there was an impending pessimism, with the LEA acting merely as 'a goalkeeper and provider of the last resort'. He saw a minimalist role emerging in which special needs, left to the whims of the market place, would revert to a service which was fragmented and based increasingly around segregation. Others were more sanguine. Moore (1993), for example, saw the development of the purchaser/provider split as positively encouraging a better level of provision as it placed the client more centrally in the debates about provision and reduced the conservative 'self-interest' of traditional providers. For Moore and others, this injection of market forces into what had previously been a restrictive monopoly situation offered the prospect of not only a better level of service for the consumer but also the dawn of a new era for the LEA. In the advocacy of this approach, they were broadly following the recommendations of the Audit Commission in suggesting the adoption of a role for LEAs as purchaser of services and monitor of quality within a competitive market environment.

GOVERNANCE WITHOUT CONTROL

The post-ERA period and its impact on the governance of special education represents, therefore, an interesting study of the need for change and adaptation in the light of a critical and changing external environment. Two factors dominate this period and are instrumental in understanding why LEAs have to examine their governance of special educational needs. First, there are the structural changes brought about by the 1988 Act. These changes were not based on the same set of liberal values which had dominated the previous periods. The introduction of a market place in education made it extremely difficult for the LEAs to exert any kind of control as individual schools were forced into competition with each other. The previous section has highlighted the difficulties LEAs faced in attempting to bring about changes within schools when there was considerable consensus around these liberal values. With this consensus effectively undermined by the legislation and with special educational needs sidelined as an issue for mainstream schools the task of the LEA was made much more complicated. Second, the post-1988 period is marked by increasing demands for 'inclusion'. These demands are increasingly orchestrated by parent groups, independent psychologists and others outside the 'professional' special education lobby which had previously dominated the agenda. These new 'voices' owed no loyalty to any previous systems and, empowered by the new legislation, were able to exert an increasing influence on policy and resourcing at a local level.

These two factors were to provide a major challenge for LEAs in providing for special educational needs. The national political context in particular was hostile with the criticisms voiced in the previous period given full vent through a series of critiques of many aspects of special needs provision. From the measured tones of various HMI reports (1989, 1990 a, b) which pointed to variance in the quality of provision to the more acerbic comments of the Audit Commission (1992 a, b; 1994), it was quite clear that a climate of concern and doubt about the capacity of the LEA to guarantee a high-quality service was being generated at a national level.

Within the literature, more specific concerns (Brown and Riddell, 1994) were being raised about the ability of LEAs to resist the influence that well-organized and politically influential pressure groups were having on the distribution of resources for special needs. In particular she highlighted (see Chapter 6) how the dyslexia lobby were apparently exerting a disproportionate influence over resource allocation in a number of LEAs. This phenomenon was reinforced by our own research (Clark *et al.*, 1995; Dyson and Skidmore, 1995) which indicated that a number of LEAs were being forced to switch part of their designated special needs resources away from support for those with mild or moderate learning difficulty and into more targeted provision for 'dyslexia'. Similarly, Gross (1996) refers to research from Lunt and Denman (1995) that 'certain types of "middle-class" disability (specific learning difficulty – SpLD in particular) have been over- represented in cases going to one or other of the pre-tribunal forms of appeal', and to Vincent (1994) who suggests that: 'apparently inequitable arrangements (are) made for children of professional middle-class parents, supported by well-organized voluntary organizations', to the detriment of pupils with moderate learning difficulties who cannot rely on such strong advocacy. Kramer (1993) describes one of the outcomes of a Special Education review as a concern of 'the undue influence of some articulate and vociferous parents . . . gaining unfairly resources for their children'. This factor is in itself not altogether surprising, given the emphasis placed by much of the educational legislation of the time on empowering parents to become more active in seeking what they regard as the most appropriate provision for their children. It does, however, illustrate the extent to which the ability to plan provision at local level is sensitive to changes in the relative influence of stakeholders. Whether central government foresaw the extent to which an Education Act aimed primarily at the creation of competition between mainstream schools would have on the overall coherence of the special education provision is unclear.

It is interesting to note how various contributors from within LEAs view their role in this particular period. Gray and Dessent (1993) for example, in discussing Nottinghamshire, describe how: 'the education committee did not consider it acceptable to be inactive in this area and thereby to risk leaving vulnerable children at the mercy of the new educational "market place".' To prevent these children falling by the wayside, they identified a number of key features which informed the Children First policy for their LEA. These included: a process of 'consultation' with mainstream schools to increase greater inclusion; better management of resources to support inclusion; the encouragement of mainstream support groups; and an increased level of training. Interestingly, this strategy was underpinned by what was described as: 'a range of . . . resources which are retained centrally . . . targeted at those pupils with the most significant needs . . . as well as supporting schools. . . .' Similarly, Kramer (1993) describes a 'review' of special education in Gwent concerned to deal with 'organisational difficulties' and 'successive budgetary overspends', together with a concern about the best use of existing resources.

It is clear, therefore, that there was mounting concern about the governance of special educational needs emanating from within the LEAs themselves. Housden (1993), for example suggests that it was not the case of there being one crisis, but that he could identify 'at least five'. In particular, Housden was concerned with the extent to which special education could still be managed at a local level in a climate of increasing self-management on the part of schools and the growth of an educational market place encouraged nationally which together made it increasingly difficult for LEAs to operate.

The response of the government was the 1993 Act and its accompanying *Code of Practice* (see Chapter 7) which was designed to regulate many aspects of the provision of special education. The *Code* and its requirements can be seen, in part at least, as an attempt by central government to address the issues raised in reports it had itself commissioned by introducing for the first time specific requirements and obligations for LEAs and schools. This regulation of the system is, at one level at least, at odds with a market-driven philosophy, but on the other hand demonstrates the extent of the difficulties in ensuring an equitable and quality provision within such a complex field as special education. For example, by identifying particular responsibilities for schools and LEAs in respect of the identification and assessment of pupils with special needs, it was attempting to ensure a degree of consistency within and between schools and LEAs. By placing specific targets on LEAs over the time limits for the completion of formal assessments, it was attempting to set a standard to which all LEAs should aspire and which in its transparency provided parents with a means of challenging what they might regard as inappropriate delays. In such a context it becomes possible to identify the framework within which LEAs seek to contribute to the governance of special education.

FUTURE ROLES AND RESPONSIBILITIES FOR LEAS

Insofar as the 1993 Act reinforced the direction set by the 1988 Act, it further reduced the traditional role of the LEA as a provider and director of resources and provision. In particular the 1993 legislation increased the pressure on LEAs to delegate to schools a greater proportion of the budget for non-statemented special needs, whilst the *Code of Practice* required them to retain sufficient services and resources to meet the needs of statemented pupils, for whom they retained statutory responsibility. The *Code* was to place responsibilities for special educational needs in mainstream schools on LEAs at a time when their actual capacity to manage and direct schools was being reduced. A certain potential for conflict is implicit in this situation, with schools subject to a range of other pressures as well as their responsibilities for special educational needs. At a time of a changing relationship between LEAs and schools in general, the case of the governance of special education provides an interesting opportunity to examine the nature of the current relationship between local and central government. Faced with a decline in their centrally held funding, and in some cases the break-up of the existing LEA structure, LEAs are nevertheless charged with a range of responsibilities:

- They retain statutory responsibility for statemented pupils.
- They are required to collaborate with mainstream and special schools in implementing the *Code of Practice*, including provision of specialist support for pupils at stage 3 in the assessment process.
- They will be required to ensure that provision for minority groups within the special needs population is maintained.
- They are charged with improving the overall efficiency of their management of resources within special education.
- They are required to liaise with GM schools in the provision of special education.

These responsibilities coincided with a number of other developments which were to impact on the provision of special education. First, there was a dramatic upsurge in the number of exclusions from mainstream schools (Imich, 1994; Stirling, 1991, 1992, 1993; Parfrey, 1994). The 1993 Act tried on the one hand to cap this by removing from schools the right to exclude a pupil on an indefinite basis. On the other hand the Act allowed LEAs to establish PRUs to accommodate pupils who had been excluded. This further illustrates the dilemma for any intermediary agency in planning for special needs, as LEAs were suddenly expected to be able to create a new form of provision whilst at the same time maintaining the existing provision for other groups. In this instance this was not the only 'new' provision that LEAs were establishing. Effective lobbying by parents empowered by the recent legislation, on behalf of the specific learning difficulties group and the recognition of ADHD as requiring a particular form of response, had all produced demands for additional 'special' provision.

The ways in which LEAs have responded to these new challenges and in particular the models of governance which were emerging in the light of the 1993 Act and the *Code of Practice* formed the basis of a substantial piece of research conducted on behalf of the Joseph Rowntree Foundation (Millward and Skidmore, 1995). This research sought to identify the extent to which LEAs were reconceptualizing their role in the light of recent changes and the extent to which new forms of governance were emerging. The research took place over the academic year 1994–5 and consisted of three stages. First, LEAs were allocated to a broad categorization frame which reflected the range of LEA types (Shire, Metropolitan Borough, former ILEA). Second, the documentation in respect of special needs produced by LEAs was analysed with a view to establishing whether any distinctive responses were emerging at a policy level. Once this had been established, it became possible to construct a smaller sample of LEAs which reflected the distinctive policy responses across the various LEA types. This small group of LEAs was then approached with a view to their participation in the project. Detailed case studies were then conducted through the interviewing of key personnel. The final stage involved the analysis of this interview data and its comparison with existing models of governance as they were reflected in the literature.

The research highlighted three major dimensions of governance: *values, roles* and *systems*. Within each of these dimensions, it was possible to identify a number of features which were indicative of a new model of governance in respect of special needs. These dimensions and underpinning features are represented diagramatically in Figure 8.1 (page 154).

The extent to which these represent a reconceptualization of the role of the LEA in the governance of special educational needs in the light of the new context forms the basis of the following section.

THE RESOURCING OF PROVISION

All the LEAs in our research expressed a concern about the overall level of funding for special education, particularly in the light of the new requirements of the *Code of Practice*; several had sought to earmark contingency funds to enable them to resource particular aspects

Figure 8.1: Models of governance

of their provision. In one Authority an emergency fund of £1 million had been set up to maintain the LEA's policy of SEN support. Another LEA with a strong commitment to inclusive education had secured £250,000 to support the implementation of the *Code*. Clearly these LEAs were continuing to experience continuing dilemmas in clarifying the relationship between what was a changing role in respect of the governance of special education and their capacity to resource a form and level of provision which reflected a previous notion of how that role should be implemented.

In an attempt to exercise the degree of budgetary control that the Audit Commission suggested was sometimes lacking, all of the LEAs were developing a form of audit model to govern the resourcing of special needs provision. This was not without difficulties and was described as having a 'difficult birth' by one interviewee as it involved the implementation of a system which was responsible for reallocating resources between schools. The adoption of these formula-based approaches to the funding of special needs is seen as a powerful tool for exerting budgetary control over what has been something of a 'black hole' in resource allocation. The system is, on the surface at least, equitable and transparent, with parents, teachers and schools having full information regarding the budgetary implications resulting from an assessment decision. Some earlier forays into this area met with initial problems in that the 'banding' systems introduced by some LEAs encouraged schools to accelerate pupils through the various levels to achieve a greater level of funding. This resulted in the resource capacity of the LEA being exceeded and in the creation of short-term resourcing problems for the schools and anxiety on the part of parents. However, once fine-tuned, these formula-based models were seen as apparently holding the key to a successful management of the resource dilemma by LEAs.

Unfortunately this has not proved so simple as at first thought, as one of the implications of the changing relationship between local and central government has been the empowerment of parents to challenge, in this case via the special needs tribunals, the placement and resource decisions of the LEAs. In a situation where the budgetary situation is marked by annual uncertainty and tight government control, there is considerable sensitivity at local level to even minor distortions to the funding profile. As Gross (1996) has pointed out, the task of tribunals is to respond to 'what is desirable', not what is 'affordable or essential' . The budgetary planning by LEAs is therefore prone to be 'blown off course' if legally-supported parental challenges upheld by the tribunals involve increased expenditure by LEAs.

MATCHING PROVISION TO CHANGING VALUES

All the LEAs in the study saw their provision for special education as indicative of the attempt to realize certain underpinning ethical commitments. Without exception, they all endorsed a notion of *equal opportunities* as central to the shaping of their management of special needs. This notion did, however, conceal a diversity of view as to whether this involved a positive commitment to what was regarded as an anti-discrimination stance in the form of an approach based on *inclusive* education, or a commitment to *equality of provision* within the area served by the LEA. This diversity can be seen as a strength of the locally organized provision. It does, however, leave the LEA open to criticism from a number of quarters. There is the likelihood of a repeat of the criticism from national surveys of the Audit Commission type which highlight inconsistency of provision. There is a similar probability that LEAs will be subject to sustained challenge from both sides of the inclusion debate for failing to provide sufficient choice. There is the danger that in accommodating one side of this debate or even one sectional interest, the overall provision will become distorted and the base level of equality of opportunity will be undermined. Clearly, at a time when LEAs are concerned about the degrees of flexibility that they have in which to operate and when the general political climate stresses the need for choice and diversity, their potential for providing a special needs provision which satisfies all sides is limited.

MANAGING A FLUCTUATING POPULATION

A number of instances were reported of LEAs seeking ways to respond to the needs of a changing population without incurring an unmanageable additional expenditure. Many of these revolved around the LEA co-ordinating groups or clusters of schools to take the initiative in responding to particular areas of special educational need. This was often the case where an LEA was seeking to reduce its out-of-authority placements as a means both of reducing expenditure and of realizing its aim to provide for all the members of its community. In this case the LEA would seek to co-ordinate the action of a number of schools to establish a particular form of provision and then to provide whatever additional support it could from the anticipated savings which were made. In doing this, the LEA was still seen as maintaining a strategic leadership role within the area of special educational needs yet at the same time it was operating as an active *partner* with the schools in the authority. This was regarded as an important dual function of the way that the LEA operated, and it was acknowledged that its realization required the steering of a careful path which was neither directive nor non-directive, but reflected more of the collegiate role described by Madden (1989). The term 'federalist ' was used on more than one occasion to describe this role. For some of the smaller LEAs and those who had been part of the former ILEA structure this involved a number of major considerations. It required agreement across schools as to the location of particular provisions involving considerable negotiation at a time when schools have a range of competing priorities. In many ways this endorsed the notion of federalism and was one very clear way in which an LEA could be seen to be exercising its 'moral authority' (Housden, 1993).

MONITORING A FLUCTUATING POPULATION

The changing nature of the special needs population and the increasing tendency to review the use of out-of-authority placements had resulted in many LEAs embracing a more active quality assurance and monitoring role. Not all LEAs were fully convinced of the purchaser/provider split advocated by the Audit Commission. They were uncertain as to the efficacy of such a precise dichotomy of function in respect of the provision and management of special education. They were, however, much clearer in their recognition of the need for the adoption of a quality assurance and monitoring role in a number of other areas. They saw a particular responsibility for pupils returning from out-of-authority placements to new provision within the LEA and for the specialist facilities developed for 'new' groups of special needs pupils (those excluded, those with ADHD, and those with specific learning difficulty for example). The nature of these populations and the likely scrutiny from parental groups made them sensitive to the need to ensure that provision was equivalent to that available elsewhere. They also recognized that the *Code of Practice* demanded a greater harmonization of processes and procedures across the LEA if they were going to be able to achieve the equality of opportunity which they all espoused as a central tenet of their policy statements. They recognized that in a situation where their own resources were limited, this demanded not simply an 'inspectorial' role but one that worked towards enhancement of the capacity of schools to self-monitor and self-evaluate. In adopting this view, LEAs were clearly in the process of establishing the parameters of a new role for themselves. A consideration of these factors will form the basis of the conclusion of this chapter.

OPTIONS FOR A FUTURE ROLE

The governance of special education is, as was stated at the outset of this chapter, complex and beset by a number of persistent dilemmas. We take the position that no central government could expect to manage that complexity without the support and active contribution of some form of intermediary agency. There are, however, a number of problems in delineating the actual role of that agency as it relates to special education.

First, as we have pointed out elsewhere (Millward and Skidmore, 1995), the capacity of any agency to act in the field of special education in the ways envisaged in the *Code of Practice* is related to financial considerations. Reforms of local government implemented from 1996 have brought into being new, small unitary authorities. These often replaced larger multipurpose county councils. Our research (Millward and Skidmore, 1995) highlighted the extent to which existing, well-established but small metropolitan boroughs, were already experiencing severe doubts about their ability to act in anything other than a minimalist way in respect of the new legislation. In particular they felt they would not be able to engage in any form of developmental work in special education and that the structure of their provision was vulnerable to decisions by individual schools to opt out of any locally agreed arrangements. They were extremely concerned that reductions in personnel at the centre were leaving them without the professional expertise to be able to provide the leadership or strategic overview necessary to manage the complexity of the field. We are also aware of how in some of these new unitary authorities it is not uncommon for special educational needs to be either a part-time or shared responsibility. There are echoes here of the pre-Warnock situation when special education was very much a backwater within local education authorities, a situation which is perhaps incompatible with the current legislative context which demands a much more proactive engagement with a field which is complex and in a stage of considerable flux.

It may be that we are being unduly pessimistic and that the breakup of the old structure paves the way for a new formulation of collaborative ventures between the emergent and existing LEAs. The function of the market may be such that the notion of purchaser/ provider transcends the relationship between schools and LEAs to incorporate a similar split between LEAs. Certain LEAs would then be able to market their services for the benefit of others, with the process of supply and demand determining the eventual cost of particular provisions. In this way a more cost-efficient special education provision which bears only a minimal relationship to local government boundaries might emerge. If this were to be the case then we see a number of issues which would need to be addressed.

We described in our earlier research in this area (Millward *et al.*, 1995) the emergence of a 'new model' of the governance of special needs. Within that new model we identified a number of key features. We suggested that the model was characterized by the notion of a three-way *collaboration* between LEAs, schools and central government. This had its genesis in the development of the *Code of Practice* and was seen by LEAs in particular as an example of 'good practice' in how all the prospective partners in the delivery of special education could co-operate to produce a policy framework which built on existing good practice and offered a realistic charter for the future. The process was described to us as one which mirrored at national level what was happening in the relationship at local level between schools and the LEAs. It was a process of policy development which also acknowledged the need for policy to be based on *consensus* building and *co-ordination* on the part of the LEA rather than on resource allocation. Without command of resources, the LEAs had to build a consensus on the overall shape and direction of the special educational provision rather than relying on command or direction. This required them to retain a strategic overview and to continue to co-ordinate a number of key functions if that provision was to operate within the nationally established framework and at the same time reflect local concerns.

It was this final concern which marked an important aspect of the model that we described – the belief that provision for special educa- tion had to a considerable extent to *reflect the needs and circumstances of the local community.* In this sense the provision of special needs was not regarded as an isolated feature of local authority provision, but an integral element in the realization of the aims and ambitions of the local community reflected by its democratically elected representa- tives. Our research indicated a diversity of interpretation of this role, reflecting the diversity in the local needs of communities. In some LEAs special education was seen as an instrument of the realization of a general policy of inclusion in which any form of segregation was seen as contrary to the desire to create a non-segregated community. This was leading to the closure of special schools and the creation of inclusive schools. In other, often geographically more dispersed LEAs, there was an equally principled response which interpreted this aspect in terms of the realization of equality of opportunity for all regardless of where in the authority an individual lived. Here special schools were seen as contributing to the achievement of equality of opportunity and not necessarily in conflict with the wider goals of integration.

Within this diversity of interpretation the unifying theme as we indi- cated above was the role of the monitoring of *quality.* Providing the 'best' possible service for their vulnerable pupils was central to the concerns of all the LEAs. This demanded the establishment of systems and procedures to monitor what was in place and to identify the potential that existed for development within a resource-limited con- text. The monitoring of quality is pivotal to the continued function of intermediary agencies in the governance of special education. It is increasingly likely that the arbitration of competing resource claims at individual pupil/parent or school level will become an increasing fea- ture of their role. Early evidence from the working of the tribunals (Lunt and Denman, 1995; Gross, 1996) suggests that LEAs are experi- encing considerable pressure from certain pressure groups over the allocation of resources. This is likely to continue in the short term. Early attempts to create a more rational means of resource allocation via audit models as a means of managing this problem experienced some difficulties. In the longer run it would appear that the principal features of the 'new' role for LEAs as we describe them will be realized as they increasingly adopt audit-based models of resourcing special education.

ISSUES AND DILEMMAS IN IMPLEMENTING THE NEW ROLE

There are a number of dilemmas which LEAs face in implementing the new role that we have described. The effect of these dilemmas is to increase the vulnerability of LEAs in the governance of special educational needs. First, the changes outlined above have given an enhanced role to a number of stakeholders who previously had only a peripheral involvement in the governance of special education. The LEA is now only one of a number of players rather than the dominant force that it used to be. The professional special education lobby who were instrumental in advocating the merger of the two systems has also been challenged by new articulate groups and individuals. Parents, either individually or via well-organized pressure groups can exert pressure on the decisions made by LEAs over individual pupils, and advocate an alternative vision of how special needs education should be realized. The tribunal system formalizes this appeal process and creates a forum in which challenges can be mounted. Where a tribunal makes a decision against an LEA this can, if there are resource implications, have the effect of threatening the overall strategy that has been devised. Similarly, the LEAs have to contend with a much more 'hands-on' approach from central government. The issuing of guidance such as the *Code of Practice* or changes to the funding arrangements demonstrate the extent to which national government can impact on the strategy that an LEA may have evolved. So, whilst the LEA has been given a clear role by the *Code of Practice* it is also more accountable to a larger number of stakeholders and has less flexibility with which to operate.

Second, the *Code of Practice* requires LEAs to operate in particular ways in respect of special educational needs. For example, they are required to ensure that schools have a recognizable special needs strategy in which there are distinctive and separate systems and procedures. This emphasis on the development of separate and distinctive special educational provision is in contrast to that of the pre-1988 period when the focus was very much more towards the enhancement of the mainstream provision in order to blur the distinctiveness of the special provision. For LEAs this represents an opportunity to develop a distinctive role which some thought had been lost. It enables them to suggest to schools models of provision which will dovetail into the systems and structures with which the LEA feels most comfortable. This can be instanced both in the general welcome with which the *Code* was greeted by LEAs (Millward and Skidmore, 1995) and by the enthusiasm (Dyer, 1995) with which many LEAs have moved towards an audit-based system for resource allocation. The audit system places the LEA in a central role for resource allocation as it enables them to control important elements of the special educational needs purse-strings. How LEAs and indeed schools respond to this emphasis on the re-establishment of a distinctive special educational needs provision and the revival of the role of the LEA will be an interesting issue for further research. It is interesting to note the effect that this trend has had in the one school that we report on in Chapter 4. However, such an optimistic view has to be set against the possibility that schools may be given increased responsibility for such issues as funding or entry criteria thus circumventing the ability of LEAs to exert influence over policy at local level.

Finally, the LEA is faced with managing its role in a situation where there is a number of conflicting values at work. The role that is suggested for LEAs is based very much on realizing the expressed interests of the community that they represent and of providing an effective provision for all of their children. This attempt to realize what we have described as the liberal values of inclusion are at one with those in guidance such as the *Code of Practice* and subsequent reports (e.g. Ofsted, 1996). Such values could, however, be described as in conflict with other equally powerful value positions and imperatives to which schools are currently required to respond. The pursuance of a high position in an examination league table is not necessarily convergent with developing an inclusive school. Inclusion may well represent the high moral ground but schools may respond at a pragmatic level and forgo the moral approval in favour of a more materially advantageous alternative. Similarly, when managing budgets there is no obligation on schools to enhance resources for special educational needs; they may well choose to resource certain pupils at the expense of others or respond to parental pressure by differentially funding provision for certain individuals at the expense of certain groups. All of these factors highlight the existence of contradictory forces at work within the new context. They suggest that a new relationship is present in the governance of special educational needs and that LEAs will continue to have a distinctive role to play. There exists, however, the potential for conflict and a risk that innovation at school level may be stifled if the LEAs interpret that role narrowly or seek to proceed without a collaborative approach.

Our view is, therefore, that the role of the local education authority will be best served by adopting a collaborative approach to the management of special education. We acknowledge that there is currently ambiguity in the relationship between local and central government as to how this might be realized and that there is a need for a period of stability in both policy and structural change. The major changes introduced by the *Code* and the reorganization of local government will need a period of consolidation in order to establish these effects. In the light of what we hope will be a systematic review of their outcomes it may well be that the present structure of LEAs may need to be reviewed. We are convinced, however, that there will continue to be a need for an intermediary agency to enable local and central priorities to be realized if the needs of a complex population of vulnerable children are to be met.

What does this analysis of the governance of special education have to contribute to our understanding of the dilemmas that are implicit in the field of special education? We would suggest there is the problem of reconciling the realization of a values position at a policy level with the actual practices that are manifest in schools and classrooms. Rhetoric in favour of inclusion is likely to be frustrated unless it is matched by the development of effective pedagogic practices which bring the values position of a policy into line with the practical needs of teachers and schools. LEAs which have forcefully articulated a values position based on greater equality and participation will have to take cognizance of the resistance that might be encountered at classroom level and to devise ways in which the problems of delivering an inclusive curriculum can be overcome. The effort by LEAs to achieve a merger of the special and mainstream systems is also likely to encounter continued resistance at school level when competing priorities and pressures have to be weighed against the somewhat intangible benefits that might accrue from adopting a values position. There is a parallel here with the role of the special needs co-ordinator seeking to argue the case for inclusion within the school. The co-ordinator has little to offer in terms of benefit to class teachers who will have to deliver these values through changes in their pedagogic practices, other than an appeal to a sense of achieving a moral outcome. Similarly, the LEA has to rely on goodwill rather than an actual ability to determine practice. It has to rely on a manipulation of the limited areas it can control; it has to negotiate; it has to encourage schools to take a broad view; it has to create a climate of trust and collaboration through which its values can be realized. It has to do so, however, in the knowledge that it is subject to more direct control from central government who in attempting to realize other values create a climate in which the LEA is further circumscribed in its ability to act. The impact of that conflict has been through the encouragement of a number of 'voices', especially those who 'consume' services, to argue for 'rights' on an individual basis thus challenging the ability of the LEA to manage services and provision on a collective basis.

The role of the LEA in the governance of special educational needs will therefore be an evolving one and may well take a number of forms. Given the recent changes in local government, there will be a need for special needs to be carefully monitored both locally and nationally if the consistency sought by the *Code of Practice* is to be realized. In particular there will be a need to ensure that in small unitary authorities there is the necessary support and professional expertise available to help in the development of an effective response for pupils with special educational needs.

The past and the future

At the outset of this book, we set ourselves the task of tracing the fate of a 'bold experiment' in special needs education. That experiment – though conceptualized somewhat differently at different times – was essentially to attempt a 'merger' of special and mainstream education: a merger which would result in the creation of mainstream schools capable of responding to the full range of student diversity and of ensuring all students access to a common, entitlement curriculum and participation in shared learning experiences. We also warned that the field of special needs education has been, in recent years, both complex and fluid, and that the best we could hope to offer was a series of 'snapshots' in the hope that, by setting these alongside each other, it might be possible to discern some overall 'moving picture'. Looking back, then, at our studies of the whole school approach, of the schools that tried to develop that approach in innovative ways, of the development of the integration – and, latterly – the inclusion movements, of the rapid emergence of specific learning difficulties, of the imposition of the *Code of Practice* (DFE, 1994a), and of the attempts by LEAs to reconstruct themselves and their roles, what can we say about the results that the bold experiment has yielded?

Perhaps the most important starting point is with the observation that a genuine experiment has, in some LEAs and schools at least, taken place. In recent years there have been attempts to develop responses to student diversity that have been characterized by all the 'boldness' that one could desire and, indeed, by considerable creativity, commitment and professional skill. The capacity of schools and LEAs to respond creatively to often difficult circumstances and to retain and act out a commitment to 'human values' is an enduring feature of the developments we have examined. Approaches to student diversity have thus been realized in some places during the late 1980s and early 1990s which, we suggest, would have been simply unthinkable in earlier times. Such approaches constitute genuine additions to the repertoire of special needs education and open up possibilities for its reconstruction as part of an overall reconstruction of education in our schools.

However, it also has to be said that such developments have been by no means the norm and that, where they have occurred, they have tended to be characterized by greater or lesser degrees of tension and limitation. Indeed it is possible to detect a pattern of failure within the 'bold experiment'. That pattern seems to have three recurrent elements:

1. In the attempted 'merger' of special and mainstream education, special education has contorted itself into a succession of new forms, without ever persuading mainstream education to do the same.
Throughout the period we have been studying, special education has reconstructed itself as the 'whole school approach', or as an approach to 'individual differences' or as 'integration' or as 'inclusion'. On each occasion, special educators have defined new roles for themselves or, 'done away with' themselves (Galletley, 1976); they have sought to acquire new forms of expertise and to make that expertise available in different places and modes; they have developed new sets of relations with their mainstream colleagues; they have devised new structures and systems; they have even agonized endlessly about what to call themselves and how to characterize their work.

Mainstream education, however, has, in many cases, remained stonily indifferent to these contortions. Special needs co-ordinators have, all too frequently, had no more impact on their colleagues' practices than their 'remedial teacher' predecessors – and even reconstructing oneself as a teaching and learning co-ordinator seems to be no guarantee of success; provision for pupils 'with special needs' has remained stubbornly 'shoddy' and widely-prescribed nostrums such as differentiation have been adopted only patchily and ineffectually; the curriculum has, if anything, become even more firmly entrenched as a 'mainstream' curriculum, structured around notions of what 'most' children need, with few if any concessions to the range of pupil diversity; and the apparently fundamental shift from integration to inclusion appears to have done little to make ordinary classrooms more hospitable places for children who experience the greatest difficulties.

Indeed, for all the rhetoric about the need to 'merge' the two forms of education, and all the calls for radical school reconstruction, it is difficult to see in this period what mechanisms and strategies special needs education has been able to develop that would allow it to impact on its 'big brother'. For much of the time, it seems to have assumed that, by placing itself in ever-closer proximity to the mainstream, it would be enabled to act upon the systems and practices therein. The reality, however, has been different. Again and again, we have seen how special educators can work alongside mainstream teachers, and pupils with special needs can be placed alongside their peers with no detectable impact on how the mainstream goes about its business. Even when – in, say, the 'innovatory' schools of Chapter 3 or in the inclusion movement – there has been a realization that mainstream education was the real target of any reconstruction, the resistance of the mainstream to such efforts has scarcely been dented. The mainstream, it appears, has remained firmly answerable to its own necessities and imperatives, and has shown little inclination to be driven by the principles and priorities of special needs education.

2. In reconstructing itself, special education has frequently simply replicated itself.
Given this failure to reconstruct mainstream education, there has been a depressing tendency for special education's convolutions to result simply in more special education. SENCOs remain special educators; support teaching and support via classroom assistants remain segregated forms of provision in integrated classrooms; differentiation appears as the 'alternative curriculum' in another guise; even inclusive education becomes, in Slee's (1996) phrase, 'a misleading veneer for old special education practices' (p. 29). Moreover, the emergence of specific learning difficulties and the imposition of the *Code of Practice* seem to have given a powerful impetus to the re-establishment of recognizable forms of 'special' provision. What seems to have happened is that special education constantly changes its *form* in order to locate itself in ever closer proximity to mainstream education, but because there is no corresponding reconstruction of the mainstream, special education retains its traditional *function* of providing shelter, support and alternative pathways in an essentially hostile and alien learning environment.

3. The attempted merger of special and mainstream education has failed to take account of the wider socio-political context.
We have referred in earlier chapters to Vislie's (1995) characterization of the integration movements in Western education systems as part of a much broader social, cultural and economic trend. Post-war economic expansion and optimism, argues Vislie, led to a flourishing of liberal values and attitudes which were in turn reflected in a whole range of social policies, including (in the UK context), the comprehensivization of mainstream schools and the development of integration

programmes. However, Vislie points out that economic expansion appears to have come to a halt and this may have consequences on the education system which are difficult to predict, but which may well reverse some of the liberal trends of recent decades.[1]

What Vislie's analysis reminds us of is the extent to which, in the UK, there has, through the 1970s and, to a large extent, the 1980s, been a congruence between developments within the field of special needs education and developments in broader areas of social and educational policy. The 1960s and 1970s, which, from our point of view, saw the development of special needs provision in mainstream schools, followed by the emergence of the whole school approach and the integration movement, also gave rise to the move towards comprehensivization, the abolition of the 11+, the exploration of mixed-ability teaching, the raising of the school leaving age, the development of alternative forms of examination to the GCE and, perhaps most important of all, extended periods of Labour government. Despite, therefore, the inevitable divergence and conflict in matters of detail, developments in special needs education were broadly in line with developments elsewhere in education. Even the advent of Conservative governments from 1979 onwards did not immediately disrupt this situation: no sudden return to selective schooling took place; the 1981 Education Act created a framework within which integration and the whole school approach could be pursued; the governments of the mid-1980s showed considerable interest in raising standards amongst low-attaining pupils (through, for instance, the Lower Attaining Pupils Project (HMI, 1990) and the Technical and Vocational Education Initiative (DES, 1989)); and even the introduction of the National Curriculum fell within an established tradition of addressing special needs issues through a rhetoric of inclusion and entitlement.

The situation following the 1988 Education Act has, we suggest, been somewhat different. We have seen how the creation of a quasi-market in education has had marked effects on the role of LEAs, the tolerance of schools towards pupils 'with special needs', and the emergence of 'new' categories of need driven by groups outside the traditional special education community, to the point where the government has felt it necessary to extend regulation across the entire special needs field. Despite the efforts that we have seen particular schools and LEAs making to maintain their liberal commitments in the face of these changes, there is little doubt that the congruence between developments in special needs education and developments elsewhere has been broken.

The problem for the professional special needs 'community' which has been responsible for promoting the 'human values' of equity and participation in recent decades is that they have had no means of resisting – let alone stopping – these changes in broader social and educational policy. That community has traditionally comprised professional educators and academics, who have enjoyed considerable autonomy in shaping special needs education in line with their own values and attitudes. An examination of the biographies of those whom we have most often referred to in this book is illuminating: Tony Dessent came up through the ranks of educational psychologists to become an LEA administrator; John Sayer wrote from his experience as a headteacher; Mel Ainscow was a headteacher and LEA adviser before entering academia; Klaus Wedell was an educational psychologist; and we ourselves represent the same pattern of professional education backgrounds leading to academic careers.

Such backgrounds are so common that they are currently taken for granted. They are, however, extraordinarily narrow; few if any of the key figures in the 'special needs community' has a background in politics, education policy-making at the national level, economics, social policy – or even, with relatively few exceptions, in mainstream education as such. It is scarcely surprising, therefore, that this 'community' has developed a rather homogeneous and, perhaps, insular set of values and attitudes. In particular, it is not surprising that it has not been able to predict or counter the changes in governance and regulation which have swept across the education system since 1988. To its credit, the inclusive education movement has, as we have seen, consistently drawn critical attention to the narrow base of the professional special needs 'community', pointing out the exclusion from that community of its supposed 'clients' – understood as people with disabilities. However, it is far from clear that the clients of the system have themselves been able to do much effectively to resist the changes of recent years, much less to reverse them.

The insularity of the professional special needs community is reflected in its concerns of recent years. Whilst special needs education has been shaped through a revolution in school governance and the creation of an educational quasi-market, the professional community has been largely preoccupied with school-level issues, whether these be issues to do with the creation of a regulatory framework for schools (Davie, 1994) or in the development of schools that are 'effective for all' (Ainscow, 1991). Even the inclusion movement seems, in practice, to have become preoccupied with the creation of inclusive *schools* rather than with any broader issues. It is, therefore, difficult in school or LEA practice, and even more difficult in the special needs literature, to find a clear articulation of the relationship between special needs education (however conceptualized), mainstream education, and broader issues of social and economic policy. Special needs education is endlessly reconstructed, but within a framework of governance, local government, economic, health and social policy which is essentially invisible. Perhaps it is only as, in recent years, this framework has imposed itself with a vengeance on special needs education that we have been in a position to see what a great omission this has been.

There is one final feature in the way special needs education has developed in recent years that we would wish to highlight. It is a feature which, we suspect, has contributed much to the insularity and naiveté of the field. There has been an almost universal acceptance among those who have advocated the values of equity and participation in these years that it was only a matter of time before special education 'did away with itself' (Galletley, 1976). Indeed, some of us have been prepared to argue (Dyson, 1990) that special education indicated a fundamental pathology within the education system, and therefore that its essential task was to reconstruct itself and the education system as a whole in such a way that the pathology was removed and special education ceased to exist – an argument which continues to recur in the special needs literature (Slee, 1996).

We still believe that such arguments have much to offer as means of critiquing the features of the education system which fail to respond effectively to the diversity of student characteristics. However, they also lead to an exceedingly optimistic account of the history of special needs education in terms of a relentless and unbroken progress towards full participation and complete equity. Writing in a US context, for instance, Wang and Reynolds (1996) assert that:

> The prominence of inclusion in current efforts for educational reform represents no simple swing of the pendulum. The history of special education shows a steady trend of progressive inclusion, beginning with total neglect, then moving to distal arrangements for a few (as in remote residential schools), to local special day schools, to special classes in regular schools, to resource rooms where students spend part of their school time – the remainder in regular classes – and, finally, to full inclusion in regular schools and classes. (pp. 20–1)

Such accounts simply do not square with the complexities and ambiguities which we have traced throughout this book. Moreover, the notion that special education would, if only the 'right' policies were implemented, 'merge' unproblematically with a reconstructed mainstream education has led in practice to an underestimation of the factors which lock the current special-mainstream divide in place. In particular, taking the notion of 'merger' as an article of faith and seeing the maintenance of separate systems as evidence of a pathology in the education system or as a form of oppression has made it difficult to see that divide as the result of anything other than the exercise of political (ill-) will on the part of self-interested and reactionary educators and policy-makers.

We believe that it is essential to set such unproblematical accounts alongside a more complex alternative. There is a small, but highly illuminating, body of work which sees educational practice in general and special needs education in particular as characterized by *dilemmas* (Berlak and Berlak, 1981; Norwich, 1993; Clark *et al.*, 1995). Such dilemmas arise because the practice of education is a complex venture which attempts to respond to essentially conflicting imperatives – to extend the capacities of the most able, for instance, whilst making provision that is equitable for all children, or to respond to children's particular interests and motivations whilst enabling them to acquire common bodies of knowledge and skill that are socially-valued. However irreconcilable such conflicting imperatives may be, educators – teachers, educational managers and policy-makers – are required to educate, and they therefore have to find a *modus vivendi* amidst these conflicts. The structures and systems they develop and the patterns of practice they evolve thus constitute their 'resolutions' of the dilemmas which confront them – resolutions which may be articulate and coherent, but which may equally, of course, be implicit and self-contradictory (Berlak and Berlak, 1981, pp. 131ff.).

One dilemma in particular is fundamental to the practice of education in modern Western societies: it is the dilemma of *commonality* versus *difference*. On the one hand, all children share many characteristics in common: learning in broadly similar ways, being engaged by broadly similar activities and so on. Moreover, modern Western societies invest this commonality with considerable value, seeing all children as entitled to participate in a recognizably similar educational process. It is, therefore, the task of schools to respond to this commonality by including all children in some broadly similar learning experiences, thus ensuring both that they are indicted into the skills and knowledge that are socially valued and that their rights and entitlements are realized. On the other hand, all children are palpably different from each other as learners, full of individual preferences and interests, setting about learning tasks in a multiplicity of different ways, and emerging from the education process with very different profiles of attainment. This individuality is also highly valued by modern Western societies, and is also seen to attract rights and entitlements which the education system must realize. As a result, it is regarded as the task of schools to respond to the individuality of learners, finding ways to offer educational experiences that are adapted to the characteristics of each and every pupil.

The dilemma for practitioners and policy-makers, of course, is that it is by no means obvious that these two imperatives – responding to commonality and responding to difference – are mutually compatible or, if they are, how that compatibility might be achieved. It is easy to see how commonality can be accommodated – by the formulation of a common curriculum, the creation of all-inclusive schools and the provision of identical learning experiences for all children. It is also easy to see that the most obvious ways of responding to difference are likely to demand precisely the opposite strategies: the formulation of a series of alternative curricula, the creation of different types of school for different children, and the provision of different learning experiences for different groups or individuals. But how, precisely, can these two very different approaches to education be reconciled so that curricula are common but multiple, schools are all-inclusive and selective, and classrooms provide learning experiences that are the same for all but different for each?

Many developments in post-war education can be seen as attempts to resolve this fundamental dilemma. The tripartite system of the 1944 Education Act, the widespread practice of ability grouping and the development of different curricula for different schools and, indeed, different groups within schools, were resolutions, as we saw in Chapter 1, that inclined towards responding to difference at the expense of commonality. Hardly surprising then, that from the 1960s onwards the education system began to incline in the opposite direction, as comprehensivization, mixed ability grouping and, latterly, the National Curriculum laid the emphasis on what children have and are entitled to in common rather that on what makes them different from each other. Hardly surprising, either, that the essentially dilemmatic nature of educational practice continues to break through the surface of these attempted resolutions, producing a picture that is messy, complex and extremely fluid. Just as grammar, technical and secondary modern schools shared some fundamental elements of a common curriculum and built upon the work of an essentially 'comprehensive' primary phase, so many comprehensive schools have retained ability grouping and the 'broad and balanced' National Curriculum is also one which is 'relevant' and 'differentiated' to the point where different children are likely to receive significantly different learning experiences. So also, in recent years, the comprehensive system has been complicated by the emergence of selective City Technology Colleges and by the impact of parental choice, whilst the National Curriculum has been 'slimmed down' to the point where it now offers alternative routes for different groups of pupils, particularly at Key Stage 4.

Although this dilemma is, we suggest, fundamental to all educational practice in modern Western societies, it becomes particularly acute wherever the education system seeks to make provision for atypical groups and individuals. In such circumstances, the attempt to respond to those atypical characteristics within a common educational framework is fraught with tension. It is not surprising, therefore, that education systems have tended to generate special forms of provision as a means of squaring this particular circle. Special education, in other words, can be seen as a particular – and particularly interesting – case of an attempt to resolve the commonality-difference dilemma. Inevitably, the attempted resolutions in this sector have closely followed those within the education system as a whole. The development, in the immediate post-war years, of a substantial special education sector based in segregated special schools was entirely in line with the prevailing emphasis elsewhere in the education system on responding to difference at the expense of commonality. In precisely the same way, the attempt to 'merge' special and mainstream education, driven by principles of access and participation, was entirely in line with the growing emphasis on commonality from the 1960s onwards. And the complexity, ambiguity and fluidity which we have seen to be characteristic of recent years is, of course, reflected elsewhere throughout the education system. Special needs education, like educational practice generally, continues to wrestle with the dilemma of commonality and difference and continues to find that dilemma intractable.

This reading of special needs education goes a long way towards explaining the complexity which we have described throughout this book. If the history of special needs education in recent years sometimes seems like a bewilderingly rapid succession of different 'approaches', that is precisely what we should expect. As the context of special needs education changes, as educators learn more about a range of strategies for organizing schools, curriculum and pedagogy; and, above all, as social values and priorities shift, so we should expect different resolutions of the commonality-difference dilemma to emerge. Similarly, if the problems that are posed for special needs education are indeed dilemmatic in form, then we should also expect that no resolution will effectively 'solve' the dilemma; the alternative 'pole' of that dilemma – the differences between children – will, we might anticipate, continually reassert itself. We should not, therefore, be surprised when 'radical' attempts to merge special and mainstream education give rise to the sorts of concerns that we saw expressed in inclusive education or 'innovatory' schools, that abolishing special education simply makes schools incapable of responding to difference. Nor should we be surprised if such radical mergers result in the reinvention and replication of special education, as schools and teachers seek to modify forms of pedagogy and organization premised on commonality in order to respond to the very real differences with which they perceive themselves to be confronted.

Finally, if special needs education is essentially dilemmatic, we should not be surprised that there is infinite scope for different interest groups to propose a multiplicity of different resolutions. The dilemma will inevitably present itself differently to groups who experience it from different positions. We might expect a liberal special needs 'community' of academics, policy-makers and managers to emphasize the high principles of commonality and to minimize the practical difficulties of responding to difference within common systems and structures; but equally, we might expect class teachers who have to manage large groups of children, or parents who are inevitably interested in their particular child, or psychologists whose profession is the study and measurement of individual difference, to formulate a range of proposed resolutions that take these interests and concerns into account. Moreover, as new 'voices' – the 'clients' of special needs education, for instance – find means of engaging with these groups, we should expect that they too will propose their own resolutions reflecting their own experiences, interests and concerns.

A MODEL OF CHANGE IN SPECIAL NEEDS EDUCATION

Setting this dilemmatic perspective alongside our earlier comments about the problems which the attempted merger of special and mainstream education has faced, makes it possible to formulate at least the beginnings of an account of how change takes place in the field of special needs education in mainstream schools. The field is characterized by a succession of proposed resolutions of the fundamental dilemma of commonality and difference. However, those proposed resolutions do not simply materialize out of the ether. Berlak and Berlak (1981), for instance, show how teachers' resolutions of the dilemmas of schooling are grounded both in their own social histories and in a range of social and institutional influences. Similarly, reviewing the impact on two schools of some of the same changes that have concerned us, Bowe and Ball (1992) show how the particular resolution that is a school's special needs policy is shaped by a series of internal and external factors: the micro-politics of the school; LEA policy and practice; central government policy and so on. The model they formulate of these 'constraints and possibilities' is presented here as Figure 9.1.

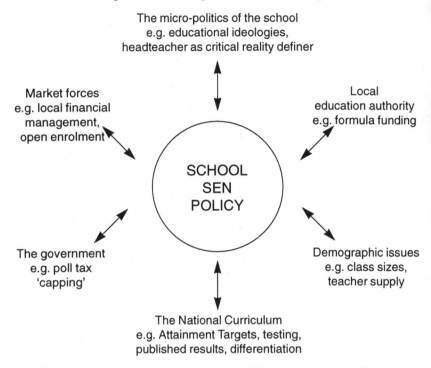

The micro-politics of the school
e.g. educational ideologies,
headteacher as critical reality definer

Market forces
e.g. local financial
management,
open enrolment

Local
education authority
e.g. formula funding

SCHOOL
SEN
POLICY

The government
e.g. poll tax
'capping'

Demographic issues
e.g. class sizes,
teacher supply

The National Curriculum
e.g. Attainment Targets, testing,
published results, differentiation

Figure 9.1: The constraints and possibilities which could affect a school's SEN provision

Reviewing the developments which we have studied in this book, it may be possible to develop a model which takes Bowe and Ball's insights further. It is evident, for instance, that the various resolutions we have traced here are grounded in the *values*, attitudes and beliefs that are prevalent in society as a whole and in the various sub-groups within society who acquire the power to involve themselves in educational issues. In the period we have studied, the 'human values' of equity and participation have been dominant in shaping special needs education – though challenges to those values seem latterly to be increasing.

Resolutions, however, are also grounded in a particular social, economic and political *context*; it is this context which empowers some groups at the expense of others; which generates resources and resource constraints that set limits to what is possible; which formulates a legislative framework within which any proposed resolution must operate or with which it must take issue; and which establishes priorities for and creates the form of mainstream education in respect of which special needs education must define itself. We have seen in earlier chapters, for instance, how economic expansion and political liberalism, comprehensivization and mixed ability teaching, and the dominance of professional voices in the control of education have created the context out of which many of the developments in special needs education emerged during the 1970s and 1980s. We have also seen how that context has changed significantly in recent years, with potentially overwhelming consequences for the direction of special needs education in mainstream schools.

At the same time, proposed resolutions are both bounded and enabled by the *technology* – which, in this instance, means the range of pedagogies, curricula and school and system organization – that they find ready to hand, or that they can generate. The resolutions stressing equity and participation which we have studied throughout this book have, therefore, depended crucially on the availability or creation of a technology which permits diverse groups of children to be educated together. Participation would have remained essentially an abstract principle without technologies of mixed-ability teaching, or special needs co-ordination, or in-class support and differentiation through which it could be realized.

These four elements – resolutions, values, contexts and technologies – are not entirely separate phenomena; rather, they continually interact with and impact upon each other in a process of mutual interdependence and causation (see Figure 9.2, page 176)[2]. If a resolution such as the whole school approach emerges out of a consensus around principles of equity and participation, then its emergence also creates the potential for many who feel some broad commitment to children 'with special needs' to prioritize those values over equally worthy principles to do with 'appropriate' education and 'meeting need'. If it is shaped by a context which includes comprehensivization, then it also makes possible the emergence within that context of a statutorily imposed National Curriculum from which children 'with special needs' are not excluded. Similarly, if it is only possible because the available technology includes a somewhat under-specified curriculum delivered through a pedagogy which was beginning to explore more flexible and 'child-centred' methods, then it also develops its own technology of support teaching and contributes to the drive for differentiation.

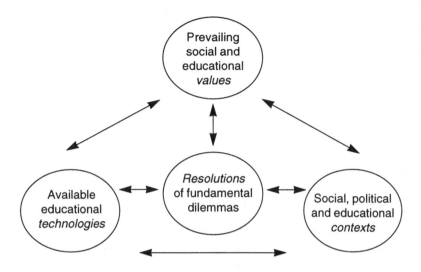

Figure 9.2: A model of change in special needs education

This interaction accounts for much of the complexity which we have seen throughout this book – a complexity which is further increased by two factors. First, the model we are proposing exists at a succession of levels within the education system. The resolutions, values, technologies and contexts at national level, for instance, are somewhat different from those which exist at local level, or within individual schools, or, indeed, individual classrooms. Second, as we have seen, those levels themselves are fragmented in complex ways: different groups and individuals, each operating with their own resolutions, values, technologies and contexts, engage with each other in national policy-making, or local administration, or within individual schools. The result of all this is precisely what we have found: within a broad overall trend towards resolutions premised on the values of access and commonality, some schools and LEAs drive towards 'radical' resolutions whilst others retain a more conservative attachment to longer-established practices; some groups (such as parts of the inclusive education movement) advocate even more radical resolutions whilst others (such as the 'dyslexia lobby') find their interests better served by revitalizing older resolutions; and some aspects of government education policy (such as the National Curriculum) respond to the more radical imperative, whilst others (such as the *Code of Practice*) simply reinforce an approach that is some two decades old.

Despite the inevitably schematic nature of this model, it does help to explain why change in the field of special needs education has been so problematic. Although any number of resolutions has been advocated and attempted in recent decades, none of them has effectively addressed the complexity of the field. In particular, the shift in values towards principles of equity and participation has, as we have seen, largely ignored both the dilemmatic nature of special needs education and the wider educational and social context within which it is located. It has failed, therefore, to take into account the extent to which its proposed resolutions might founder on the dual rocks of the irreducibility of 'difference' and the overwhelming impact of the world outside special needs education. It has, in this, not been helped by the tendency of many advocates of these principles to focus almost exclusively on one or other aspect of the field in isolation, rather than engaging with its full complexity. As we have pointed out elsewhere (Clark, Dyson and Millward, 1995; Clark *et al.*, 1995a and c; Skidmore, 1996), different elements of an overview exist scattered amongst a series of accounts which are essentially reductionist in effect. Some commentators advocate changes in school organization or classroom practice without considering the broader context of such changes; others focus on questions of value, or on a critical analysis of the socio-political context of special needs education but have nothing to say about the technology which might realize the resolutions they advocate. Currently, there exist few means for these scattered elements to be brought together, so that they illuminate and inform each other; and even if there were such means, so few commentators acknowledge the dilemmatic nature of special needs education that it is doubtful whether anything like a complete account would be produced.

The consequence of all this for policy-makers and practitioners in this field – and thus ultimately for children 'with special needs' – is that they are the recipients of much exhortation and, indeed, a good deal of sermonizing, little of which matches the complexity of the situations they see themselves as experiencing. In the final part of this chapter, therefore, we propose to explore some of the implications of our analysis for these groups.

THE FUTURE OF SPECIAL NEEDS EDUCATION: LESSONS FOR PRACTICE

Our first point is that the very complexity and fluidity which is the theme of our analysis has some immediately practical implications. Special needs education is a field which is inherently unstable. It is not, in the mid-1990s, the same field as it was in the mid-1980s or 1970s, in terms of values, resolutions, contexts or technologies. There is, therefore, no reason to suppose that it will be the same field in the middle of the next decade. The implication is that there are no absolutes in this field; in particular, the resolutions that are advocated now – be they the 'received' resolutions such as that proposed by the *Code of Practice*, or 'radical' resolutions such as inclusive education – will almost certainly not be the resolutions that are being advocated then. As values, technologies and contexts change, as different groups seek and win power within special needs education, so old resolutions will appear limited and new resolutions will come to take their place. Moreover, because each term of our model will inevitably shift, those new resolutions will not simply be 'better' ways of achieving old aims, but ways of achieving something subtly or markedly different in a subtly or markedly different situation.

Alongside these shifts over time which our model predicts, there are the spatial shifts which occur in the practice of special needs education from school to school and classroom to classroom. Resolutions which are advocated at the national level will necessarily be mediated be the contexts, technologies and values of different schools. There is, therefore, a real sense in which special needs education is and must be different wherever it is practised; or, to use Fulcher's (1993) terminology, in which special education policy is formulated through 'contests' in each separate 'site'. For all these reasons, it follows that those engaged in the practice of special needs education would do well to retain both a critical scepticism about resolutions that are currently advocated, an inquiring spirit into that which might be possible, and an awareness of their location in a particular time and place. There is every reason why they should both value the local resolutions which they are able to formulate and realize, and should view the relationship of national to local resolutions in terms of dialogue rather than of unproblematic implementation.

This view is strengthened by what we see as the relationship between values and resolutions. The field of special needs education is necessarily shot through with questions of ethics and values. In whatever way that field has been conceptualized throughout its existence, those conceptualizations inevitably raise questions about what we regard as the aims of education, how we define educational success and failure, and how we choose to respond to difficulties and failures in our education system. Special needs education is thus an essentially ethical activity, and those engaged in it are obliged to address these ethical questions directly. However, our model suggests that there is no single straight line between the formulation of principles and values and their realization in particular practices. No set of values, however compelling, will entirely overcome the fundamental dilemma to which special needs education has been a response, nor will it automatically call into being the technology which will enable its realization, nor will it create a context which is supportive of such a realization. The complex interactions which our model posits suggest that sets of values and principles can never be more than one factor in determining action within this field – and, moreover, a factor which is itself recursively shaped by the other components with which it interacts. There is, therefore, a particular onus on those involved in this field not only to act *in accordance with* explicitly-formulated values and principles, but also to *explore* what those values and principles might mean *in their particular circumstances*.

We regard such a caveat as being particularly important at the current time because so much debate within the field is structured around notions of rights and entitlements. The danger is that strong positions on such rights and entitlements are taken unproblematically to mandate one and only one course of action, and that any deviation from these is construed as resistance, reaction or, at worst, oppression. Our view is rather that practitioners and policy-makers need to engage with and understand the interactions between the four terms of our model, so that their values shape – but do not determine – the resolutions that emerge, and are in turn shaped by the attempted implementation of those resolutions.

THE FUTURE OF SPECIAL NEEDS EDUCATION IN MAINSTREAM SCHOOLS

Everything we have said about the fluidity and complexity of change in special needs development makes us cautious either of predicting the way that practice and provision will change in coming years or of prescribing with any confidence the ways in which we feel they *ought* to change. We confess to some ambivalence about the continual advocacy of new 'approaches' which continues to be characteristic of this field. Such advocacy, we suspect, all too often overlooks the real complexity of this field, substituting exhortation and an attempt to seize the moral high ground for open-minded engagement with the dilemmas and constraints which face practitioners and policy-makers 'on the ground'. On the other hand, the advocacy of alternative approaches founded on unequivocal commitment to particular value positions undoubtedly has the effect of problematizing current practice and opening up a debate about alternative possibilities. What we hope to do in the remainder of this chapter, therefore, is to outline what seem to us to be interesting and important possibilities without falling into the trap of advocating over-simplistic solutions.

Systemic change

Perhaps the most important feature of our model in terms of the future of special needs education is its essentially *systemic* nature – that is, the interaction of different elements within the model to shape and limit each other. The clear implication is that attempts to manage change in special needs education simply by manipulating one or other element in the model are highly unlikely to be successful; either they will produce little noticeable change, or the change they produce will be different from that which is intended. As a result, those who seek to promote change need, on the one hand, to accept an inevitable messiness and incompleteness in that process and, on the other hand, to work to bring about change across all elements of our model. In particular, we believe that we need a debate about special needs education which will be much wider than that which has hitherto taken place. Fundamental debates about educational governance and democracy, about the purposes of education, about the nature of curriculum or about the nature of learning have, in recent years, slipped off the special needs agenda – if ever they were truly present. In their place, we (and we do indeed include much of our own work in this criticism) have tended to have a narrower preoccupation with the nature of school and classroom organization, as though wide-ranging change could be brought about by restructuring schools or redefining roles. What we believe is now urgently needed is to open up these fundamental debates as a first step towards more meaningful change.

Values

We have seen how developments in special needs education have been driven by the 'human values' of equity and participation. From our position as liberal-minded citizens of a Western democracy, we find such values unexceptionable. However, we also find them bland and ill-defined. Two particular problems seem to us unresolved in such a position. The first is the definition of what counts as 'participation'. Is it mere physical presence alongside one's peer group? Is it participation in common learning and/or social activities? Is it some sort of shared learning in the sense of engaging in the same learning experiences or acquiring the same knowledge or skills as one's peer group? We have seen throughout this book how apparent examples of participation can be highly ambiguous: do we want to count presence in a mainstream lesson and participation in activities which are either too difficult or so 'watered down' as to be trivial as genuine participation? If not, what does participation 'really' look like, and how do we know it when we see it?

The second problem is related to this. If participation is a central value in the development of special needs education, is it the *over-riding* value? As Slee (1996) asks in respect of inclusive education:

> The epidemic ravages of ADD/ADHD ... like the discovery of other learning disabilities ... together with the expansion of special needs categories ... would suggest that regular schools are unsatisfactory for an expanding section of their current population. Is the claim for a place for disabled children in dysfunctional regular schools a proper claim to be making? (p. 25)

In other words, is participation in *any* form of mainstream education good enough, or are there other values that come into play at this point and which are concerned with some notion of what constitutes 'quality' education? If so, do we actually know what we understand by the notion of quality education, and what do we do if it turns out *empirically* to be difficult or impossible to reconcile quality with participation? As Zigmond and Baker (1995) and Gerber (1995) point out, special education has always claimed (rightly or wrongly) to provide quality education for certain children, in being more individually-appropriate – and yet this sort of quality at least seems to have an unfortunate habit of evaporating in any attempted 'mergers' with mainstream education.

The notion of quality begs a further set of fundamental questions about what we regard as the *aims* of education. After all, a 'quality' education which aimed at teaching children basic literacy skills might look very different from one which aimed at turning them into economically successful adults or one which aimed at developing their individual personal qualities. In the wake of Warnock's declaration that 'the purpose of education for all children is the same; the goals are the same' (DES, 1978, 1.4), debates around the nature of these goals have surfaced from time to time in the special needs literature (Dyson, 1985; Galletley, 1985; Dumbleton, 1990; White, 1991) – but all too rarely. Our preoccupation with the structure of provision and with the realization of the principle of participation has contributed to the marginalization of such debates – together, in recent years, with the formulation of a National Curriculum prescribing aims which, however confused, have been almost impossible to challenge effectively. In particular, there has been a tendency to overlook the strong tradition within special education of attempting to define a set of aims in distinction to those accepted within mainstream education. Although such attempts have, by their very nature, been premised on segregated models of provision, they nonetheless beg the question as to whether the unproblematical acceptance, in the interests of participation, of the current aims of mainstream education is one that can and should be sustained. Given the endemic confusions in the National Curriculum – as evidenced, for instance, by the injections of vocationalism in recent curriculum reviews (Dearing, 1994/1996), the time may be ripe for the resuscitation of a debate around the aims and purposes of schooling.

We make no pretence to being in a position to resolve these complex issues. This is in part because of the lack of debate from which the special needs community has suffered in recent years. However, it is also because of the relationship in which questions of value stand to the other elements in our proposed model. Because educational values are realized, not in the abstract but in relation to proposed resolutions of real dilemmas, in a given educational and social context, and through a particular set of technologies, the meaning of a value position only becomes clear as that position is worked out in practice. In other words, in our field at least, educational value positions are not absolutes with unequivocal practical implications, but are broad principles which interact with and are defined and redefined by their attempted realization. It seems that it is something of this sort which Booth (1996) is hinting at in respect of inclusive education:

> . . . there is a danger in using 'inclusive education' to describe an ideal state or aim. There is a temptation to think that there is a practice of inclusive education that we can study. This search for 'good practice' is a chimera. There are very few, if any, schools in England which include all the children from a neighbourhood, defined as the catchment area of the school. I prefer to think of integration or inclusion in education as an unending *set of processes*, rather than a state. Inclusion implies change. To say that inclusion is occurring means that the participation of some students in mainstream schools has increased. It comprises two linked processes: it is the process of increasing the participation of students in the cultures and curricula of mainstream schools and communities; it is the process of reducing the exclusion of students from mainstream cultures and curricula. (p. 89; emphases in original)

Such a view of inclusive education seems to us to open up more possibilities than the simple advocacy of absolute positions. Moreover, if the principle of inclusion is set alongside the principle of quality and some notion of what constitutes the purposes of education, and if all three are defined in their interaction with each other and with the process of their realization in practice then we have the possibility for the sort of fundamental debate which we regard as an essential part of any future developments.

Contexts

If there has been a single underlying failure of attempts to change special needs education in recent decades, it has been the assumption that such change could be brought about without reference to the various contexts in which special needs education was nested. The emphasis on restructuring special needs provision in order to 'merge' it with mainstream education has distracted attention from the overwhelming determining effect on special needs education, first of the nature of mainstream schooling, and second of the political context of education, particularly as embodied in its systems of governance. If, therefore, we are to avoid further stalled 'approaches' which simply replicate the practices of special education in ever-closer proximity to the mainstream, then it is essential that we pay attention to these determining contexts.

As we have seen in Chapter 5, the inclusive education movement has re-emphasized something that has been evident throughout the period we have studied, *viz.* that any reform of special education which aims at increasing participation and access has to begin with the reform of *mainstream* education (Vislie, 1995; Dyson and Millward, 1997). Despite the limitations and difficulties of their approaches, this lesson had to a significant extent been learned by the 'innovatory' schools of Chapter 3, which were beginning to find structures and processes which would allow them to engage in the reconstruction of mainstream schooling as a means of increasing participation by all their students. Moreover, there is now a substantial theoretical literature and a growing body of empirical evidence (Ainscow, 1991/1994; Skrtic, 1991; Villa *et al.*, 1992; Rouse and Florian, 1996) which addresses the question of what mainstream schools might look like as they become more capable of responding to student diversity. There is, then, much that we can say about how mainstream schools can become more flexibly organized, more collaborative and more problem-focused as a means of avoiding the witting and unwitting exclusion of some pupils from participation in their cultures and curricula.

Where this literature is limited, however, is in its excessively managerial orientation and its consequent failure to address aspects of schooling which are not in the direct control of school managers. Two of these are, we believe, particularly significant. The first, as we saw in Chapter 5, is the nature of the school curriculum. It is evident that, insofar as the curriculum is content-heavy, organizes skills and knowledge hierarchically, and requires children to progress through this hierarchy sequentially, it is also inherently segregatory in its effect (Dyson, Millward and Skidmore, 1994; Ware, 1995). Since some children will 'master' content more slowly than others and make more limited progress through the hierarchy of knowledge, the attainments of children, and the learning experiences which are necessary for them to 'progress' will begin to diverge. Under such circumstances, whilst participation in common social experiences may continue to be valuable, participation in shared learning experiences comes to seem increasingly inefficient and unsustainable.

Up to a point, the resolution of this dilemma is dependent on the availability of an appropriate technology – that is, on some technique of 'differentiation' which allows pupils whose attainments are widely different to be educated alongside each other. However, such a resolution amounts to a somewhat limited form of participation. Anything more seems to require the development of a curriculum in which all pupils can participate regardless of their level of attainment. Ware (1995) suggests that such a curriculum must be based on constructivist principles, whilst Dyson *et al.* (1994) confirm that it requires a fundamental rethinking of the nature of knowledge and learning. Certainly, we suggest that a debate is urgently needed about the nature of a common curriculum – a debate which has effectively been outlawed in the UK in recent years by the imposition of an apparently unchallengeable National Curriculum. The elements of such a debate are, perhaps, not too far away. We note with interest, for instance, the efforts of colleagues working in the education of children 'with severe learning difficulties' to develop a meaningful curriculum within a common framework (Sebba, Byers and Rose, 1993; Coupe-O'Kane, Porter and Taylor, 1994; Nind and Hewett, 1994; Rose *et al.*, 1994), the emergence of 'thinking skills' as a common element in the curricula of certain schools (Adey and Shayer, 1994), the implications of the TVEI flexible learning initiative for curriculum as well as pedagogy (Nash, 1993), and the considerable amount of work that was done on notions of common curriculum before these were overtaken by the National Curriculum (DES, 1977). Whilst none of these may offer a ready-made answer, it may well be that the curriculum scene is not quite so devoid of possibilities as it initially seems.

The second aspect which urgently needs to be addressed is the wider social and political context of schooling. One unfortunate consequence of the dominance in educational thinking of the effective schools movement, and of the acceptance of its more attractive elements by the professional special needs community in recent years (e.g. Rouse and Florian, 1996) is what we referred to earlier as the excessive managerialism of much of the literature, indicated by the assumption that individual schools, through the actions of their managers, can control their own destinies. This is misleading in at least two respects. First, schools are located within particular socio-economic contexts which have significantly determining effects on how they go about their work, what they can expect to achieve and, indeed, what might count as 'effective' in their situations (Proudford and Baker, 1995; Reynolds, 1995). Reliance on the actions of school managers within individual schools alone seems particularly misplaced where schools are located in areas of significant social deprivation. Regardless of how 'effective' the school may become, it seems unlikely that it will overcome the endemic social problems which its pupils face both during their school careers and afterwards. As Reynolds (1995) points out, these issues are particularly significant in the field of special educational needs, given the known link between 'incidence' of 'special needs' and poverty. At the very least, some concerted action between education and other social and (crucially) *economic* agencies aimed at addressing these underlying problems seems to be called for. Unfortunately, the evidence suggests that the means of bringing such action about are not immediately to hand (Atkins, Dyson and Easen, 1995), and, certainly, any debate around these issues seems to be conspicuous by its absence from the special needs literature.

The assumption that schools control their destinies has been further exposed in recent years by the changes in governance which we examined in Chapters 7 and 8. The erosion of LEA control and the creation of a quasi-market in education have had major (and largely negative) implications for special needs education. In particular, the management – albeit sometimes ineffective in practice – of the education system in the interests of some notion, albeit somewhat vaguely defined, of equity and participation has been replaced by the dominance of those 'consumers' who are most articulate, aware and active in their manipulation of the system. There is, therefore, it seems to us, a need to rethink the nature of educational governance to overcome these problems.

This need is made particularly acute because the marketization of education has been accompanied within the special needs field by the emergence of powerful 'voices' from outside the traditional community of special needs professionals demanding to have their say in the future of policy and provision. We have seen throughout this book how the values and principles of the professional special needs community have dominated developments in this field over recent decades. That domination may well have presented itself as benign, but it has by no means always been perceived as such from the outside. Parents (in the case of the 'dyslexia lobby'), activists in the disability movement (in the case of inclusive education) and politicians (in the case of the *Code of Practice*) have, in recent years, all sought to influence the development of special needs education in directions which are far from identical with those which the professional community has pursued. The question therefore arises as to which of these competing 'voices' is to have the final say over the direction of special needs education, and what sort of engagement is possible between their very different positions.

One answer to this question is to settle the matter through the exercise of power: politicians gain such legitimacy as they have through an electoral system which gives them considerable power over special needs education; other groups can engage in 'contests' in particular 'sites' to enable their voices to be heard above those of others (Fulcher, 1993). The problem with such a conflictual model, of course, is that the distribution of power does not necessarily coincide with any notions of legitimacy or equity other, perhaps, than those of the powerful. We have seen, for instance, how a determined group such as the 'dyslexia lobby' can effectively reshape special needs education in certain sites at the expense of other groups which might widely be regarded as equally, if not more, 'needy'.

Slee (1996) hints at an alternative by advocating a 'dialogue' (p. 19) between different voices. Unfortunately, a good deal of work is necessary if we are to develop this hint, since we seem in the UK at least to be singularly lacking in means of facilitating such a dialogue and bringing it to a productive conclusion. The erosion of the LEA, which has traditionally played the role of the representative of the community as a whole, and the establishment of a quasi-market allowing the voice of the aware and articulate parent-consumer to be heard above all others have considerably weakened such capacity for dialogue as we may have had. We believe, therefore, that there is an urgent need for the revitalization of democratic structures in the governance of education. Such structures will serve the dual purposes of facilitating the involvement of as many stakeholders as possible in policy-making and of protecting the interests of those who are unable or unwilling to be so involved. We share the concerns of some (Thomas, 1992) that the management of special needs education by 'old-style' (i.e. pre-1988) LEAs often achieved neither of these purposes, but instead operated as a self-interested and self-perpetuating bureaucracy. Nonetheless, we agree with Housden (1993) that it is only the LEA which seems likely to offer a 'moral authority' which will, on the one hand, offset the inevitably narrow interests of individual schools and, on the other, balance the competing claims of different stakeholders. We have seen in Chapter 8, for instance, how some LEAs are beginning to redefine their role in terms of partnership with their schools and (albeit to a lesser extent) with their communities. We have, moreover, in the case of

Newham (Corbett, 1994) an example of an LEA paying careful attention to the radical agenda of inclusion, and in the case of many other authorities, examples of LEAs working in close partnership with a potentially hostile dyslexia lobby and other special interest groups. In other words, as Brighouse (1996) makes clear, it is by no means inevitable that revitalized LEAs will revert to centralizing and self-aggrandizing type.

Moreover, recent years have seen the emergence of structural changes which promise to make LEAs more permeable to a range of influences. For all the damaging effects of the marketization of education, for instance, it has brought with it a significant change in the balance of power between schools and LEAs and a devolution to school level of responsibilities that were formerly held by the LEA. It has also brought with it an increased sensitivity on the part of schools to their communities – or at least to the potential 'consumers' within those communities. Although there is a danger in such changes of schools exercising an even stronger and narrower self-interest than old-style LEAs, there is also the potential for permeating central policy-making with the experience of lower levels of the system where the contact with children, parents and communities is more immediate. The 'partnership' models of governance that are emerging in some LEAs (McConnell and Stephens, 1993) may thus be developed to produce a more responsive and, in Slee's terms, dialogical education service. In the same way, the emergence of 'clusters' of schools collaborating to develop special needs provision offers the potential both of giving schools a wider 'whole community' responsibility and of devolving aspects of decision-making from an inevitably remote LEA centre (Gains, 1994; Lunt *et al.*, 1994).

None of these developments offers a complete and unproblematic answer to the question of educational governance, but they do suggest a possible way forward. That way forward combines the devolution of some elements of power downwards through the system whilst involving lower levels of the system (notably schools) in sharing previously centralized responsibilities. In this way, power and responsibility permeate the entire local system rather than remaining centralized in county or city hall. It may thus be possible to create a system of governance which is responsive to those 'voices' which are able to make themselves heard, protective of those who do not make themselves heard, and capable of arbitrating in some principled and transparent manner between the claims that are made by each of these competing voices.

Technologies

There is a sense in which the technologies of special needs education – notably pedagogy and school organization – are the elements of our model which have been most fully developed over recent years. Certainly, considerable energy has been expended on exploring and extending techniques of support teaching and differentiation, or the roles of the special needs co-ordinator, or the systems and structures through which special needs education is managed and delivered in the school. However, we detect a limitation in some of this endeavour which, we suggest, will need to be addressed in coming years: although many technological developments have taken place, these developments have tended, like Sayer's (1994/1987) 'garden shed extensions', to be additions to the existing structures of mainstream education rather than radical reconstructions of the ways in which teaching and learning happen in schools. In particular, the principal structure of mainstream schooling, the classroom of thirty or so children, led and instructed by a single teacher, tends to have been taken for granted and the greatest efforts have been placed into trying to find ways – support teaching, group work, differentiation and so on – to inject an element of flexibility into this structure.

Whilst we recognize the contribution which such efforts have made towards enabling mainstream schools to respond to the diversity of their pupil populations, we wonder whether they will need to be redirected if any further progress is to be made in this direction. We say this for two reasons. First, there may be some natural limits to the capacity of the classroom and class teacher structure to respond to diversity. As McIntyre (1993) suggests, it is a structure which is essentially based on the values and assumptions of the newly-industrialized Victorian society, and which carries with it certain tendencies for the complexity of teaching and the diversity of students to be simplified. Second, there may also be some natural limits to the willingness and capability of teachers working within this structure to orient themselves towards the diversity of their pupils. The ecology of the classroom is such that teachers are inevitably placed in a position of having to be at least as much concerned with classroom management – in the sense of organizing and controlling pupil activity – as with any notions of learning or responding to individual difference (Brown and McIntyre, 1992).

It is not surprising, moreover, if many mainstream teachers tend to be sceptical about 'inclusion' initiatives which require them to respond to an even greater range of diversity (Vlachou and Barton, 1994). Such initiatives commonly carry with them the expectation that, in order to respond to this increased range of diversity, classroom teachers will abandon the methods which have served them well in establishing control over their pupils' activities, and embrace other techniques which require them to surrender greater or lesser elements of that control. There are, of course, some particularly talented, highly-motivated and well-supported teachers who are able and willing to rise to this challenge. However, it seems probable that, until it is possible to develop a technology which enables the majority of 'good enough' mainstream teachers to respond to the diversity of their pupils, the progress of any initiatives aimed at increasing the participation of the full range of children in mainstream schools and classrooms will be extremely limited.

The implication would seem to be that we need to look at technologies which do not depend (entirely, at least) upon the traditional classroom structure for their capacity to respond to pupil diversity. Some recent literature, for instance, has begun to explore the possibility of developing such responses through a radical restructuring of schools (Ainscow, 1991/1994; Skrtic, 1991; Villa and Thousand, 1995; Villa *et al.*, 1992). Much of this has tended to focus on the restructuring of working relationships amongst staff rather than of the organization of teaching and learning as such, on the assumption that if teachers work together in 'problem-solving teams', the necessary technologies of teaching will inevitably emerge. It may be, however, that there are elements of the necessary technology more immediately to hand. Initiatives such as Flexible Learning (Nash, 1993), the development of resource and drop-in centres (Clark *et al.*, 1995) or the approaches to specific learning difficulties provision reported in Chapter 6 leave the mainstream classroom intact as the location of most teaching and learning. However, they surround the classroom with a range of alternative forms of provision to which children have flexible access. There is a sense in which such provision is not 'inclusive', since all children do not participate in it all of the time. However, neither is it 'exclusive' or segregatory in any usual meaning of these terms in that a wide range of children *may* have access to it, and it does not necessarily interfere with their participation in the mainstream curriculum to any marked degree – indeed, it may be an integral part of the 'delivery' of that curriculum.

Insofar as such forms of provision constitute genuine responses to diversity rather than the reinvention of segregation, they depend on a distinction between presence in a mainstream classroom, and inclusion in a mainstream curriculum under the same general conditions as all other children. This distinction may, of course, prove in practice to be a deceptive one, but it may also prove to be an important one for the further development of initiatives aimed at facilitating participation and access. Moreover, given what we have said about the interdependence of the various elements in our model, the capacity of the developments we are advocating to promote participation will depend both on how we come to define the mainstream curriculum in years to come and, crucially, on how we come to understand the 'human values' which this provision seeks to realize.

TOWARDS A RESOLUTION?

What we have proposed in this chapter makes no pretence to be a fully-fledged resolution of the dilemmas of special needs education. Rather than advocating in detail yet another 'approach', we have tried to open up a range of possibilities and issues which have been relatively under-explored in recent years. This is, we believe, consistent with our view that special needs education has, historically, been generated by the continuing attempts to resolve dilemmas that are fundamentally irresolvable.

Underlying our position is a commitment to the 'human values' which have underpinned special needs education throughout the period we have studied. Principles of equity, participation and inclusion seem to us, from our position as professional educators in a late twentieth-century Western democracy, to be entirely worth pursuing. However, in contradistinction, we suspect, to many others in this field, we see such values as neither unproblematic in themselves nor as leading, in any unequivocal way, to particular forms of provision. A major task of coming years, is to explore the meaning of such principles in the light both of their attempted realization and of their interrelationship with other values to which we might wish to adhere. We also believe that we are now in a position to understand some of the limitations in previous attempts to realize these principles. In its continual attempts to reconstruct itself, special needs education has focused too narrowly on its own structures and concerns. We now urgently need to broaden those concerns so that they include the nature of mainstream schooling, of the mainstream curriculum, of the governance of education, and of the education service as a whole as part of overall social policy.

In recent years, there has been much concern with the question of whether it is possible to construct an approach to diversity which will take us 'beyond special needs' – a concern to which we admit to having contributed ourselves (Dyson, 1990a and b; Dyson and Gains, 1993). As we have reviewed in the course of this book attempts to explore this question over the last two decades, we are forced to the inevitable conclusion that it is the wrong question to ask. Of course, it matters greatly whether our schools are capable of responding to diversity so that all children learn effectively. It also matters whether that response is made at the expense of the participation of all members of our society in the central social institution of the 'community' school offering a common set of experiences in shared classrooms. The question, therefore, of whether a whole school approach or an 'innovatory' approach, or 'inclusive education' or some other approach will achieve the optimum realization of these two imperatives is an important one.

However, in the final analysis the answer to that question depends crucially on the answers to far more fundamental questions – questions to do with what we believe education to be about, what we believe children should learn, what kind of society we wish to create and, ultimately, who the 'we' is who should debate and decide these things. These questions are complex and contentious – but they are the ones that all those involved in what we currently call 'special needs education' must now ask.

NOTES

1 Wang and Reynolds (1996) offer a similar analysis of the recent history of special education in the USA, arguing that the economic expansion which sustained the growth of special education programmes is at an end, and that the current period of recession could easily reverse previous trends.
2 Readers might wish to compare this model and, in particular, the posited relationship between 'technology' and values with Pacey's (1983) model of technology practice.

Bibliography

Adey, P. and Shayer, M. (1994) *Really Raising Standards: Cognitive Intervention and Academic Achievement*. London: Routledge.

Ainscow, M., Booth, T. and Dyson, A. *Tales of Innocence and Experience from Richard Lovel High School*, Inclusion and Exclusion an International Comparison, Cambridge, UK.

Ainscow, M. and Tweddle, D. A. (1979) *Preventing Classroom Failure: An Objectives Approach*. Chichester, Wiley.

Ainscow, M. (Ed.) (1991) *Effective Schools for All*. London, David Fulton.

Ainscow, M. (1994) *Special Needs in the Classroom: A Teacher Education Guide*. London, Jessica Kingsley Publishers/UNESCO Publishing.

Ainscow, M. and Sebba, J. (Eds) (1996) 'Developments in Inclusive Education', *Cambridge Journal of Education* Vol. 26 No. 1.

Allan, J., Brown, S. and Munn, P. (1991) *Off the Record: Mainstream Provision for Pupils with Non-Recorded Learning Difficulties in Primary and Secondary Schools*. Edinburgh, Scottish Council for Research in Education.

Andrews, G. (1989) 'The management of support services: conflicts and tensions in the role of the support teacher', in T. Bowers (Ed.), *Managing Special Needs*. Milton Keynes, Open University Press.

Armstrong, D. (1995) *Power and Partnership in Education: Parents, Children and Special Educational Needs*. London, Routledge.

Atkins, M., Dyson, A. and Easen, P. (1995) 'Conceptualisations of professional practice and interprofessional collaboration', in *European Conference on Educational Research*, University of Bath, UK, September 1995.

Audit Commission and HMI (1992a) *Getting the Act Together: Provision for Pupils with Special Educational Needs: A Management Handbook for Schools and Local Education Authorities*. London, HMSO.

Audit Commission and HMI (1992b) *Getting in on the Act: Provision for Pupils with Special Educational Needs: the National Picture*. London, HMSO.

Audit Commission (1994) *The Act Moves On Progress in SEN*. HMSO. November (1994).

Augur, J. and Briggs, S. (Ed.) (1992) *The Hickey Multisensory Language Course*. London, Whurr.

Baker, J. M. and Zigmond, N. (1995) 'The meaning and practice of inclusion for students with learning disabilities: Themes and implications from the five cases', *Journal of Special Education*, 29(2), 163–80.

Ball, S. J. (1993) 'The market as a class strategy in the UK and US', *British Journal of Sociology of Education* 14(1), 3–19.

Ballard, K. (1994) *Disability, Family, Whanau and Society*. Palmerston North, New Zealand Dunmore Press.

Ballard, K. (1995) 'Inclusion, Paradigms, Power and Participation' in Clark, C., Dyson, D. and Millward, A. (Eds) *Towards Inclusive Schools?* London, Fulton.

Ballard, K. (1996) 'Inclusive Education in New Zealand', *Cambridge Journal of Education* Vol. 26 No. 1, 33–45.

Bangs, J. (1993) 'Support Services – Stability or Erosion?' *British Journal of Special Education* Vol. 20 No. 3, 105–107.

Barton, L. (1994) 'Disability, Difference and the Politics of Definition', *Australian Disability Review* No. 3, 8–22.

Barton, L. (1995) 'The politics of education for all', *Support for Learning*, 10(4), 156–60.

Barton, L. and Landman, M. (1993) 'The Politics of Integration: Observations on the Warnock Report', in Slee, R. (Ed.), *Is There a Desk With My Name On It? Politics of Integration*. London: Falmer.

Barton, L. and Oliver, M. (1992) 'Special Needs: Personal Trouble or Public Issues' in Arnot, M. and Barton, L. (Eds) *Voicing Concerns: Sociological Perspectives on Contemporary Educational Reforms*. Wallingford, Triangle.

Bennett, N., Desferges, C., Cockburn, C. and Wilkinson, B. (1984) *The Quality of Pupil Learning Experiences*. London, Lawrence Erlbaum.

Berlak, A. and Berlak, H. (1981) *Dilemmas of Schooling: Teaching and Social Change*. London, Methuen.

Best, R. (1991) 'Support Teaching in a Comprehensive School', *Support for Learning* Vol. 6 No. 1, 27–31.

Best, R. (1994) 'Teachers' Supportive Roles in a Secondary School: A Case Study and Discussion', *Support for Learning* Vol. 9 No. 4, 171–78.

Bines, H. (1986) *Redefining Remedial Education*. Beckenham: Croom Helm.

Bines, H. (1995) 'Special educational needs in the market place', *Journal of Education Policy*, 10(2), 157–72.

Bines, H. and Loxley, A. (1995) 'Implementing the Code of Practice for Special Educational Needs', *Oxford Review of Education*, 21(4), 381–94.

Booth, T. (1983) 'Integration and participation in comprehensive schools', *Forum*, 25(2), 40–2.

Booth, T. (1995) 'Mapping Inclusion and Exclusion: Concepts for All' in Clark, C., Dyson, D. and Millward, A. (Eds), *Towards Inclusive Schools?* London: Fulton.

Booth, T. (1996) 'A perspective on inclusion from England', *Cambridge Journal of Education* 26(1), 87–99.

Bowe, R. and Ball, S. J., with Gold, A. (1992) *Reforming Education and Changing Schools*. London, Routledge.

Bowers, T. (1995) 'Touched by the invisible hand?', *Support for Learning*, 10(3), 113–18.

Brennan, W. K. (1974) *Shaping the Education of Slow Learners.* London, Routledge and Kegan Paul.

Brennan, W. K. (1979) *The Curricular Needs of Slow Learners: Report of the Schools Council Curricular Needs of Slow-learning Pupils Project (Schools Council Working Paper 63).* London, Evans/Methuen Educational.

Brighouse, T. (1996) *A Question of Standards: The Need for a Local Democratic Voice.* London, Politeia.

British Dyslexia Association (BDA) (1995a) *Dyslexia? Your First Questions Answered.* Reading, BDA.

British Dyslexia Association (BDA) (1995b). SEN Tribunal Notes. *Friends*, July 1995, 7.

Brown, M. (1996) 'Supporting learning through a whole school approach', in G. Reid (Ed.), *Dimensions of Dyslexia: Assessment, Teaching and the Curriculum.* Edinburgh, Moray House Publications.

Brown, S. and McIntyre, D. (1992) *Making Sense of Teaching.* Buckingham, Open University Press.

Brown, S., Riddell, S. and Duffield, J. (1991) 'Parental power and SEN: the case of specific learning difficulties', *British Education Research Journal*, 20, 327–44.

Brown, S .and Riddell, S. (1994) *Special Educational Needs in the 1990s: Warnock in the Market Place.* Routledge.

Burroughs, S. (1989) 'Dilemmas in the role of the support teacher', in R. Winter (Ed.), *Learning from Experience: Principles and Practice in Action Research.* London, Falmer.

Carroll, H. M. C. (1972) 'The remedial teaching of reading: an evaluation', *Remedial Education*, 7(1), 10–15.

Clark, C., Dyson, A. and Millward, A. (1995) 'Towards inclusive schools: Mapping the field', in C. Clark, A. Dyson, and A. Millward (Eds), *Towards Inclusive Schools?* London, David Fulton.

Clark, C., Dyson, A., Millward, A. and Skidmore, D. (1995) 'Dialectical analysis, special needs and schools as organizations', in C. Clark, A. Dyson, and A. Millward (Eds), *Towards Inclusive Schooling?* London, David Fulton.

Clark, C., Dyson, A., Millward, A. and Skidmore, D. (1995) *Innovatory Practice in Mainstream Schools for Special Educational Needs.* London, HMSO.

Clark, C., Dyson, A., Millward, A. and Skidmore, D. (1995c). 'Theorising Special Education', in *International Special Education Congress*, Birmingham, UK.

Clayton, T. (1992) 'Support for special needs', *Support for Learning* 7(4), 152–5.

Coles, G. (1987) *The Learning Mystique: A Critical look at 'Learning Disabilities'.* New York, Pantheon.

Collins, J. E. (1972) 'The Remedial Education hoax', *Remedial education*, 7(3), 9–10.

Collet, R. (1988) in Sykes, S. *TES* 10/6/88 No.3254.

Cooper, P. and Ideus, K. (1995) 'Is attention deficit disorder a Trojan Horse?', *Support for Learning* 10(1), 29–34.

Copeland, I. (1991) 'Special Education Needs and the Education Reform Act 1988'. *British Journal of Educational Studies* Vol. 39 No. 2, 190–206.

Copeland, I. (1993) 'Is There a Sociology of Special Education and Integration?' *European Journal of Special Needs Education* Vol. 8 No. 1, 1–13.

Corbett, J. (1994) 'Challenges in a competitive culture: A policy for inclusive education in Newham', in S. Riddell and S. Brown (Eds), *Special Educational Needs Policy in the 1990s: Warnock in the Market Place*. London, Routledge.

Corbett, J. (1996) *Bad Mouthing: the Language of Special Needs*. London: Falmer.

Coupe-O'Kane, J., Porter, J. and Taylor, A. (1994) 'Meaningful content and contexts for learning', in J. Coupe-O'Kane and B. Smith (Eds), *Taking Control: Enabling People with Learning Difficulties*. London, David Fulton.

Crisfield, J. and Smythe, I. (Ed.) (1993) *The Dyslexia Handbook 1993/4*. Reading, British Dyslexia Association.

Croll, P. and Moses, D. (1985) *One in Five – The Assessment and Incidence of Special Educational Needs*. London, Routledge & Kegan Paul.

Davie, R. (1994) 'A consortium for children', *Therapeutic Care and Education*, 3(3), 206–17.

Dearing, R. (1994) *The National Curriculum and its Assessment: Final Report*, London School Curriculum and Assessment Authority.

Dearing, R. (1996) *Review of Qualifications for 16–19 year olds: Summary Report*, March 1996. London, School Curriculum and Assessment Authority.

Dennison, P. E. and Hargrove, G. (1985) *Personalized Whole Brain Integration*. California, Educational Kinesthetics.

DES (1967) *Units for Partially Hearing Children*, Education Survey No. 1. London, HMSO.

DES (1968) *Blind and Partially Sighted Children*, Education Survey No. 4. London, HMSO.

Department of Education and Science (DES) (1972) *Children with Specific Learning Difficulties (The Tizard Report)*. London, HMSO.

Department of Education and Science (DES) (1975) *A Language for Life (The Bullock Report*. London, HMSO.

Department of Education and Science (DES) (1977) *Curriculum 11–16*. London, HMSO.

Department of Education and Science (DES) (1978) *Special Educational Needs: Report of the Committee of Enquiry into the Education of Handicapped Children and Young People* The Warnock Report. London, HMSO.

Department of Education and Science (DES) and the Welsh Office (1987) *The National Curriculum 5–16: A consultation document*. London, DES.

Department of Education and Science (DES) (1989a) *A Survey of Pupils with Special Educational Needs in Ordinary Schools: A Report by H.M. Inspectorate*. London, DES.

Department of Education and Science (DES) (1989b) *A Report by HM Inspectors on Special Education within the Technical and Vocational Education Initiative*. London, DES.

Department of Education and Science (DES)(1989c) *Discipline in Schools:*

Report of the Committee of Enquiry Chaired by Lord Elton. London, HMSO.

Department For Education (DFE) (1993) *Draft Code of Practice on the Identification and Assessment of Special Educational Needs.* London, Department for Education.

Department for Education (DFE) (1994a) *Code of Practice on the Identification and Assessment of Special Educational Needs.* London, DFE.

Department for Education (DFE) (1994b) *Pupils with Problems.* London, DFE.

Dessent, T. (1987) *Making the Ordinary School Special.* London, Falmer.

Diamond, C. (1993) A reconsideration of the role of SEN support services: Will they get in on the Act?, *Support for Learning,* 8(3), 91–8.

Dumbleton, P. (1990) 'A philosophy of education for all?', *British Journal of Special Education* 17(1), 16–18.

Dyer, C. (1988) 'Which support? An examination of the term', *Support for Learning,* 3(1), 6–11.

Dyer, C. (1995) 'The Code of Practice through LEA eyes', *British Journal of Special Education,* 22(2), 48–51.

Dyson, A. (1985) 'A curriculum for the "Educated Man"?', *British Journal of Special Education,* 12(4), 138–9.

Dyson, A. (1990a) 'Effective learning consultancy: a future role for special needs co-ordinators?', *Support for Learning,* 5(3), 116–27.

Dyson, A. (1990b) 'Special educational needs and the concept of change', *Oxford Review of Education,* 16(1), 55–66.

Dyson, A. (1992) 'Innovatory mainstream practice: what's happening in schools' provision for special needs?', *Support for Learning,* 7(2), 51–7.

Dyson, A. (1993) 'Do we need special needs co-ordinators?', in J. Visser and G. Upton (Eds), *Special Education in Britain After Warnock.* London, David Fulton.

Dyson, A. (1995). *Provision for Pupils with Specific Learning Difficulties in Cleveland Secondary Schools: A Cost Benefit Analysis.* Special Needs Research Group, University of Newcastle upon Tyne for Cleveland LEA.

Dyson, A. (1995) 'Thriving on chaos? Co-ordinators, conflict and uncertainty', in P. Stobbs, T. Mackey, B. Norwich, and N. Peacey (Eds), *Schools' SEN Policies Pack.* London, National Children's Bureau.

Dyson, A. (1996) *Managing SEN Policy in Cleveland Primary and Secondary Schools: Individual Education Plans.* Middlesbrough, Cleveland LEA.

Dyson, A. and Gains, C. (1993) 'Special needs and effective learning: towards a collaborative model for the year 2000', in A. Dyson and C. Gains (Eds), *Rethinking Special Needs in Mainstream Schools: Towards the Year 2000.* London, David Fulton.

Dyson, A. and Gains, C. (1995) 'The role of the special needs co-ordinator: Poisoned chalice or crock of gold?', *Support for Learning,* 10(2), 50–6.

Dyson, A., Lin, M. and Millward, A. (*in press*) *Individual Education Plans.* Special Needs Research Centre, University of Newcastle upon Tyne for Cumbria, Durham, Gateshead and Sunderland LEAs.

Dyson, A. and Millward, A. (1997) 'The reform of special education or the transformation of mainstream schools?', in S. J. Pijl and C. Meijer (Eds), *Inclusive Education. A Global Agenda*. London, Routledge.

Dyson, A., Millward, A. and Skidmore, D. (1994) 'Beyond the whole school approach: an emerging model of special needs practice and provision in mainstream secondary schools', *British Educational Research Journal*, 20(3), 301–17.

Dyson, A. and Skidmore, D. (1994). *Provision for Pupils with Specific Learning Difficulties in Secondary Schools: A Report to SOED*. Special Needs Research Group, Department of Education, University of Newcastle upon Tyne.

Dyson, A. and Skidmore, D. (1995) 'Provision for pupils with Specific Learning Difficulties: an emerging model in Scottish Secondary Schools', *Scottish Educational Review*. 20 (2) 123–37.

Dyson, A. and Skidmore, D. (1996) 'Contradictory models: the dilemma of specific learning difficulties', in G. Reid (Ed.), *Dimensions of Dyslexia*. Edinburgh, Moray House Publications.

Dyson, A. and Wood, B. (1994). *A Survey of Provision for Pupils with Specific Learning Difficulties in Middle and High Schools Maintained by [One] LEA*. Department of Education, University of Newcastle upon Tyne.

Employment Department (1991) *Flexible Learning: A framework for Education and Training in the Skills Decade*. Sheffield, Employment Department.

Eraut, M., Nash, C., Fielding, M. and Attard, P. (1991) *Flexible Learning in Schools*. Sheffield, Employment Department.

Evans, R., Docking, J., Bentley, D. and Evans, C. (1995). *Special Educational Needs: Review of Policy and Practice in Five Authorities*. Roehampton Institute London Research Centre.

Ferguson, N. and Adams, M. (1982) 'Assessing the advantages of team teaching in remedial education: The remedial teacher's role', *Remedial Education* 17(1), 24–30.

Fish, J. (1989) *What is Special Education?* Milton Keynes, Open University Press.

Fletcher-Campbell, F., with Hall, C. (1993) *LEA Support for Special Needs*. London, NFER-Nelson.

Ford, J. Mongon, D. and Whelan, M. (1982) *Special Education and Social Control*. Routledge and Kegan Paul.

Freeman, J. (1996) *Highly Able Girls and Boys*. London, NACE/DFEE.

Fulcher, G. (1989) *Disabling Policies? A Comparative Approach to Education Policy and Disability*. Lewes, Falmer Press.

Fulcher, G. (1993) 'Schools and contests: a reframing of the effective schools debate?', in R. Slee (Ed), *Is there a Desk With My Name On It? The Politics of Integration*. London, Falmer Press.

Fullan, M.G. (1991) *The Meaning of Educational Change* London. Cassell

Gains, C. W. and McNicholas, J. A. (Ed.) (1979) *Remedial Education: Guidelines for the Future*. London, Longman.

Gains, C. W. and McNicholas, J. A. (1979) 'Summary: Guidelines for the future', in C. W. Gains and J. A. McNicholas (Eds), *Remedial Education: Guidelines for the Future*. London, Longman.

Gains, C. W. (1980) 'Remedial education in the 1980s', *Remedial Education*, 15(1), 5–9.

Gains, C. (1994) 'Editorial: new roles for SENCOs', *Support for Learning*, 9(3), 102.

Gains, C. (Ed.) (1994) 'Collaborating to Meet Special Educational Needs', v. 9, no. 2

Galletley, I. (1976) 'How to do away with yourself', *Remedial Education*, 11(3), 149–52.

Galletley, I. (1985) 'Vocationalism must come first', *British Journal of Special Education* 12(4), 140–1.

Galloway, D. and Goodwin, C. (1987) *The Education of Disturbing Children: Pupils with Learning and Adjustment Difficulties*. London, Longman.

Garner, M., Petrie, I. and Pointon, D. (1990) *LEA Support Services for Meeting Special Educational Needs: SENNAC survey*. Stafford, Flash Ley Resource Centre.

Garner, P. and Sandow, S. (1995) 'Towards the Inclusive School' in Garner, P. and Sandow, S. (Eds), *Advocacy, Self Advocacy and Special Needs*. London, Falmer.

Gerber, M. M. (1995) 'Inclusion at the high-water mark? Some thoughts on Zigmond and Baker's case studies of inclusive educational programs', *Journal of Special Education* 29(2), 181–91.

Golby, M. and Gulliver, R. J. (1979) 'Whose remedies, whose ills? A critical review of remedial education', *Remedial Education* 11(2), 137–47.

Goodman, J. F. and Bond, L. (1993) 'The individualized education program: A retrospective critique', *Journal of Special Education*, 26(4), 408–22.

Gray, and Dessent, T. (1993) 'Getting our Act Together', *British Journal of Special Education*, Vol. 20 No. 1, 9–12.

Green, A. and Steedman, H. (1993) *Educational Provision, Educational Attainment and the Needs of Industry: A Review of Research*. London, National Institute of Economic and Social Research.

Gross, J. (1996) 'The weight of the evidence: Parental advocacy and resource allocation to children with statements of special educational need', *Support for Learning*, 11(1). 3–12.

Gulliford, R. (1979) 'Remedial work across the curriculum', in C. Gains and J. A. McNicholas (Eds), *Remedial Education: Guidelines for the Future*. London, Longman for the National Association for Remedial Education.

Gulliford, R. (1971) *Special Educational Needs*. London, Routledge & Kegan Paul.

Hanko, G. (1995) *Special Needs in Ordinary Classrooms: from staff support to staff development* (3rd ed.). London, David Fulton.

Hart, S. (1986)'In class support teaching: tackling Fish', *British Journal of Special Education* Vol. 13 No. 2, 51–8.

Hart, S. (1986) 'Evaluating support teaching', *Gnosis* September 1986, 26–31.

Hart, S. (1992) 'Differentiation – way forward or retreat?', *British Journal of Special Education* 19(1), 10–12.

Her Majesty's Inspectorate (HMI) (1990) *Education Observed 12: The Lower-Attaining Pupils' Programme 1982–88.* London, HMSO.

Her Majesty's Inspectorate (HMI) (1990) *Special Needs Issues: A Survey by HMI.* London, HMSO.

Her Majesty's Inspectorate (HMI) *Special Needs and the National Curriculum, 1990–91: A Report by HM Inspectorate.* London, HMSO.

Her Majesty's Inspectorate (HMI) (1990) *Standards in Education, 1988–89: The Annual Report of HM Senior Chief Inspector of Schools.* London, DES.

Her Majesty's Inspectorate (HMI) (1991) *Standards in Education, 1989–90: The Annual Report of HM Senior Chief Inspector of Schools.* London, Her Majesty's Inspectorate and the Department of Education and Science.

Her Majesty's Inspectorate (HMI) (1992) *Special Needs and the National Curriculum, 1990–91: A Report by HM Inspectorate.* London, HMSO.

HM Inspectors of Schools: Audit Unit (1993) *Standards and Quality in Scottish Schools 1991–92: A Report by HM Inspectors of Schools.* Edinburgh, Scottish Office Education Department.

Hinson, M. (1985) 'Teachers' involvement in curriculum change', in C. Smith (Ed), *New Directions in Remedial Education.* Lewes, Falmer.

Hornsby, B. and Shear, F. (1975) *Alpha to Omega: the A–Z of Teaching Reading.* London, Heinemann.

Housden, P. (1993) *Bucking the Market, LEAs and Special Needs.* Stafford, NASEN.

Housden, P. (1994) 'The Management of Education and Training', *Education Review* Vol. 8 (1), 35–9.

Imich, A. J. (1994) 'Exclusions from school: current trends and issues', *Educational Research Journal* Vol. 36 No. 1 Spring 1994, 3–11.

Irlen, H. (1991) *Overcoming Dyslexia and Other Reading Disabilities through the Irlen method.* New York, Avery.

Kramer, J. (1993) Gwent Reviews its Needs. *British Journal of Special Education,* Vol. 20 No. 4, 136–40.

Lewis, A., Neill, S. R. S. J. and Campbell, R. J. (1996). *The Implementation of the Code of Practice in Primary and Secondary Schools: A National Survey of Perceptions of Special Educational Needs Co-ordinators.* University of Warwick for the National Union of Teachers.

Lewis, G. (1984) 'A supportive role at secondary level', *Remedial Education,* 19(1), 7–11.

Lovell, K., Johnson, E. and Platts, D. (1962) 'A summary of a study of the reading ages of children who had been given remedial teaching', *British Journal of Educational Psychology,* 32, 66–71.

Lovey, J. (1996) 'Concepts in identifying effective classroom support', *Support for Learning,* 11(1), 9–12.

Lunt, I. and Denman, B. (1995) 'More or less appealing Act?', *Educational Psychology in Practice* Vol. 10 , 238–47.

Lunt, I. and Evans, J. (1994) 'Dilemmas in special educational needs: some effects of local management of schools', in S. Riddell and S. Brown (Eds), *Special Educational Needs Policy in the 1990s: Warnock in the Market Place.* London, Routledge.

Lunt, I., Evans, J., Norwich, B. and Wedell, K. (1994) *Working Together: Inter-School Collaboration for Special Needs*. London, David Fulton.

Lunzer, E. and Gardiner, K. (Eds) (1979) *The Effective Use of Reading*. London, Heinemann.

Luscombe, J. (1993) 'Rethinking the role of the special needs co-ordinator: Devolving the remedial department', in A. Dyson and C. Gains (Eds), *Rethinking Special Needs in Mainstream Schools: Towards the Year 2000*. London, David Fulton.

McLaughlin, M. (1995) 'Defining Special Education: A Response to Zigmond and Baker'. *Journal of Special Education* Vol. 29 No. 2, 200–207.

Maclure, S. (1989) *Education Reformed* (2nd Edition). London, Hodder and Stoughton.

McConnell, E. and Stephens, J. (1993) 'Oxfordshire schools in partnership', in S. Ransom and J. Tomlinson (Eds), *Autonomy and Interdependence in the New Governance of Schools*. London, Longman.

McIntyre, D. (1993) 'Special needs and standard provision', in A. Dyson and C. Gains (Eds), *Rethinking Special Needs in Mainstream Schools: Towards the Year 2000*. London, David Fulton.

Madden, M. (1989) *New networks for old. TES* 1/9/89.

Millward, A. and Skidmore, D. (1995) *The Role of Local Education Authorities in the Management of Special Needs*. York, Joseph Rowntree.

Mintzberg, H. (1979) *The Structuring of Organisations*. Englewood Cliffs, NJ, Prentice Hall.

Mintzberg, H. (1983) *Structure in Fives: Designing Effective Organisations*. Englewood Cliffs, NJ, Prentice Hall.

Mittler, P. (1993) 'Special needs at the crossroads', in Visser, J. and Upton, G. (Eds) *Special Education in Britain after Warnock*. London, David Fulton.

Mittler, P. (1995) 'Special Needs Education: An International Perspective', *British Journal of Special Education* Vol. 22 No. 3, 105–108.

Montacute, C. (1993) 'The self-destructing SEN department', *Managing Schools Today* 2(9), 44–5.

Moore, J. (1993) 'How will the "self-managing school" manage?', in A. Dyson and C. Gains (Eds), *Rethinking Special Needs in Mainstream Schools: Towards the Year 2000*. London, David Fulton.

NARE (1985) *Guidelines 6: Teaching Roles for Special Educational Needs: a Statement by the National Association for Remedial Education*. Stafford, NARE Publications.

Nash, C. (1993) 'Flexible learning', in A. Dyson and C. Gains (Eds), *Rethinking Special Needs in Mainstream Schools: Towards the year 2000*. London, David Fulton.

National Curriculum Council (NCC) (1989) *Curriculum Guidance 2: A Curriculum for All*. York, National Curriculum Council.

National Curriculum Council (NCC) (1989a) *Circular Number 5: Implementing the National Curriculum – Participation by Pupils with Special Educational Needs*. York, National Curriculum Council.

Newton, M. J. and Thomson, M. E. (1982) *Aston Index (Revised)*. Wisbech, Cambs., Learning Development Aids.

Nind, M. and Hewett, D. (1994) *Access to Communication: Developing the Basics of Communication with People with Severe Learning Difficulties through Intensive Interaction*. London, David Fulton.

Norwich, B. (1993) 'Ideological dilemmas in special needs education: practitioners' views', *Oxford Review of Education*, 19(4), 527–46.

Ofsted (1996) *The Implementation of the Code of Practice for Pupils with Special Educational Needs*. London, HMSO.

O'Hanlon, C. (1988) 'Alienation within the profession ; special needs or watered down teachers? Insights into the tension between the ideal and the real through action research', *Cambridge Journal of Education*, 18(3), 297–311.

O'Hanlon, C. (1988) 'Alienation Within the Profession; Special Needs or Watered Down Teachers? Insights into the Tension Between the Ideal and the Real Through Action Research', *Cambridge Journal of Education* 18(3), 297–311.

Oliver, M. (1990) *The Politics of Disablement*. London, Macmillan.

Oliver, M. (1992a) 'Intellectual masturbation: a rejoinder to Soder and Booth', *European Journal of Special Educational Needs* 7 (1), 20–8.

Oliver, M. (1992b) 'Changing the Social Relation of Research?', *Disability, Handicap and Society*. Vol. 7 (2), 101–14.

Pacey, A. (1983) *The Culture of Technology*. Oxford, Basil Blackwell.

Parfrey, V. (1994) 'Exclusions: failed children or systems failure?', *School Organisation* Vol. 14 No. 2, 107–20.

Pickup, M. (1995) 'The role of the special educational needs co-ordinator: developing philosophy and practice', *Support for Learning*, 10(2), 88–92.

Proudford, C. and Baker, R. (1995) 'Schools that make a difference: a sociological perspective on effective schooling', *British Journal of Sociology of Education* 16(3), 277–92.

Reid, G. (1994) *Specific Learning Difficulties (Dyslexia): A Handbook for Study and Practice*. Edinburgh, Moray House Publications.

Reid, J. (1977) 'Dyslexia: a problem of communication', in J. F. Reid and H. Donaldson (Eds), *Reading: Problems and Practices*. London, Ward Lock Educational.

Reid, R., Maag, J. W. and Vasa, S. F. (1993) 'Attention Deficit Hyperactivity Disorder as a disability category: A critique', *Exceptional Children*, 60(3), 198–214.

Reynolds, D. (1995) 'Using school effectiveness knowledge for children with special needs – the problems and possibilities', in C. Clark, A. Dyson, and A. Millward (Eds), *Towards Inclusive Schools?* London, David Fulton.

Riddell, S. and Brown, S. (Eds) (1994) *Special Educational Needs Policy in the 1990s: Warnock in the Market Place*. London, Routledge.

Riddell, S., Brown, S. and Duffield, J. (1994a) 'Conflicts of policies and models: The case of specific learning difficulties', in S. Riddell and S. Brown (Eds), *Special Educational Needs Policy in the 1990s: Warnock in the Market Place*. London, Routledge.

Riddell, S., Brown, S. and Duffield, J. (1994b) 'Parental power and special educational needs: the case of specific learning difficulties', *British Educational Research Journal*, 20(3), 327–44.

Riddell, S., Duffield, J., Brown, S. and Ogilvy, C. (1992) *Specific Learning Difficulties: Policy, Practice and Provision: a Report to SOED*. Department of Education, University of Stirling.

Roaf, C. and Bines, H. (1989) *Needs, Rights and Opportunities. Developing Approaches to Special Education*. London, Falmer Press.

Robinson, J. (1974) 'Special Educational Needs After the 1993 Reforms', *Education and the Law*, Vol. 6 No. 1, 3–14.

Rose, R., Fergusson, A., Coles, C., Byers, R. and Banes, D. (Eds) (1994) *Implementing the Whole Curriculum for Pupils with Learning Difficulties*. London, David Fulton.

Rouse, M. and Florian, L. (1996) 'Effective inclusive schools: A study in two countries', *Cambridge Journal of Education* 26(1), 71–85.

Russell, P. (1990) 'The Education Reform Act: The implications for special educational needs', in M. Flude and M. Hammer (Eds), *The Education Reform Act, 1988: Its Origins and Implications*. London, Falmer.

Russell, P. (1994) 'The Code of Practice: New partnerships for children with special educational needs', *British Journal of Special Education*, 21(2), 48–52.

Sandow, S., Stafford, D. and Stafford, P. (1987) *An Agreed Understanding? Parent-professional communication and the 1981 Act*. Windsor, NFER-Nelson.

Sapon-Slavin, M. (1996) 'Full Inclusion as Disclosing Tablet: Revealing the Flaws in Our Present System', *Journal of Theory into Practice* Vol. 35 No. 1, 35–41.

Sayer, J. (1994/1987) *Secondary Schools for All? Strategies for Special Needs* (2nd. edition). London, Cassell.

Schön, D. A. (1983/1991) *The Reflective Practitioner: How Professionals Think in Action*. Aldershot, Avebury.

Scottish Consultative Council on the Curriculum (SCCC) (1993) *Support for Learning: Special Educational Needs Within the 5–14 Curriculum*. Dundee, SOED.

Scottish Education Department (SED) (1978) *The Education of Pupils with Learning Difficulties in Primary and Secondary Schools in Scotland: A Progress Report by HM Inspectors of Schools*. Edinburgh, HMSO.

Scottish Office Education Department (SOED) (1993) *Standards and Quality in Scottish Schools 1991–92: A Report by HM Inspectors of Schools*. Edinburgh, HMSO.

Sebba, J., Byers, R. and Rose, R. (1993) *Redefining the Whole Curriculum for Pupils with Learning Difficulties*. London, David Fulton.

Simpson, J. (1993) 'Rethinking the role of the special needs co-ordinator: The Quality Assurer', in A. Dyson and C. Gains (Eds), *Rethinking Special Needs in Mainstream Schools: Towards the year 2000*. London, David Fulton.

Skidmore, D. (1996) 'Towards an integrated theoretical framework for research into special educational needs', *European Journal of Special Needs Education* 11(1), 33–47.

Skrtic, T. M. (1991) *Behind Special Education: A Critical Analysis of Professional Culture and School Organization*. Denver, Love.

Slee, R. (1995) *Changing Theories and Practices of Discipline* London, RKP.

Slee, R. (1996) 'Inclusive education in Australia? Not yet!', *Cambridge Journal of Education* 26(1), 19–32.

Sleeter, C. E. (1986) 'Learning disabilities: the social construction of a special education category', *Exceptional Children*, 53(1), 46–54.

Smyth, J. (1991a) 'Teachers' Work and the Politics of Reflection: or, Reflection on a Growth Industry'. Paper presented to Conference: Conceptualising Reflection in Teacher Development, University of Bath.

Smyth, J. (1991b) *Teachers as Collaborative Learners*. Milton Keynes, OUP.

Stainbeck, S. and Stainbeck, W. (Eds), (1992) *Curricular Considerations in Inclusive Classrooms: Facilitating Learning for all Students*. Baltimore, Paul H. Brookes.

Stirling, M. (1991) 'Absent Without Leave', *Special Children* 52, 10–13.

Stirling, M. (1992) 'How many pupils are being excluded?', *British Journal of Special Education*, 19(4), 128–30.

Stirling, M (1993) Second Classes for a Second class? *Special Children* 66. 15–18.

Stradling, R., Saunders, L. and with Weston, P. (1991) *Differentiation in Action: A whole-school approach for raising attainment*. London, HMSO.

Susman, J. (1994) 'Disability, stigma and deviance', *Social Science and Medicine*, 38(1), 15–22.

Swann, W. (1985) 'Is the integration of children with Special Needs Happening?: an analysis of recent statistics of pupils in special schools' *Oxford Review of Education*, Vol. 11 No. 1, 3–18.

Swann,W. (1988) 'Trends in Special school placement to 1986: measuring, assessing and explaining segregation', *Oxford Review of Education*, Vol. 14 No. 2, 139–60.

Swann, W. (1992) 'Hardening the hierarchies: the national curriculum as a system of classification', in T. Booth, W. Swann, M. Masterton, and P. Potts (Eds), *Curricula for Diversity in Education*. London, Routledge.

Swann, W. (1992) *Segregation Statistics*. London, Centre for Studies on Integration in Education.

Tansley, A. E. and Gulliford, R. (1960) *The Education of Slow Learning Children* (2nd edition). London, Routledge and Kegan Paul.

The Hertfordshire Association, NASUWT, (1995). *Special Education Needs: A report on the Code of Practice and the work of SENCOS*. NASUWT.

Thomas, G. (1992) 'Local authorities, special needs and the status quo', *Support for Learning* 7(1), 36–40.

Thomas, G. (1992) *Effective Classroom Teamwork: Support or Intrusion?* London, Routledge.

Thompson, D. and Barton, L. (1992) 'The wider context: a free market', *British Journal of Special Education* 19(1), 13–15.

Tomlinson, S. (1982) *A Sociology of Special Education*. London, Routledge & Kegan Paul.

Tomlinson, S. (1985) 'The expansion of special education', *Oxford Review of Education*, 11(2), 157–65.

Uldvari-Solner, A. and Thousand, J. (1995) Effective Organisational Instruction: Curricula Practice in Inclusive Schools, in Clark, C., Dyson, D. and Millward, A. (Eds), *Towards Inclusive Schools*. London, David Fulton.

Villa, R. and Thousand, J. S. (Eds) (1995) *Creating an Inclusive School*. Alexandria, Va., Association for Supervision and Curriculum Development.

Villa, R. A., Thousand, J. S., Stainback, W. and Stainback, S. (Eds) (1992) *Restructuring for Caring and Effective Education: An Administrative Guide to Creating Heterogeneous Schools*. Baltimore, Paul H. Brookes.

Vincent, C., Evans, J., Lunt, I. and Young, P. (1995) 'Policy and practice: the changing nature of special educational provision in schools', *British Journal of Special Education* 22(1), 4–11.

Vincent, C., Evans, J., Lunt, I., Steedman, J. and Wedell, K. (1994) 'The market forces? The effect of local management of schools in special educational needs provisions', *British Educational Research Journal*, 20(3), 261–78.

Vislie, L. (1995) 'Integration policies, school reforms and the organisation of schooling for handicapped pupils in western societies', in C. Clark, A. Dyson, and A. Millward (Eds), *Towards Inclusive Schools?* London, David Fulton.

Visser, J. (1986) 'Support: a description of the work of the SEN professional', *Support for Learning* 1(4), 5–9.

Vlachou, A. and Barton, L. (1994) Inclusive education: teachers and the changing culture of schooling', *British Journal of Special Education*, 21(3), 105–7.

Walberg, H. J. (1993) 'Learning "disabilities" revisited', *European Journal of Special Needs Education*, 8(3), 289–302.

Wang, M. C. and Reynolds, M. C. (1996) 'Progressive inclusion: Meeting new challenges in special education', *Theory into Practice*, 35(1), 20–5.

Ware, L. (1995) 'The aftermath of the articulate debate: the invention of inclusive education', in C. Clark, A. Dyson, and A. Millward (Eds), *Towards Inclusive Schools?* London, David Fulton.

Wedell, K. (1988) 'The new act: A special need for vigilance', *British Journal of Special Education*, 15(3), 98–101.

Wedell, K. (1993) Editorial, *British Journal of Special Education*, 20(4), 119.

Weston, P. (1992) A decade for differentiation, *British Journal of Special Education* 19(1), 6–9.

Westwood, P. (1975) *The Remedial Teacher's Handbook*. Edinburgh, Oliver & Boyd.

Wheal, R. (1995) 'Unleashing individual potential: A team approach', *Support for Learning*, 10(2), 83–7.

White, J. (1991) '"The goals are the same. . . ." Are they?', *British Journal of Special Education*, 18(1), 25–6.

Widlake, P. (1975) 'Remedial education at the crossroads', *Remedial Education*, 10(3), 103–7.

Wolfendale, S. (1987) *Primary Schools and Special Needs: Policy, Planning and Provision.* London, Cassell.

Zigmond, N. and Baker, J. M. (1995) 'Concluding comments: Current and future practices in inclusive schooling', *Journal of Special Education* 29(2), 234–50.

Index